BOURGEOIS UTOPIAS

BOURGEOIS UTOPIAS

The Rise and Fall
of Suburbia

ROBERT FISHMAN

Basic Books, Inc., Publishers

NEW YORK

Library of Congress Cataloging-in-Publication Data

Fishman, Robert, 1946–
  Bourgeois utopias.

  Bibliographic notes: p. 209
  Includes index.
  1. Suburbs.   2. Suburban life.   3. Suburban homes.
I. Title.
HT351.F575   1987   307.7′4   87–47508
ISBN   0–465–00748–1   (cloth)
ISBN   0–465–00747–3   (paper)

For
Clifford and Carole,
Mitchell and Lois,
Joan and Gregg

CONTENTS

Illustrations follow page 116

PREFACE

THIS BOOK began as an attempt to get away from utopia. My first book had dealt with three twentieth century planners whom I called "urban utopians": Ebenezer Howard, Frank Lloyd Wright, and Le Corbusier. They believed that planning must begin with the uncompromising rejection of all previous urban forms and seek the creation of a new utopian city based on advanced technology, aesthetic harmony, and social justice. They disagreed vehemently about the form of the ideal twentieth century city, but they agreed on one crucial point: the ideal city would have no place for suburbia. With passion and eloquence they attacked the suburban ideal, and their arguments were taken up by some of the most influential architects and planners of their time.

I felt inspired by these three planners' utopian visions, but I could not help reflecting that their designs for ideal cities remained largely on paper and were often disappointing when built; meanwhile, the suburban ideal was winning enough support from ordinary people in the real world to transform the structure of the modern city. This obvious fact suggested that a study of the history of suburbia would teach some vital lessons which were necessarily absent from my first book. What are the true sources of new urban forms which prove to be effective? What are the real forces that shape urban growth? What are the mechanisms whereby new ideas are transmitted to those who have the power to transform the built environment? In particular, who invented suburbia and why? What explains its extraordinary hold over the middle-class mind?

The answers to these questions took me further in time and space than I had anticipated, back to the suburbs of eighteenth century London and to myriad other suburbs which followed; but I soon realized that behind the practical work of speculative builders and land developers I was attempting to document there lay a powerful cultural ideal. Suburbia, I came to believe, must be understood as a utopia in its own right. Its power derived ultimately from the capacity of suburban design to express a complex and compelling vision of the modern family freed from the corruption of the city, restored to harmony with nature, endowed with wealth and independence yet protected by a close-knit, stable community. Unlike the planners' utopias, it was not the work of an individual genius developing his ideas in isolation. Suburbia was, rather, the collective creation of the Anglo-American middle class: the bourgeois utopia.

I realize that the words "bourgeois" and "utopia" do not couple easily. "Bourgeois" connotes a hard-headed materialism and a disdain for ideals that seem to be the exact opposite of utopianism. This paradox is indeed at the heart of my analysis of suburbia. Where other modern utopias have been collectivist, suburbia has built its vision of community on the primacy of private property and the individual family. Suburbia has founded its hopes for community stability on the shifting sands of land speculation and based its reconciliation of man and nature on the capacity to exclude the urban world of work which is the ultimate source of its wealth. Lewis Mumford perhaps best expressed the paradox of the bourgeois utopia in *The Culture of Cities* (1938), where he describes suburbia as "a collective effort to live a private life."

Cultural forms flourish on their contradictions, and the very impossibility of the suburban vision impelled a series of architects and designers to attempt ever more imaginative embodiments of the bourgeois utopia. These designs, together with the efforts of thousands of land speculators, builders, investors, and homebuyers, constitute the "rise of suburbia." From a marginal form intended for a restricted elite of eighteenth century London merchants, suburbia grew to become the residence of choice for the Anglo-American middle class, and an urban form capable of re-shaping the whole modern metropolis.

This remarkable growth is also at the heart of my concept of "the fall of suburbia." I am not predicting a return to the cities, nor do I foresee grass growing in the gently-curving streets of abandoned subdivisions, nor the wind whistling through empty shopping malls. My point is almost the opposite. The massive postwar decentralization of the most vital urban functions has profoundly transformed the basic urban ecology in which suburbia developed over its two-hundred-year history. As a result, the original concept of suburbia as an unspoiled synthesis of city and countryside has lost its meaning. No longer can a purely residential "bourgeois utopia" define itself in relation to a centralized urban core, for the suburban periphery has become the favored locale for our most advanced and important enterprises. If anything, suburbia has succeeded too well. It has become what even the greatest advocates of suburban growth never desired—a new form of city.

In acknowledging the generous assistance I have received while writing this book, I am pleased to begin with Martin Kessler, president and editorial director of Basic Books. His advice and encouragement—above all, his unswerving belief in this project—made the book a reality.

I was fortunate to be a member of a faculty seminar on the culture of cities organized by Thomas Bender at the New York Institute for the Humanities. The meetings brought me into frequent contact with a remarkable group of scholars whose ideas and discussion provided an impressive education in cities and in culture: Marshall Berman, Christine Boyer, Peter Buckley, Elizabeth Kendall, Linda Nochlin, Anson Rabinbach, Wolfgang Schivelbusch, Carl Schorske, Richard Sennett, Christina Spellman, Susan Squier, William Taylor, and Anthony Vidler.

In addition I acknowledge the essential material support that I received from the Andrew W. Mellon Foundation and the Rutgers Research Council.

Preface

The superb urban history collections at three notable libraries greatly enhanced the documentary scope of this book: the Guildhall Library, London; the Local History Collection and Archives of the Manchester Central Library; and the Special Collections Department at the University of California, Los Angeles. My extended stay in Los Angeles was made possible by the hospitality of my aunt and uncle, Dorothy and Herman J. Fishman.

Donald J. Olsen generously shared with me his profound knowledge of European cities and Sir John Summerson directed me toward important material in the Public Record Office I would never have found on my own.

Andrew Lees and Lynn Hollen Lees contributed advice, information, encouragement, and above all, friendship; to thank them I can only repeat what George Bernard Shaw said of two other distinguished urban historians, Sidney and Beatrice Webb: "Each of them is a force; and their marriage was an irresistible reinforcement."

My greatest debt is to my late friend and colleague Louis Forman (1913–1987). His love of teaching and learning was a constant inspiration to me throughout the writing of this book.

BOURGEOIS UTOPIAS

Introduction

> Our suburban architecture . . . reveals the spirit and character of modern civilization, just as the temples of Egypt and Greece, the baths and amphitheaters of Rome, and the cathedrals and castles of the Middle Ages help us to comprehend and penetrate the spirit of previous civilizations.
>
> —CÉSAR DALY, 1864[1]

EVERY CIVILIZATION gets the monuments it deserves. The triumph of bourgeois capitalism seems most apparent in the massive constructions of iron and steel that celebrate the union of technology and profit: the railroad terminals, exposition halls, suspension bridges, and skyscrapers. One does not look to suburbia for the modern equivalents of the Baths of Caracalla or Chartres cathedral.

But if, like Daly quoted above, we are seeking the architecture that best reveals "the spirit and character of modern civilization," then suburbia might tell us more about the culture that built the factories and skyscrapers than these edifices themselves can. For suburbia too was an archetypal middle-class invention, perhaps the most radical rethinking of the relation between residence and the city in the history of domestic architecture. It was founded on that primacy of the family and domestic life which was the equivalent in bourgeois society of the intense civic life celebrated by the public architecture of the ancient city. However modest each suburban house might be, suburbia represents a collective assertion of class wealth and privilege as impressive as any medieval castle. Most importantly, suburbia embodies a new ideal of family life, an ideal so emotionally charged that it made the home more sacred to the bourgeoisie than any place of worship. The hundred years of massive suburban development that have passed since Daly wrote can only confirm his judgment that the true center of any bourgeois society is the middle-class house. If you seek the monuments of the bourgeoisie, go to the suburbs and look around.

Suburbia is more than a collection of residential buildings; it expresses values so deeply embedded in bourgeois culture that it might also be called the bourgeois utopia. Yet this "utopia" was always at most a partial paradise, a refuge not only from threatening elements in the city but also from discordant elements in bourgeois society itself. From its origins, the suburban world of leisure, family life, and union with nature was based on the principle of exclusion. Work was excluded from the family residence; middle-class villas were segregated from working-class housing; the greenery of suburbia stood in contrast to a gray, polluted urban environment. Middle-class women were especially affected by the new suburban dichotomy of work and family life. The new environment supposedly exalted their role in the family, but it also segregated them from the world of power and productivity. This self-segregation soon enveloped all aspects of bourgeois culture. Suburbia, therefore, represents more than the bourgeois utopia, the triumphant assertion of middle-class values. It also reflects the alienation of the middle classes from the urban-industrial world they themselves were creating.

In this book I wish to understand the significance of suburbia both for modern culture and for the modern city first by tracing this urban form back to its origins in the late eighteenth century and then by showing the evolution of the suburban tradition of design to the present. I adopt this historical method in part because, like so many great inventions, suburbia has always seemed contemporary. In the United States, people are often surprised to learn that suburbs existed before 1945. Even César Daly was unaware that the mid-Victorian English suburbs he observed were the product of an urban evolution that was already a century old at the time he wrote.

Only by examining the eighteenth century origins of suburbia can one grasp its radical departure from all previous traditions of urban structure as well as its crucial role in reshaping the modern city. In order to clarify this "suburban revolution" in metropolitan structure I must first define the precise meaning of the "suburb." The word means literally "beyond the city," and thus can refer to any kind of settlement at the periphery of a large city. A former mill town in the process of being swallowed up by an expanding metropolis, or a newly built industrial area on the urban fringes—these, strictly speaking, are as much "suburbs" as the most affluent bedroom community.

In this book, however, I am concerned only with the middle-class suburb of privilege, and I shall use the words "suburb" and "suburbia" to refer only to a residential community beyond the core of a large city. Though physically separated from the urban core, the suburb nevertheless depends on it economically for the jobs that support its residents. It is also culturally dependent on the core for the major institutions of urban life: professional offices, department stores and other specialized shops, hospitals, theaters, and the like. The true suburb, moreover, is more than a collection of dense city streets that have reached the edge of the built-up area. The suburb must be large enough and homogeneous enough to form a distinctive low density environment defined by the primacy of the single family house set in the greenery of an open, parklike setting.

I should emphasize that the suburb, in my definition, is not necessarily a separate political unit. In selecting a site for a nineteenth century suburb, developers carefully considered such questions as topography or access to the central city, but virtually ignored whether an attractive location was within or outside the political jurisdiction of the central city. Only in the twentieth century did a separate political identity become important in maintaining a separate social or design identity. Even today almost all large cities have suburbs as I define them within their borders.

Suburbia can thus be defined first by what it includes—middle-class residences—and second (perhaps more importantly) by what it excludes: all industry, most commerce except for enterprises that specifically serve a residential area, and all lower-class residents (except for servants). These social and economic characteristics are all expressed in design through a suburban tradition of both residential and landscape architecture. Derived from the English concept of the picturesque, this tradition distinguishes the suburb both from the city and from the countryside and creates that aesthetic "marriage of town and country" which is the mark of the true suburb.

One need only contrast this definition with the realities of the eighteenth century city to see how radically suburbia contradicted the basic assumptions that organized the premodern city. Such cities were built up on the principle that the core was the only appropriate and honorific setting for the elite, and that the urban peripheries outside the walls were disreputable zones, shantytowns to which the poorest inhabitants and the most noisome manufactures were relegated.

In London—a typical premodern city in this respect and one with a special relevance to this study—income and social standing declined markedly as one moved from the center to the outskirts. These social distinctions were enshrined in the language itself. From its earliest usage in the fourteenth century until the mid eighteenth century, a "suburbe"—that is, a settlement on the urban fringe—meant (in the definition of the *Oxford English Dictionary*) a "place of inferior, debased, and especially licentious habits of life." The canon's yeoman in Chaucer's *Canterbury Tales* says of himself and his master, a crooked alchemist, that they live "in the suburbes of town. We lurk in corners and blind alleys where robbers and thieves instinctively huddle secretly and fearfully together. . . ."[2]

In Shakespeare's London so many houses of prostitution had moved to these disreputable outskirts that a whore was called "a suburb sinner," and to call a man a "suburbanite" was a serious insult.[3] One nineteenth century writer has described the inhabitants of the suburb of Cripplegate in the seventeenth century as

> a population of tanners and skinners, catgut makers, tallow melters, dealers in old clothes, receivers of stolen goods, charcoal sellers, makers of sham jewelry, coiners, clippers of coin and silver refiners, who kept their melting-pots ready day and night for any silver plate that might come to hand, toilers in noisome trades and dishonest dealers. . . . Forgers of seals, of bills, of writs, professional pick-purses, sharpers and other thieves, conjurors, wizards and fortune tellers, beggars and harlots found a refuge here.[4]

If the modern suburb can be defined as a peripheral zone in which people of means choose to live, then such a district was literally unthinkable in the premodern city, a contradiction in the basic terms that defined urban structure.

Indeed, even the concept of a residential district from which commerce and industry had been excluded was inconceivable for the premodern city. The basic principle of a city like London before 1750 was that work and residence were naturally combined within each house. Almost all middle-class enterprises were extensions of the family, so that it was not only the Spitalfields weaver who lived with his loom or the grocer who lived above his shop. The banker conducted business in his parlor, the merchant stored his goods in his cellar, and both housed and fed their apprentices along with their families.

This intimate connection of work and residence explained the universal attraction of the wealthy bourgeoisie to the urban core. When workplace and residence are combined, the best location for transacting one's business determined the location of one's house. In a mercantile city this location was almost invariably the most crowded district of the urban core.

I should emphasize here that even the relatively wealthy core areas were never upper-class neighborhoods in the modern sense. Just as the idea of a district devoted to a single function—a residential district or a business district—was foreign to the premodern city, so too was a single-class district. John Strype describes the privileged parish of St. Giles in the Fields as possessing "a mixture of rich inhabitants, to wit, of the Nobility, Gentry, and Commonality, but, withal, filled with abundance of poor."[5]

The wealthy might, at best, occupy large townhouses that fronted on the principal streets. But the poor inevitably crowded into the narrow alleyways and courtyards that existed literally in the backyards of the rich. This "medley of neighborhood," as Strype put it, was accepted without question. The poor were often servants in nearby houses, or workers in the multitude of small workshops found throughout the city. As one eighteenth century writer observed, "Here lives a personage of high distinction; next door a butcher with his stinking shambles! A Tallow-chandler shall be seen from my Lord's nice Venetian window; and two or three brawny naked Curriers in their Pits shall face a fine Lady in her back Closet, and disturb her spiritual Thoughts."[6] Here indeed we find the "mixed uses" frequently romanticized by twentieth century "postsuburban" planners. These mixed uses often had a functional basis, as when workshops clustered around the homes of merchants who dealt in their products. Sometimes they seem bizarre, as when a notorious "crime district" called Alsatia could be found adjoining the Temple, the center of English law.[7] In any case, the basic principles of the modern suburb had no precedents in the premodern city.

The suburb as we know it, therefore, did not evolve smoothly or inevitably from the premodern city; still less did it evolve from those disreputable outlying districts which originally bore the name of "suburbes." The emergence of suburbia required a total transformation of urban values: not only a reversal in the meanings of core and periphery, but a separation of work and family life and the creation of new forms of urban space that would be both class-segregated and wholly residential.

Who then invented suburbia and why? To ask the question is to formulate a major thesis of this book, which is that suburbia was indeed a cultural creation, a conscious choice based on the economic structure and cultural values of the Anglo-American bourgeoisie. Suburbanization was not the automatic fate of the middle class in the "mature industrial city" or an inevitable response to the Industrial Revolution or the so-called transportation revolution.

Yet, if suburbia was an original creation, it was not the product of an architect of genius who conceived the modern suburb in a single vision, which then gradually inspired the design profession and eventually the middle class. Indeed, in this history of suburban design, professional architects and city planners play a remarkably limited role.

Suburbia, I believe, was the collective creation of the bourgeois elite in late eighteenth century London. It evolved gradually and anonymously by trial-and-error methods. Wealthy London bankers and merchants experimented with a variety of the traditional housing forms available to them to create an original synthesis that reflected their values. Suburbia was improvised, not designed. Its method of evolution paralleled that of the contemporaneous Industrial Revolution, then taking place in the north of England, which also proceeded by trial-and-error adaptation. In both cases one senses the power of a class with the resources and the self-confidence to reorder the material world to suit its needs.

The motives that inspired the creation of suburbia were complex, and I shall try to untangle them in the next chapter. Here I would emphasize only one, which seems to me the most crucial. The London bourgeoisie who invented suburbia were also experiencing a new form of family, which Lawrence Stone has called "the closed domesticated nuclear family." Inner-directed, united by strong and exclusive personal ties, characterized in Stone's phrase by "an emphasis on the boundary surrounding the nuclear unit," such families sought to separate themselves from the intrusions of the workplace and the city. This new family type created the emotional force that split middle-class work and residence.[8]

The bourgeois residence was now freed from traditional patterns to be redesigned as a wholly domestic environment—the

9

home of a family that acted primarily as an emotional rather than an economic unit. This home, moreover, need not be restricted to the crowded districts of the urban core, as the logic of business location had formerly dictated. It was free to seek a more appropriate setting beyond the city in the picturesque villages that surrounded London. There, within easy commuting distance to the city by private carriage, these merchants and bankers could construct their "bourgeois utopia" of leisure, neighborliness, prosperity, and family life.

To this strong cultural impetus to suburbanization was soon added an equally strong economic motive. The suburban idea raised the possibility that land far beyond the previous range of metropolitan expansion could be transformed immediately from relatively cheap agricultural land to highly profitable building plots. This possibility provided the great engine that drove suburban expansion forward. For reasons that I hope to make clear in chapters 3 and 4, builders in both England and the United States adapted more easily to the needs of suburban development than they did to the more difficult challenge of creating middle-class districts within the city. Suburbia proved to be a good investment as well as a good home.

Middle-class suburbanization thus entered into the structural logic of the expanding Anglo-American city. It formed an integral part of what Frederick Law Olmsted perceived to be "the most prominent characteristic of the present period of civilization . . . the strong tendency of people to flock together in great towns."[9] Suburbia might appear to be a flight from the city but, seen in a larger, regional context, suburbanization was clearly the outer edge in a wider process of metropolitan growth and consolidation that was draining the rural areas and small towns of their population and concentrating people and production within what H. G. Wells called "the whirlpool cities."[10]

In 1800 only 17 percent of the English people lived in settlements larger than 20,000 people.[11] Cities were then places for highly specialized forms of consumption, manufacture, and trade. The real work of the world took place in the villages and in the countryside. By 1890, however, 72 percent of the English population lived in districts classified as "urbanized."[12] In the United States in 1800 less than 4 percent of the population lived in cities of 10,000 people or more; by 1890 that figure had reached 28 percent.[13] Behind these statistics lies a fundamental shift in the role of the modern city. Where premodern cities had been parasitic on the larger societies, the new industrial metropolis emerged as the most efficient and productive site for the most characteristic modern industries.[14]

As such "whirlpool cities" as London, Manchester, and New York came to dominate the world economy, their attraction grew ever more powerful. In these centers of exchange and information, crowding seemed to work; in other words, intense congestion led not to chaos and decline but to further expansion. In the nineteenth century the expression "urban crisis" referred to the explosive growth of the great cities, and to horrified critics it seemed that almost the whole population of modern nations would soon be sucked into the already crowded urban centers.[15]

Inevitably, these whirlpool cities had to expand physically, to break the barriers of size that had always constrained urban growth. The only question was if they would grow in the traditional manner, with the wealthy massed at the core and the poor pushed ever farther into the periphery; or if the middle class would use their wealth and resources to seize the unspoiled land at the urban fringe for their suburban "bourgeois utopia," forcing the working class into an intermediate "factory zone" sandwiched between the central business district and the suburbs.

Broadly speaking, continental and Latin American cities opted for the traditional structure, while British and North American cities followed the path of middle-class suburbanization. This distinction, still fundamental in so many of the world's great cities, had nothing to do with the supposed backwardness of continental cities as compared to their Anglo-American counterparts. Paris in the nineteenth century became far more intensively industrialized than London, and the French capital developed a network of omnibuses, streetcars, and railroads that matched the transportation facilities in any English or

American city. Yet the Parisian middle class remained loyal to the central city; the transportation system in Paris was used to move Parisian industry and its workers to the suburbs, and every further advance in transportation and industry has meant moving factories and the working class even farther from the city while the Parisian middle class has solidified its hold on the urban core.

However "objective" the "industrial city" might appear in diagrams from the Chicago School of sociology, its form rests ultimately on the values and choices of the powerful groups within the city. The decision of the bourgeoisie in Manchester and the other early industrial cities in the 1840s to suburbanize created the basic structure of the Anglo-American industrial city, while the decision of the comparable group in Paris of the 1850s and 1860s (aided by considerable governmental aid and intervention) to live in apartment houses in the center created the modern continental-style city.

In both cases the key actor was that elite of the middle class, the bourgeoisie. By "bourgeoisie" I mean that part of the middle class which through its capital or its professional standing has attained an income level equal to the landed gentry, but whose daily work in urban offices ties it to a middle-class style of life. Their personal resources permit them to create new patterns of living, while the values they share with the rest of the middle class makes them the model for eventual emulation by the less prosperous. The history of suburbia must therefore be a cultural and social history of the Anglo-American bourgeoisie. They are the pioneers whose collective style and choices define the nature of suburbia for their era.

For these English and American bourgeois pioneers, the "frontier" was inevitably the urban periphery, with its relatively cheap, undeveloped land. In continental cities massive governmental intervention—the nineteenth century versions of urban renewal—opened the possibility of reshaping the urban core for bourgeois uses. In England and the United States, laissez-faire urban economics turned the core into a tangle of competing uses. Only the periphery was sufficiently undefined to permit innovation. Indeed, the fate of the periphery was ultimately decisive in defining the whole structure of the Anglo-American city. In this Darwinian struggle for urban space, the bourgeoisie sought not only land for their commercial and industrial enterprises but also land for their dreams: their visions of the ideal middle-class home. These dreams are now deep in the structure of the twentieth century city.

This history of suburbia is thus a history of a vision—the bourgeois utopia—which has left its mark on thousands of individual suburbs, each with its own distinctive history. But I believe that all these communities can be linked to a single suburban tradition of architectural and social history. In attempting to outline the principal stages in the evolution of this tradition, I have been forced to depart from the usual method of suburban history, which is to examine one community over time. No single suburb adequately represents all the stages of suburban evolution, so I have selected a series of communities that seem best to embody the suburban idea at each crucial point of innovation.

These suburbs are not typical of their time but rather exemplary. Built rapidly in periods of unusual growth and prosperity, they incorporate in their design a creative response to contemporary changes in the structure and economy of modern cities. Unconstrained by previous building, responding to new social and cultural forces, these communities are truly "of their time." Through a series of often uncoordinated decisions by developers, builders, and individuals, a new style arises, which is then copied in hundreds of other suburbs. These exemplary suburbs create the image that, at any particular time, defines the suburban tradition. This image then becomes an active force in urban history, shaping subsequent decisions by speculators and home buyers that transform the urban landscape.

The first models for this process—and consequently the inevitable starting point for this book—were those earliest of modern suburbs which took shape on the outskirts of London in the second half of the eighteenth century. They not only defined the essential suburban image for all subsequent development but, in their strict segregation of class and function, they also implied a new structure for the modern city.

These implications were first worked out in practice not in London itself but in the early nineteenth century industrial cities of northern England. The suburbs of Manchester, which form the second group of exemplary suburbs, were the necessary catalyst in reshaping the whole structure of the modern industrial city. For the first time one sees a middle class that is wholly suburbanized; and, as necessary correlates, a central business district devoid of residents and a crowded, smoky factory zone between the central business district and suburbia. Frenzied land speculation, bitter class conflict, and the alluring image of the bourgeois utopia combined to restructure the basic components of the city.

By the 1840s Manchester had established a model for middle-class suburbanization that was to endure fundamentally unchanged for a century. In the 1850s and 1860s this suburban model established itself outside the rapidly growing cities of the United States but was decisively rejected in France. There, as we have seen, the bourgeoisie maintained their hold on the urban core. This dichotomy creates an important problem for any history of suburbia: why did this bourgeois utopia take hold only among the "Anglo-Saxon" bourgeoisie, when the equally bourgeois French followed a very different vision?

The answer hinges both on long-term differences between French and Anglo-American images of the city and on the specifics of Eugène-Georges Haussmann's massive rebuilding of Paris. In any case, the great apartment houses along the new boulevards of Paris—as well as their counterparts in Vienna's Ringstrasse—created a powerful counterimage that shaped the continental city into a structure diametrically opposed to that of the English city. At the same time, and for equally strong cultural and economic reasons, the American middle class adopted the English model of bourgeois suburbanization so decisively that ever since Americans have been convinced that it was they who invented suburbia.

Indeed, after 1870 the site of the "exemplary" suburb shifted decisively to the United States. It happened not because of any loss of enthusiasm for the suburban ideal in England. The slowing of the British economy, first apparent in the late nineteenth century, combined with the explosive growth of the American industrial city, meant that English suburbs were more constrained by the past, while the United States was forced to innovate.

The suburbs that arose outside the American industrial cities at the end of the nineteenth century were the classic embodiments of the whole history of suburbia. They not only summed up the design tradition now more than a century old, but they provided the model that all subsequent suburbs have attempted to imitate. Structurally, these suburbs were at once separate from the industrial city and yet, through the streetcar and the steam railroad, easily accessible to it. Socially, they housed a powerful and self-conscious bourgeoisie that combined the old business and professional elite with the "new middle class" anxious to establish its separateness from the immigrant cities. In design, the substantial houses set in open, tree-shaded lots summed up that blend of property, union with nature, and family life which defines the suburban tradition. I have chosen the suburbs of Philadelphia to exemplify this era—though the suburbs of Boston, New York, Baltimore, St. Louis, and especially Chicago would have served just as well.

If there is a single theme that differentiates the history of twentieth century suburbia from its nineteenth century antecedents, it is the attempt to secure for the whole middle class (and even for the working class as well) the benefits of suburbia, which in the classic nineteenth century suburb had been restricted to the bourgeois elite alone. Inevitably, this attempt was to change the basic nature both of suburbia and of the larger city. For how can a form based on the principle of exclusion include everyone?

This paradox is exemplified in the history of Los Angeles, the suburban metropolis of the twentieth century. From its first building boom in the late nineteenth century, Los Angeles has been shaped by the promise of a suburban home for all. The automobile and the highway when they came were no more than new tools to achieve a suburban vision that had its origins in the streetcar era. But as population spread along the streetcar lines and the highways, the "suburbs" of Los Angeles began to lose contact with the central city, which so diminished in importance that even the new highways bypassed it. In the 1920s, a new urban form evolved in which the industries, specialized shopping, and offices once concentrated in the urban core spread over the whole region. By the 1930s Los Angeles had become a sprawling metropolitan region, the basic unit of which was the decentralized suburb.

This creation of a suburban metropolis signaled a fundamental shift in the relationship of the urban core and its periphery, with implications extending far beyond Los Angeles. As we have seen, the suburb emerged during the era of urban concentration, when the limitations of communications and transportation combined to draw people and production into the crowded core. By the 1920s an interrelated technology of decentralization—of which the automobile was only one element—had begun to operate, which inexorably loosened the ties that once bound the urban functions of society to tightly defined cores. As the most important urban institutions spread out over the landscape, the suburb became part of a complex "outer city," which now included jobs as well as residences.

Increasingly independent of the urban core, the suburb since 1945 has lost its traditional meaning and function as a satellite of the central city. Where peripheral communities had once excluded industry and large scale commerce, the suburb now becomes the heartland of the most rapidly expanding elements of the late twentieth century economy. The basic concept of the suburb as a privileged zone between city and country no longer fits the realities of a posturban era in which high tech research centers sit in the midst of farmland and grass grows on abandoned factory sites in the core. As both core and periphery are swallowed up in seemingly endless multicentered regions, where can one find suburbia?

This problem forms the heart of my concluding chapter, "Beyond Suburbia: The Rise of the Technoburb." Kenneth Jackson in his definitive history of American suburbanization, *Crabgrass*

Frontier, interprets post–World War II peripheral development as "the suburbanization of the United States," the culmination of the nineteenth century and early twentieth century suburban tradition.[16] I see this development as something very different, the end of suburbia in its traditional sense and the creation of a new kind of decentralized city.

Without anyone planning or foreseeing it, the simultaneous movement of housing, industry, and commercial development to the outskirts has created perimeter cities that are functionally independent of the urban core. In complete contrast to the residential or industrial suburbs of the past, these new cities contain along their superhighways all the specialized functions of a great metropolis—industry, shopping malls, hospitals, universities, cultural centers, and parks. With its highways and advanced communications technology, the new perimeter city can generate urban diversity without urban concentration.

To distinguish the new perimeter city from the traditional suburban bedroom community, I propose to identify it by the neologism "technoburb." For the real basis of the new city is the invisible web of advanced technology and telecommunications that has been substituted for the face-to-face contact and physical movement of older cities. Inevitably, the technoburb has become the favored location for those technologically advanced industries which have made the new city possible. If, as Fernand Braudel has said, the city is a transformer, intensifying the pace of change, then the American transformer has moved from the urban core to the perimeter.[17]

If the technoburb has lost its dependence on the older urban cores, it now exists in a multicentered region defined by superhighways, the growth corridors of which could extend more than a hundred miles. These regions, which (if the reader will pardon another neologism) I call techno-cities, mean the end of the whirlpool effect that had drawn people to great cities and their suburbs. Instead, urban functions disperse across a decentralized landscape that is neither urban nor rural nor suburban in the traditional sense. With the rise of the technoburb, the history of suburbia comes to an end.

CHAPTER 1

London: Birthplace

of Suburbia

LIKE written constitutions, the novel, steam engines, and so many other innovations that have reshaped our lives, the middle-class residential suburb was a product of the eighteenth century. Its form and function reflect many of the most pervasive cultural elements in eighteenth century civilization, but the suburb also reflects the specific conditions of the city in which it was born. Perhaps inevitably, London was the site of this innovation in urban form: for London was the first of H. G. Wells's "whirlpool cities."[1]

London had become the largest city in Europe by the end of the seventeenth century, and its predominance over its great continental rivals—Paris, Naples, and Amsterdam—increased markedly during the eighteenth century. While, for example, Paris reached 500,000 people by 1700 but hardly grew in the next hundred years, London went from 575,000 in 1700 to 675,000 in 1750 and reached 960,000 by 1800. Indeed, London's population exceeded 1.1 million in 1800, if one counts the whole metropolitan area now known to demographers as "greater London."[2]

Perhaps even more impressive than these figures were the economic and political supremacies that made them possible. For London was the focus of a worldwide network of ocean-going trade routes, which made the city the international center of long-distance trade and banking. It was also the political capital of the British Empire and its center for the production and consumption of luxury goods. With this combination of functions (along with a prosperous hinterland that kept the city well supplied with food and fuel), London became the first modern city to overcome the barriers to growth that had kept the medieval and early modern cities in check.

The modern suburb was a direct result of this unprecedented urban growth. It grew out of a crisis in urban form that stemmed from the inability of the premodern city to cope with explosive modern urban expansion. It also reflected the unprecedented growth in the wealth and size of an upper-middle-class merchant elite. This London bourgeoisie had attained the critical mass in numbers, resources, and confidence to transform the cities of their time to suit their values.

The growth of eighteenth century London was initially a source of pride to its citizens. Only gradually did its consequences become clear. John Strype wrote in 1720 that London "may boast itself to be the largest in extent, and the fairest built, the most populous, and best inhabited, and that by a civil, rich, and sober People, of any [city] in the world. And for a general trade throughout the Universe, all others must give her precedence."[3] Daniel Defoe in 1724 described viewing London from a small hill outside the city and suddenly seeing "a fair prospect of the whole city of London itself; the most glorious sight without exception that the whole world at present can show, or perhaps ever could since the sacking of Rome in the European and the burning of the Temple of Jerusalem in the Asian part of the world."[4] Defoe found London remarkable especially for its size, that "prodigy of buildings" which unfolded to his glance. Reading his description today, however, we are astonished at how small in area this city of 600,000 people was; how closely it hugged the north and south banks of the Thames around its original center; how easily Defoe can take it in as a whole from his vantage point.

For example, a person standing in the heart of the city at St. Paul's Cathedral was no more than half a mile—perhaps a twenty minute walk—from open fields in what is now Bloomsbury. And the countryside was even closer from other districts. Eighteenth century maps show clearly the dense mass of the city suddenly giving way to open fields. This stark contrast is something more than the necessary condition of a "walking city" in which the lack of mechanical transportation limited its size. For even the slowest walker could have lived beyond the early eighteenth century limits of the city and commuted by foot to the center. London was not limited by any weakness in foot power, or hemmed in by walls, as continental cities still were. Its growth, I believe, was restricted by the invisible walls of a premodern urban ecology, a set of social and economic barriers to expansion.

The central principle of this premodern ecology was that the wealthiest members of the community lived and worked closest to the historic core, while the poorest people were pushed to the periphery. Indeed, the word "suburb," as we have seen, referred exclusively to these peripheral slums, which surrounded all large towns. These suburban poor lacked the means to expand their shantylike "suburbs" into the surrounding countryside. So London was like an increasingly overpacked container, continually bulging but never able to expand efficiently.

Since the Middle Ages, the mercantile center of London had been the mile-square "City of London." And, within that center, the mercantile elite occupied virtually the same narrow streets as their medieval counterparts. Lombard Street, named for the Italian bankers who dominated medieval English finance, was still the home of London's leading bankers in the eighteenth century—as it remains the London headquarters of the great international banking corporations today. This conservatism was something more than blind traditionalism. London thrived as a center of trade: in other words, as a center of information. Its leading merchants depended on rapid knowledge of markets throughout the world, a knowledge that was available to them only through a multitude of face-to-face contacts. The concentration of England's leading merchants in the few intensely crowded acres at the heart of the City (and just blocks from the port) was a highly efficient mechanism for promoting this exchange of information.

Thus, for the elite, crowding was productive. But it meant that not only their working lives but also their family lives were spent in the most congested part of the kingdom. As late as the middle of the eighteenth century, it was taken for granted that "home" and "work" were virtually inseparable. Even the wealthiest bankers conducted their business from their homes; great merchants lived, in effect, above the shop, with goods stored in their cellars and apprentices living in the attics. This identity of home and work was the basic building block of eighteenth century urban ecology. It seemed to be so deeply ingrained in the lives of the London bourgeoisie that any fundamental separation of home and work was deemed impossible. So, the elite of bankers and merchants who traded with the whole world found their domestic lives restricted to a few blocks in the most congested area in the kingdom.[5]

The rich, at least, could afford the high costs of living in the core. The poor, often forced to crowd whole families into a single, stifling room, naturally sought the cheaper land and rents on the outskirts—but their expansion was limited. Neither the government nor private landowners had any desire to see the "disreputable" suburbs expand. Instead, the authorities attempted to respond to these conditions by prohibiting new building on the outskirts. In 1580 a royal proclamation forbade all new building within three miles of the city; and within that zone subdivision of existing houses into rooms for the poor was also forbidden.[6]

These decrees were periodically reissued in the seventeenth century, good evidence that they were often ignored. But far more effective than this governmental action was the reluctance of landowners to subdivide their properties for so despised a population. The land around London's edges was generally held in large tracts by aristocratic landowners or powerful institutions. They restricted their conversion of agricultural land into building land to speculations likely to attract a wealthy clientele, most notably the elegant new squares that were rising in the West End of London.

For the suburban poor, the limitations on growth meant that their districts were at least as crowded as the center. Some expansion did occur, especially in the south and east, where cottages pushed out along the roads toward such villages as Islington—themselves filling up—which lay just a few miles outside the city. But the description in the 1580 proclamation against urban expansion remained descriptive of suburbs "where there are great multitudes of People brought to inhabit in small rooms; whereof a great part are seen very poor; yea such as must live by Begging or by worse means; and they [are] heaped up together, and in a Sort smothered with many Families of Children and Servants in one House or small Tenement."[7] When the city as a whole grew slowly or not at all, this crowding was the problem of the poor alone. But when London began its explosive growth, the peripheral areas acted like an inelastic container for the rapidly expanding core. Inevitably, all districts grew more crowded, including the areas of privilege at the center.

I should emphasize here that even the relatively wealthy core areas were never upper-class neighborhoods in the modern sense. Just as the idea of a district devoted to a single function— a residential district or a business district—was foreign to the premodern city, so too was a single-class district. In the medieval city, still relatively uncrowded, the presence of highly valued open space—monastic gardens or private courtyards—mitigated the crowding of narrow streets and a dense population. But as London grew, these precious spaces were usually filled by buildings. By the mid eighteenth century the city was clearly approaching an ecological crisis. The few examples of improvements—such as the filling in of the Fleet Ditch, a stream that had become a noisome sewer—could hardly keep pace with the difficulties. The streets, for example, were drained only by a "kennel" or ditch running down the middle, which was usually filled with rubbish and worse. A visitor to London in 1765 noticed that

> In the most beautiful part of the Strand [then London's most fashionable street] . . . I have, during my whole stay in London, seen the middle of the street constantly foul with a dirty puddle to the height of three or four inches; a puddle whose splashings cover those who walk on foot, fill coaches where their windows happen not to be up, and bedaub all the lower parts of such houses as are exposed to it.[8]

One can readily imagine the state of less fashionable streets.

Thus the economics of the great city were attracting an increasingly wealthy elite to an urban core that was, at best, crowded, dirty, noisy, and unhealthy. In other centuries these conditions might have been tolerated even by the elite. The eighteenth century, however, was an "age of improvement" in which leaders were constantly seeking a better order for life, whether in government, manufacturing, or cities. In retrospect we can see that there were two alternative models for this improvement. The first was for the elite to take possession of an area at or close to the core and rebuild it according to the most elegant eighteenth century models. The second was the far more radical decentralization of bourgeois residence that we have come to call suburbanization.

So deeply held were the traditional ideas of urban form—most notably, the identification of the elite with the urban core—that for most of the eighteenth century only the reconstruction of the core seemed possible and likely. An excellent model for such a reconstruction was at hand in the London square. In the early seventeenth century Inigo Jones brought back from Italy the idea of a rectangular piazza or square made up of elegant townhouses of unified design, an embodiment of order, space, and commodiousness in a disorderly city. He designed Covent

Garden for the Earl of Bedford in 1630; the houses there were intended not for the merchants of the City but for members of the aristocracy and gentry who came to London from their main residences in the country for the spring Season to conduct parliamentary business and social pleasure.[9]

During the Restoration the London square took hold both as an architectural model and as the favored means of development for the aristocratic landowners who wished to increase their revenues from the land they owned in Bloomsbury or Westminster. The squares were successful in attracting the aristocracy or gentry for which they were designed; yet it took at least fifty years for Jones's concept of order and cleanliness to be understood and acted upon. The Bedford estate saw no better use for the open space in the center of Covent Garden than to rent it for a market so that, in Thomas Babington Macaulay's words, "fruit women screamed, carters fought, cabbage-stalks and rotten apples accumulated in heaps at the thresholds of the Countess of Berkshire and of the Bishop of Durham."[10]

Even as the new squares were built in Westminster—then the western edge of the city and the site of both Parliament and the royal palace—they could not keep out the city around them. St. James's Square, Macaulay reports, "was a receptacle for all the offal and cinders, for all the dead cats and dead dogs of Westminster."[11] It was not until the 1720s and the 1730s that the great aristocratic estates mastered the design formulas of the city square, including unified house facades—often with a central pediment to give each side of the square a "palace facade"—and an elegant open space with an enclosed formal garden at its center.

These squares were built for the aristocracy and landed gentry, but it seemed inevitable that similar squares and streets closer to the City would become the homes of the merchant elite. John Gwynn, author of *London and Westminster Improved* (1766), put forward a plan for what we would today call urban renewal that illustrates very well the conventional expectations of his time. He proposed to cut long, straight streets through the dense urban fabric of the City, streets that would serve both for communication and as suitable locations for the merchants' townhouses. These "spacious, elegant" streets, Gwynn believed, would keep the merchants in the core where they belonged, away from the Westminster squares of "persons of quality, whose manner of living and pursuits are totally unsuitable to men of business," and also in close contact with the working poor.

> In settling a plan of large streets for the dwelling of the rich, it will be found necessary to allot smaller spaces contiguous, for the habitations of useful and laborious people, whose dependence on their superiors requires such a distribution; and by adhering to this principle, a political advantage will result to the nation; as this intercourse stimulates their industry, improves their morals by example and prevents any particular part from being the habitation of the indigent alone, to the great detriment of private property.[12]

In rebuilding the core, Gwynn also proposed a limit on building at the periphery. Thus, he writes, "a most elegant line would be formed round the metropolis, and the adjacent fields compose a beautiful lawn, and make an agreeable finish to the extreme parts of town."[13]

Gwynn's plans aptly illustrate the hold of traditional ideas of urban form on even the most ambitious improvers. He takes for granted the idea of keeping the merchants at the core; preserving mixed neighborhoods; and even limiting the size of the metropolis. It is in this context that we can understand the true originality of the suburban idea: for the modern suburb involved discarding the old preference for center over periphery; radically disassociating home and work environments; creating neighborhoods based both on the idea of a single class and on that of a single (domestic) function; and, finally, creating a new kind of landscape in which the clear line that Gwynn and others had hoped to draw between city and country becomes thoroughly blurred in an environment that combines the two.

All these transformations were involved when, in the mid eighteenth century, the London merchant elite began to convert their combined homes and offices at the core into offices only; and then to move with their families not to adjacent urban squares but as much as five miles outside the city to spacious villas in the quiet agricultural settlements that ringed London. As we can now appreciate, this flight from the city was in fact a new and highly potent form of urban expansion.

The merchant elite leaped over the belt of poverty that had constrained the metropolis and used their wealth to establish a new kind of rapidly expanding urban periphery, which we now call suburbia. They realized that, with their private carriages and ample funds, they were no longer limited to the area traditionally considered the city. On the relatively inexpensive land still a surprisingly short commute to the core, they could build a world of privilege, leisure, and family life that reflected their values.

As I have already emphasized, this radical rethinking of the meaning of the city and of domesticity was not the work of a single architect of genius, who proposed a new model and then convinced his clients of its worth. Rather, suburbia was a collective creation of the city's bourgeois elite, a gradual adoption of a new way of living by a class that had the wealth and confidence to remake the world to suit its values.

It was, indeed, this class that was transforming society in so many other ways as it reshaped the world to fulfill its needs. Suburbia was only one characteristic bourgeois invention, but one that has had a remarkable influence on the modern world. To understand suburbia—both in its earliest eighteenth century form and in its twentieth century incarnations—we must now look closely at the class that created it.

The London Bourgeoisie and Their City

Every true suburb is the outcome of two opposing forces, an attraction toward the opportunities of the great city and a simultaneous repulsion against urban life. This conflict, now deeply embedded in suburban design, first arose out of the tensions in the eighteenth century London bourgeoisie's feelings toward their metropolis. Every year made the city more important economically, yet, in the course of the eighteenth century, the very bourgeoisie who profited most from London's centralization came to hate and fear the social consequences of city life.

Suburbia can never be understood solely in its own terms. It must always be defined in relation to its rejected opposite: the metropolis. If the eighteenth century creators of suburbia bequeathed to their successors their positive ideal of a family life in union with nature, they also passed on their deepest fears of living in an inhumane and immoral metropolis. Buried deep within every subsequent suburban dream is a nightmare image of eighteenth century London.

But before elaborating this bourgeois critique of the city, we must first define the London "bourgeoisie" itself. I use the term to designate those most prosperous members of the middle class whose businesses and capital accumulation—at least £25,000 to more than £100,000—gave them an income comparable to the rural squirearchy and even to some of the aristocracy, yet who maintained the living and working habits of the urban middle class.[14] The London bourgeoisie stood at the apex of a great middle-class hierarchy which stretched upward from the mass of humble shopkeepers and artisans who formed its base. Higher on the scale were the proprietors of fashionable shops whose expensive stock could attract aristocratic patronage; and those master craftsmen who, with apprentices and journeymen, manufactured and sold those articles of luxury or skill which made London craftsmanship world famous. The greatest of these craftsmen-businessmen certainly belonged to the bourgeoisie: for example, Thomas Chippendale, who designed, built, and sold his famous furniture in his own house (and three adjacent houses) on St. Martin's Lane.[15]

Nevertheless, a member of the London bourgeoisie was characteristically a merchant engaged in overseas trade and the financial operations that accompanied it. Sugar from the West Indies, tea from China, spices from India, furs from North

America, naval stores from Russia and the Baltic—these were among the immensely profitable items that filled bourgeois storehouses. A relatively small circle of entrepreneurs controlled the vast revenues that derived ultimately from Britain's naval and colonial supremacies. This group was confined to those who held directorships in one of the chartered companies, such as the East India Company; to members of the prestigious "livery companies" of the City; to those elected to be one of the 24 aldermen or 200 common councilmen of the City; and to those who intermarried among other London merchant families or their counterparts in the provinces.[16]

This merchant elite often possessed yearly incomes of more than £10,000—incomes worthy of an aristocrat and enough to make even the mothers of Jane Austen's heroines take notice. It is important to note, however, that in Jane Austen's world of the rural elite a gentleman's income came largely from the rents of land he owned, and thus it was virtually guaranteed. But the merchant's capital was constantly at risk, which required his constant presence in London.

As London emerged as the world city of the eighteenth century, its port had become a unique center for the all-important exchange of information. The very density of the City permitted and encouraged that intense face-to-face contact which—in the absence of timely and reliable published information—enabled London merchants to find out about market conditions throughout Britain and the world in advance of their competitors elsewhere. Within the crowded streets of the City there existed a unique store of expertise: shipping, insurance, brokerage, commercial banking. To be a merchant meant to be in constant, informal touch with all these potential sources of useful information. Even a location half a mile from the City drastically diminished one's potential contacts. Thus there was a strong attraction—H. G. Wells's whirlpool effect—drawing merchants from lesser cities into the metropolis and drawing all London merchants as close to the crowded center as possible.

If a seemingly inevitable logic drew merchants' premises as close as possible to the center, an equally compelling logic associated the family with the workplace. Even for the wealthy elite of merchants and bankers, the family was not simply (or perhaps even primarily) an emotional unit. It was at least equally an economic unit. The merchant's capital was essentially a family resource; his work force was his family—including his wife and older children—as well as apprentices who lived in the house and were treated like children. Virtually every aspect of family life was permeated by the requirements of the business.

This interpenetration is most clearly visible in the active role played by women in London commercial life. A wife's daily assistance in the shop was vital for smaller businesses, and even the most opulent merchants were careful to give their wives a role sufficiently prominent that they could participate in and understand the source of their income. As Daniel Defoe explains this practice in his *English Tradesman*, the worst threat to the family was the husband's death. Only if the wife had the competence to carry on the business could the capital be passed down to the next generation. Defoe therefore recommends the closest cooperation between husband and wife at the same time that he criticizes the merchant who is "foolishly vain of making his wife a gentlewoman," keeping her out of the counting room.[17]

The typical merchant's townhouse, therefore, was surprisingly open to the city. Commercial life flowed in freely, so that virtually every room had some business as well as familial function. From the front parlor where customers were entertained and deals transacted, to the upper stories where the apprentices slept and the basement where goods were stored, there was little purely domestic space. As apprentices, teenage boys were inevitably drawn into this system, either within their own homes or as part of another family; at the same time, teenage girls were taught the necessary skills for playing their part in their future husband's business.

The whole family, not just the adult men, were thus firmly anchored to the business life of the urban core. And, if the commerce of the city entered freely into the house, the family members were all in their various ways deeply immersed in the wider life of communication and sociability that took place outside the home. The tavern or coffee house were at least as important to the merchant as his own home. Each group had its own gathering place where, in the midst of conversation, crucial information was exchanged and deals transacted. Lloyd's of London, for example, began as just such a coffee house on Tower Street, where insurance brokers customarily met.[18]

Beyond this business-related activity, there was a surprising amount of social interaction that took all the family members out of the house and also deeply enmeshed them in London life. The men had their drinking clubs which met regularly in the private rooms of the taverns; and even the apprentices had a kind of teenage culture organized around their own drinking and boating clubs. Defoe was (or affected to be) scandalized by the freedom with which fathers allowed their sons and apprentices to go out at night to taverns, a freedom that he explained by the constant presence of the fathers at these same taverns.[19]

For women, the comparable institution was "visiting," which took them to friends' houses throughout the city for tea and conversation. Even teenage girls were allowed a similar freedom to move through the city on their own "visits" (if Defoe, who condemned the practice, can be believed).[20] In addition, the three legitimate London theaters—Drury Lane, Covent Garden, and the Haymarket—were patronized by the middle class, who also were among the dancers at such elegant ballrooms as the Carlisle House in Soho Square and the Pantheon on Oxford Street.[21]

Children too were allowed to seek their amusements in the streets and other public places of the city. Their games were street games, their entertainment provided by puppeteers and Punch-and-Judy shows. Far from isolating children from the raucous London world, parents often took them to adult theaters and pleasure grounds.[22]

At the summit of this intense London social life were the two amusement gardens at Vauxhall and Ranelagh. These privately owned establishments provided landscaped grounds for strolling, elegant cafés for dining, and halls and bands for dancing. The eighteenth century had not yet experienced that essentially Victorian segregation of social life that restricted each class to its equals and completely excluded the disreputable. At Ranelagh and Vauxhall middle-class women mingled with duchesses and whores. These gardens were pure public space: places to see and be seen, and to enjoy the spectacle of London life. Here density and communication became aestheticized; the city was revealed to itself as a scene to be enjoyed.[23]

This involvement on many levels with the city seemed to overcome the dangers and the discomforts of urban living and to preclude any "bourgeois flight." Perhaps even more than men, middle-class eighteenth century women had seized the "freedom of the city" to make themselves at home in both the counting house and the ballroom. And both men and women benefited from the extraordinary openness of the city, the remarkable range of experiences that were possible. Not all of these experiences were purely frivolous. It was, after all, Samuel Johnson's London (and James Boswell's). Many of the men's clubs encouraged serious conversation and learning; middle-class women read the classics, played the harpsichord or the violin; indeed, according to one censorious moralist, some shopkeeper's wives even studied philosophy.[24] One can understand why John Gwynn's "improvements" of 1766 called for the bourgeoisie to remain in the city and in close touch with its varied population.

Nevertheless, the mid eighteenth century saw a crucial change in bourgeois attitudes toward the city that led directly to suburbanization. This growing repulsion was not, I think, the inexorable result of any drastic social change in the city itself. Despite the population growth and resulting overcrowding, London remained a city of commerce and small workshops. The Industrial Revolution, just beginning in the north of England, essentially bypassed London until the middle of the nineteenth century. Crime was serious, but there is no evidence that it was increasing dramatically; the lighting of streets at night had somewhat increased safety. Transportation within and outside the city remained restricted to stage coaches and private carriages traveling on still primitive roads.[25] There was nothing in the eighteenth century comparable in severity to those awful seventeenth century disasters: the Great Plague of 1665 and the Fire of 1666.

The crucial changes occurred instead within bourgeois culture, within that complex of attitudes which defined the meaning of the city. The most important of them concerned the family; but I would also point to a subtle yet pervasive shift in the relation of the middle class to the rest of the city population. Anyone looking at eighteenth century life must be struck by what Ian Watt has called "the combination of physical proximity and vast social distance."[26] English society was still something of a caste society in the sense that social distance was so marked that the privileged felt no need to protect themselves further from the poor by physical distance. That the richest bankers in London lived literally surrounded by poor families did not in the least diminish the bankers' status. One might even say that in a caste society the rich need the constant and close presence of the poor to remind them of their privileges.

In the course of the eighteenth century, this attitude slowly began to move closer to the nineteenth century idea that social distinctions require physical segregation. Part of the change was no doubt due to differing personal habits of the rich and poor, especially over personal cleanliness, that great divide of disgust which would culminate in the Victorian adage George Orwell reports hearing when he was young: "The lower classes smell."[27] One can sense the mingled sexual and social unease in the passage quoted in the introduction about the proximity of "two or three brawny naked curriers" disturbing a lady's spiritual thoughts.

In any case, it is one of the paradoxes of urban history that the extremely unequal cities of the eighteenth century tolerated a great measure of close physical contact between rich and poor; whereas the more "equal" cities of the nineteenth and twentieth centuries were increasingly zoned to eliminate such

contacts. For our purposes, the newly felt need for social segregation made the crowded, intensely mixed neighborhoods of
the urban core appear all the more unpleasant and threatening
to the bourgeoisie. Social segregation destroyed many of the
most prized sites of eighteenth century urban social life: the
pleasure gardens lost patronage largely because the respectable
no longer wished to mix with "low" company. And the desire
for segregation fueled that search for single-class neighborhoods
securely protected from the poor which was to become a powerful motive in the spread of suburbia.

Even more fundamental was the profound change in the
bourgeois family, which began as early as the last quarter of
the seventeenth century and fully emerged in the mid eighteenth century. Lawrence Stone, in his important book *The
Family, Sex and Marriage in England, 1500–1800,* has called this
new bourgeois form "the closed domesticated nuclear family."
He refers essentially to the emergence of the family as the primary and overwhelming emotional focus of its members' lives.
For Stone, this "modern" family is not a natural biological unit
that has remained constant through history but the product of
a long historical evolution. From medieval times to the sixteenth
century, he argues, the family was "open" in the sense that
"outside" influences from neighbors and kin outweighed internal ties among the "nucleus" of father, mother, and children.
In the older family,

> members of the nuclear family were subordinated to the will of its
> head, and were not closely bonded to each other by warm affective
> ties. They might well feel closer to other members of the kin, to
> fellow members of a guild, or to friends and neighbors of the same
> sex whom they met daily in an ale-house. . . . [The family] was also
> very short-lived, being frequently dissolved by the death of husband
> or wife, or the death or early departure from the home of the
> children. So far as the individual members were concerned, it was
> neither very durable, nor emotionally or sexually very demanding.[28]

By the eighteenth century, however, one can see among the
urban bourgeoisie (and also, more slowly, the rural gentry) a

new intensity in the relations of father, mother, and children. The increasing personal autonomy that merchant capitalism both encouraged and required led to the diminishing importance of kin groups and to greater opportunities for both men and women to select their own mates on the basis of romantic attraction. Husbands and wives grew closer and more equal: the "companionate marriage." Increasing longevity led to longer marriages and to a greater emotional investment in children now more likely to survive. All these trends deeply intensified the emotional bonds that united family members. The result was Stone's "closed, domesticated nuclear family"; closed in around itself, separated from its environment, focused especially on mutual intimacy and on child raising.

The importance of this new kind of family for this book is that the essential principles of the closed family contradicted the basic principles of the eighteenth century city. Just as the traditional urban ecology was unable to cope with the demands of modern growth, so the traditional urban form and domestic architecture were contrary to the needs of the new family. As we have seen, even the most opulent merchant's house was essentially open to the city; it provided little or no privacy for the emergence of a closed sphere of emotional intimacy. Further, the constant presence of urban amusements drew the family away from its domesticated attachments and into the older, wider networks of urban amusements.

This contradiction between the city and the new family was further sharpened by a religious movement that took hold with special strength among the upper middle class of London: the Evangelical movement. It first arose in the early eighteenth century as a response within the Anglican church to John Wesley's renewed emphasis on personal salvation. By the second half of the eighteenth century, however, the emphasis of its leaders had shifted to promoting a new ideal of conduct that emphasized the role of the family. One might call the Evangelicals the ideologists of the closed, domesticated nuclear family.[29]

"God Almighty has set before me two great objects," wrote William Wilberforce, the leading Evangelical author in 1787, "the suppression of the slave trade and the reformation of manners."[30] The role of Wilberforce and his fellow Evangelicals in the abolitionist movement is still justly celebrated. Their role in "manners" is less well remembered, though G. M. Young has observed that "the imponderable pressure of the Evangelical discipline . . . at every turn controlled and animated" English culture.[31] The Evangelicals were the most influential group in creating that complex of attitudes which we now call Victorianism, but which in fact originated in the late eighteenth century. Members of the Established church but uncertain of its efficacy, the Evangelicals taught that the most secure path to salvation was the beneficent influence of a truly Christian family. Anything that strengthened the emotional ties within the family was therefore holy; anything that weakened the family and its ability to foster true morality was anathema.

Chief among the enemies of the family was the city, with its social opportunities. Wilberforce's "reformation of manners" was essentially a broad attack on all forms of urban pleasures. He himself, a member of Parliament and wealthy heir of a distinguished mercantile family from Hull, resigned all his memberships in London clubs immediately after his conversion to the Evangelical cause in 1784. Attendance at the theater, he advised, was "most pernicious" and "directly contrary to the laws of God."[32] As to "balls, concerts, cards, etc.," they might be tolerated "not as amusements to be enjoyed, but temptations to be undergone."[33] The Evangelical movement went on to attack street fairs, taverns, ballrooms, pleasure gardens—the whole range of urban amusements, even the lottery. Whatever they could not close down entirely they attempted to prohibit on Sunday.

Perhaps the most significant aspect of Evangelical ideology was the attitude toward women. On the one hand, they gave to women the highest possible role in their system of values: the principal guardian of the Christian home. On the other, they fanatically opposed any role for women outside that sphere. Wilberforce and his fellow Evangelicals were the first to my knowledge to reverse the traditional medieval notion that women were the "weaker vessel," creatures whose passions overpowered their wills, Eves and Jezebels quicker to sin than men. Women, as Wilberforce asserted to the contrary, were "naturally more disposed to Religion than men."[34]

This natural disposition was a sign of providence, for men's work necessarily exposed them to the evils of the city. Women, however, could and must escape this taint by restricting themselves to the home and devoting themselves to their God-given functions: the education of children and the emotional and religious support of their husbands. "This more favorable disposition to Religion in the female sex," writes Wilberforce,

> was graciously designed also to make women doubly valuable in the wedded state: and it seems to afford to the married man the means of rendering an active share in the business of life more compatible, than it would otherwise be, with the liveliest devotional feelings; that when the husband should return to his family, worn and harassed by worldly cares or professional labors, the wife, habitually preserving a warmer and more unimpaired spirit of devotion, than is perhaps consistent with being immersed in the bustle of life, might revive his languid piety.[35]

This restriction of women to the home was in fact an elevation to the only real priesthood that the Evangelicals recognized. "It is sure[ly] no mean or ignoble office which we would allot to the female sex," Wilberforce proclaimed, "when we . . . make them as it were the medium of our intercourse with the heavenly world."[36]

For women, these "faithful repositories of the religious principle," nothing was more degrading than contact with either the business or the social world. It was treason to their higher natures. Wilberforce reserved his special scorn for those young women hurrying "night after night to the resorts of dissipation," despising "the common comforts of the family circle."[37]

Wilberforce and his fellow Evangelical Hannah More were constantly concerned to redefine the education and values of eighteenth century bourgeois women to make them fit their new ideal. More had been a popular playwright and famous wit until her own conversion to Evangelical principles led her to despise her former life and to publicize this version of feminine virtue. In her *Strictures on Feminine Education*, More argues that the only valid education for women leads to skills in "home enjoyment," that capacity to please one's husband at home in order to overcome a man's natural passion for outside amusements. More advised women to overcome a man's passion for clubs with "a passion of a different nature, which Providence has kindly planted within us; I mean, by inspiring [a man] with the love of fireside enjoyment." Once this preference for "the almost sacred quiet of a virtuous home" had been instilled by a wife, a man's heart "would compare its interesting domestic scene with the vapid pleasures of public resort, till it would fly to its own home, . . . not from duty but delight."[38] More further develops her ideas in her very popular *Cælebs in Search of a Wife*, a novel in which a man who has accepted Evangelical principles goes in search of the perfect Evangelical woman. This book is a kind of tract directed against what More calls "the exhibiting, the displaying" woman. As the young suitor says of his ideal, "she is *not* a professed beauty; she is *not* a professed genius, she is *not* a professed philosopher, she is *not* a professed anything. . . . She is, from nature—a woman, gentle, feeling, animated, modest. —She is, by education, elegant, informed, enlightened. —She is, from religion, pious, humble, candid, charitable."[39]

In practice this portrait means a woman entirely concerned with her home, as skillful in household management as in teaching the young, and constantly striving to better the moral and religious states of the whole family. She must be sufficiently well informed to be a good companion to her husband, but not so well educated that she might seek to display outside the home what she has learned. "You will want a COM-PANION," says one character in *Cælebs* to the young man seeking a wife. "An ARTIST you may hire."[40] An Evangelical wife's only "outside" interest is charity work among the local poor. "I have often heard it regretted," More declared, "that ladies have no stated employment, no profession. It is a mistake, *Charity is the calling of a lady; the care of the poor is her profession.*"[41]

If the eighteenth century city was poorly adapted to the needs of the "closed, domestic nuclear family," it was even more at odds with the heightened Evangelical interpretation of the "closed" family and the sheltered woman. When Wilberforce spoke of the devoted wife reviving the languid piety of her harassed husband when he returned home from work, he ignored the fact that, for most of his readers, home and work were still under the same roof. A wife was immersed in the very same "bustle of life" as her husband. Hannah More's "sacred quiet of a virtuous home" was broken by the bargaining of customers in the front parlor, the rough language of apprentices upstairs, the merriment of the tavern at the corner, the hammerings of the workmen in the shop next door; the presence, within blocks, of theaters, ballrooms, and worse.

This contradiction between the city and the Evangelical ideal of the family provided the final impetus for the unprecedented separation of the citizen's home from the city that is the essence of the suburban idea. The city was not just crowded, dirty, and unhealthy; it was immoral. Salvation itself depended on separating the woman's sacred world of family and children from the profane metropolis. Yet this separation could not jeopardize a man's constant attendance at his business—for hard work and success were also Evangelical virtues—and business life required rapid personal access to that great beehive of information which was London. This was the problem, and suburbia was to be the ultimate solution.

CHAPTER 2

Building the

Bourgeois Utopia

T HE London bourgeoisie did not suddenly abandon their city townhouses for a wholly new form of residence, the suburb. There was a crucial intermediate stage: the weekend villa. From the early eighteenth century it was the custom for the London middle class to own a "villa" or "box" in the picturesque countryside around the metropolis and for the whole family to "retire" there each Saturday afternoon, returning Monday morning. The modern suburb began when the merchant elite shifted its primary residence to the weekend villa, allowing the women and children of the family to remain wholly separate from the contagions of London while the merchants themselves commuted daily from their villas to London by private carriage.

The weekend villa was thus the crucial bridge between traditional bourgeois living patterns and the new era of suburbanization. It made possible a gradual transition between old and new, because innovation was limited to adapting already existing structures to new functions. What I have termed the "collective creation" of suburbia by the bourgeoisie was accomplished through what the anthropologist Claude Lévi-Strauss has called *bricolage*, after the way a handyman or *bricoleur* creates a new structure with whatever materials are already at hand.[1]

The various kinds of weekend houses were the ready-made materials from which the bourgeoisie created suburbia. We must therefore look closely at this transitional stage, because its forms amount to a kind of "deep structure" in the language of suburban design. Suburbia has inherited its characteristic design from the range of architectural styles, landscaping, and cultural associations that defined the eighteenth century merchant's villa.

The origins of the English bourgeois villa go back as far as the sixteenth century, when merchants like Thomas Gresham, with close connections at court, built elaborate mansions in the countryside outside London while retaining their traditional residences in the City. Gresham's Osterley Park clearly imitates the elaborate mansions of those aristocrats whose principal income or power derived from their position at court and who had therefore built their seats not in the midst of their ancestral acres but in close proximity to the palaces of Westminster.[2] After the disruptions of the Civil War, the Plague, and the Fire in the seventeenth century, the custom of owning a villa spread to the merchant elite who had no particular contact with the court. "How many noble seats, superior to the palaces of sovereign princes, in some countries, do we see erected within a few miles of this city, by tradesmen," Daniel Defoe exulted with some exaggeration.[3] The villas he referred to were not in fact like palaces; nevertheless, they possessed the same substantial size and comfort as the houses of the rural landowning elite. And, except for the summer, these houses were used only from Saturday afternoon to Monday morning.

We can best comprehend the scale of the more elaborate merchant's villas from an advertisement that appeared in the London *Daily Advertiser* of 1774:

A very valuable estate, suitable for a Merchant or any genteel Family, in a most delightful and healthful situation at Layton, near Walthamstow, in Essex, about five miles from Town, being on a rising ground and commands a fine prospect: consisting of a spacious and substantial Brick Mansion, Wings adjoining with a large Court Yard, Coach-yard, two excellent six-stall stables, and other stabling for eight horses. Four Coach Houses, large Kitchen and Pleasure Gardens, with fine shady Walls, Shrubberies handsomely laid out, the Walls and Garden well stocked with choice Fruit Trees, Fishponds and Canals . . . likewise a good Farm Yard detached from the Mansion with a large barn etc., the whole containing 33 acres and a half.[4]

The appeal is obvious: here a merchant can be an aristocrat on weekends. The advertisement exactly defines the style of the eighteenth century rural elite: the large house on a hill with a view; horses, gardens, food from one's own farm. The great distinction is that, with a true country house belonging to the rural gentry or aristocracy, this establishment would be the headquarters for large landholdings, not thirty-three and a half but hundreds of acres, usually leased to working farmers. The rents from these broad acres would provide the basic income to support such an aristocratic country house.

For the merchant's villa, however, we have the form of the aristocratic country house without its economic underpinnings. Everything pleasurable and prestigious has been retained; only the income producing acreage is missing. The merchant's earnings from the counting house support a (weekend) life-style wholly at odds with the urban culture that generated that income. One might treat this phenomenon as an example of bourgeois subservience to aristocratic styles, that disposition to "love a lord" of which the English middle class has been frequently accused. There was indeed a large portion of envy of the "country gentleman" in these weekend villas, an envy that was perhaps inevitable in view of the rural elite's tight hold on power and prestige within eighteenth century English society.

Yet, the meaning of the eighteenth century bourgeois villa was more complex than simple imitation of the aristocracy. As

Nicholas Rogers has shown in his study of the eighteenth century London bourgeoisie, the mid eighteenth century merchant displayed a far greater loyalty to the merchant's calling than did his predecessors of the late seventeenth century. Far fewer used the fortune they had accumulated in trade to buy a large country estate—and the massive, expensive land holdings that went with it—in order to retire from business and set themselves or their children up as genuine landed gentlemen living on agricultural rents. Instead, they kept their capital in trade and themselves in London, using the profits from the booming business to maintain what Rogers calls an "urban genteel style," which included the pleasures of London, visits to spas like Bath—and a villa.[5]

In this context we can see the weekend villa as an attempt by the London bourgeoisie to appropriate the prestige and the pleasures of the aristocracy while keeping their class pride—and their merchant's capital—intact. There was no need to sell out to the aristocracy in order to enjoy (at least intermittently) the finest fruits of the aristocratic life. They could remain merchants and yet possess a country house typical of the most genteel society: hence their obstinate pride in deserting these opulent estates in order for the whole family to return to London on Monday morning. The habit affirmed their identity. Defoe, for example, praises a merchant who settled his family in a villa during the summer, but stayed in London himself. Each afternoon he went out to the country for dinner with his family, and each evening he returned to London to make sure that the apprentices had closed up properly and were out of mischief.[6]

By the mid eighteenth century, the ownership of a substantial weekend villa was routinely mentioned as one of the defining characteristics of London's most substantial merchants. "In all seasons," wrote one visitor, "the London merchants generally retire to the country on Saturdays, and do not return till Monday at Change-time."[7] We can gauge the strength of the movement by that surest of tests: imitation. More modest shopkeepers strove to secure the modest "boxes" that lined the roads out of the city. "A London tradesman is as well acquainted with Turnham-Green or Kentish-Town [both then agricultural villages that were among the favored sites for villas] as Fleet Street or Cheapside," wrote one observer in 1754.[8]

There is good evidence that many eighteenth century contemporaries saw this middle-class move into the countryside as a kind of presumption. The London satirists, fierce defenders of established values, could only see a clumsy imitation of aristocratic fashions by plebeians incapable of understanding them. The "citizen in his villa" became a favorite target, as prints depicted grossly overweight merchants and their wives clumsily ill at ease in villas that combined every current fashion without an ounce of true taste.

One writer describes an imaginary visit to such a villa. He portrays it as "pleasantly situated about three miles from London, on the side of a public road, from which it is separated by a dry ditch, over which is a little bridge consisting of two narrow planks, leading to the house. The hedge on the other side of the road cuts off all prospect whatever, except from the garrets, from whence indeed you have a beautiful vista of two men hanging in chains on Kennington Common." After a brief tour of the garden, the visitor is ushered into the house, where he sees in the parlor a portrait of the lady of the house "in the habit of a shepherdess, smelling to a nosegay, and stroking a ram with gilt horns."[9]

A poem with a similar theme recounts the saga of the City merchant "Sir Thrifty" who is pressed by his wife (envious of their neighbor Sir Traffick's country house) to purchase a house so that

> . . . ev'ry trav'ller in amaze,
> Should on our little mansion gaze,
> And pointing to the choice retreat
> Cry, "That's Sir Thrifty's country-seat."

Inevitably, Sir Thrifty yields, not only purchasing the house but allowing his wife to renovate it in the latest (1750s) styles: chinoiserie and "Gothick."

The trave'ller with amazement sees
A temple, Gothic or Chinese,
With many a bell and tawdry rag on,
And crested with a sprawling dragon.
A Wooden arch is bent astride
A ditch of water four feet wide;
With angles, curves, and zig-zag lines,
From Halfpenny's exact designs. . . .
    The villa thus completely graced,
All own that Thrifty has a taste;
And Madam's female friends and cousins,
With Common-council-men by dozens
Flock ev'ry Sunday to the seat,
To stare about them and to eat.[10]

On a somewhat more serious note, Samuel Johnson recounts the story of a modest tradesman who "thought himself rich enough to have a lodging in the country, like the mercers of Ludgate Hill. . . . I found him at Islington, in a room which overlooked the high road, amusing himself with looking through the window, which the clouds of dust would not suffer him to open. He embraced me, told me I was welcome into the Country, and asked me, if I did not feel myself refreshed."[11] Johnson goes on to reflect on the vanity of human wishes.

These satires had no effect on the middle-class conquest of the land around London. The bourgeoisie overlooked or ignored the old division between town and country that had reserved the enjoyment of the latter to a landed elite. Nor did they consider that their occupations made them unworthy of a house that resembled the models of both ancient and modern prestige. As one defender of aristocratic privilege wrote,

If the taste for building increases with our opulence for the next century, we shall be able to boast of finer country-seats belonging to our shopkeepers, artificers, and other plebeians, than the most pompous descriptions of Italy or Greece have ever recorded. We read, it is true, of country-seats belonging to Pliny, Hortensius, Lucullus and other Roman [patricians]. . . . But . . . could any of their shoemakers or tailors boast a Villa?[12]

Such talk did not deter the bourgeoisie. They had won the trade of the whole world, and they saw no reason why they should not possess the most pleasant sites of the London countryside.

The aristocratic country seat was thus appropriated by the bourgeoisie as raw material in the *bricolage* that created suburbia. The real meaning of these estates—the supremacy of a landed elite deriving its income from agricultural rents—was transformed into something very different: the right of a merchant class to enjoy the same genteel culture as the aristocracy. Yet the influence of the aristocratic country houses survives even today in the basic suburban image of the substantial house surrounded by its own land; and, perhaps more deeply, in the implication that the land around a suburban house is not simply pretty space but the sign of superior social and economic status.

There was, however, another image central to the *bricolage* that built suburbia: the classical villa. As the references to Pliny, Hortensius, and Lucullus in the quotation above show, the eighteenth century could not think of a house in the country without recalling those classical antecedents—the villas of ancient Rome—and attempting to imitate them. This villa ideal overlapped to some degree with the country house ideal, but the attempt to revive something approaching the classical villa in the countryside outside London helped to define more sharply the distinctive style of the merchants' estates and, ultimately, the style of suburbia.

Indeed, there was some real connection between the *villae suburbanae* that ringed ancient Rome as early as the first century B.C. and the eighteenth century London villas. The Romans had established the pattern of a wealthy urban elite building opulent pleasure houses set in gardens in the picturesque countryside outside the city.[13] The villa idea was revived in the Renaissance, as merchants from each Italian city-state built their versions of classical villas outside the city, while retaining their palazzos within the walls. "The Florentines . . ." wrote the Venetian ambassador Foscari in 1530, "have built so many palaces, all so magnificent and sumptuous, outside the city, that together they would make a second Florence."[14]

The summit of Renaissance villa design was reached by Andrea Palladio (1508–80), whose name became synonymous in England with the purest classicism. He worked largely in the Venetian terra firma, the territory on the Italian mainland along the Brenta River that belonged to Venice. Some of his villas were built on large landholdings that Venetian capitalists bought to diversify their investments beyond trade; but the most famous, the Villa Rotonda, was a true *villa suburbana* designed for elegant leisure.[15] The house is the ultimate expression of civilization conceived as order: the plan a perfect square; each of the four facades with identical columned porticoes and pediments; all of the interior rooms arrayed symmetrically; and the whole surmounted by a perfectly circular dome set precisely over the middle of the square. A belvedere set on a hill, the Villa Rotonda looked out on an equally well ordered nature, the result of centuries of careful farming. Palladio's villas defined the villa ideal of the civilized house set in the midst of nature, designed for a leisurely contemplation that would combine the natural and the civilized virtues. "The ancient sages," Palladio wrote, "commonly used to retire to such places, where being oftentimes visited by their virtuous friends and relations, having houses, gardens, and such like pleasant places, and above all their virtues, they could easily attain to as much happiness as could be attained here below."[16] The path from the Villa Rotonda to the suburban tract house is a long and twisted one, but we cannot understand the latter without realizing that some small vestige of the former's ideal of the "civilized house in nature" survives in even the most modest suburban development.

The Palladian ideal was introduced into England first by Inigo Jones and then by Lord Burlington, who purchased Palladio's plans to the Villa Rotonda and built a free copy for himself at Chiswick in the heart of London's emerging suburban belt.[17] Equally influential was Alexander's Pope's villa at Twickenham on the Thames. Renaissance Italian in style, it inspired so many imitators (mostly wealthy merchants) that Horace Walpole was led to call the Thames "our Brenta."[18]

Yet the Palladian ideal underwent some crucial changes in its English incarnation, and they came eventually to be incorporated into suburbia. First, the rigors of Palladio's classicism were noticeably reduced in domestic design, and the English evolved a house type the "mellow and undated rightness"[19] (in Nikolaus Pevsner's phrase) of which has remained a touchstone for suburban architecture. The English Palladian house—known also as "Georgian," especially in the United States—was a substantial brick structure with a flat rectangular facade. Windows symmetrically placed around a central doorway give a properly balanced look to the facade. The massive columns and portico of the Villa Rotonda have shrunk to classical detailing on the facade: a central pediment set into the roof line (sometimes supported by columns) crowns the center of the facade, while the ornamented doorway with its pedimented entry and flanking columns proclaims the proper architectural taste of the owners.

Inside, a central hall is well-lit by a "Palladian window" on the landing of the staircase leading to the upper two stories. On the ground floor, large, well-lighted rooms lead off the hall: perhaps a formal drawing room on one side, a front parlor or library and a rear dining room on the other. The kitchen was either in the basement, as in the London townhouse, or in a separate wing in the rear. Although suburban design would soon provide more ornate and imaginative alternatives to the formality of the Palladian house, its elegant simplicity has never been forgotten.

If English Palladian house design remained relatively formal, the eighteenth century English garden constituted a radical break with Italian villa precedents and presented an important new concept of nature, one that would become the heart of suburban landscape architecture. For the Italian Renaissance, nature had nothing in common with "wilderness." Their ideal garden was as symmetrical and as formal as their villas. As James Ackerman has noted, "Nature was anathema to the Renaissance Italian except as ordered by man."[20] The aim of their plantings was to make "greenery behave in as elegant and unnatural fashion as a courtier at the Vatican."[21]

In the early eighteenth century a new ideal of landscape arose in England based on the idea of nature as *variety*. The straight lines and right angles of the old gardens would be replaced by gentle curves, the symmetries replaced by carefully planned irregularities. Trees, shrubs, and flowers would be allowed to "be themselves," to grow in their natural shape and to be planted in scatterings which sought to imitate the unaided work of nature. Instead of the strictly-delimited world of the Renaissance garden, the ideal was of an encompassing world of greenery and variety that extended into the most distant prospect.

To be sure, this new aesthetic had rules almost as rigid as the old. Its name the "picturesque" betrays its origins not in the direct appreciation of "nature" but in the imitation in real gardens and parks of the landscapes found in certain painters of the seventeenth century, most notably Claude Lorrain. Claude did not work "from nature" but from an idealized view of the classical age, which he sought to capture on his canvases. His was a vision of what Kenneth Clark has called "the most enchanting dream which has ever consoled mankind, the myth of the Golden Age in which man lived on the fruits of the earth, peacefully, piously, and with primitive simplicity."[22] This vision certainly enchanted and consoled the English upper classes. With the encouragement of cultural leaders like Pope and Lord Burlington and the genius of such landscape architects as William Kent, Lancelot "Capability" Brown, and Humphry Repton, the great landowners set out to create "parks" around their country houses that matched the ideal. All the resources of advanced agriculture were called into play to produce the appearance of unspoiled nature. The fences that had kept the animals out of the park were eliminated by narrow, hidden ditches called ha-has, which created the illusion of vast stretches of unfenced nature. Trees were cut down to create a "prospect"; others planted where nature was judged to be too monotonous; rivers were diverted to form ponds and winding streams in more propitious locations; and everywhere the straight was made crooked and the symmetrical irregular.

Raymond Williams has aptly judged the economic context of

this fashion for "picturesque," naturalistic landscapes when he remarks,

> The mathematical grids of the enclosure awards, with their straight hedges and straight roads, are contemporary with the natural curves and scatterings of the park scenery. And yet they are related parts of the same process—superficially opposed in taste only because in one case the land is being organized for production, where tenants and laborers will work, while in the other case it is being organized for consumption—the view, the ordered proprietary repose, the prospect.[23]

Land organized for consumption—here is the social basis of this style of landscape design and the source of its deep appeal for suburbia. It is as much a manmade landscape as the city; both are, in Le Corbusier's phrase, "the grip of man upon nature." But the picturesque landscape has been carefully designed to represent the consumption of the property by the viewer/owner, and this passive enjoyment is precisely the relationship of suburbia to its environment. The aesthetic of the picturesque has thus become the design language in which the idea of "a natural setting" has been expressed in the suburban setting, so much so that today we can hardly conceive of a suburb without the winding lanes and "scatterings of park scenery" that derive from it.

Nevertheless, if the picturesque was destined to become the language of the suburban landscape, it took a long process of assimilation for a form originally deployed on the broad acres of parks that surrounded an aristocratic country house to be adapted for use on the subdivided landscape of the modern suburb. Indeed, one might say that the whole design history advanced in this book from John Nash's Park Village (1824) and Victoria Park, Manchester (1837) through Frederick Law Olmsted's Riverside, Illinois (1868) and such twentieth century automobile suburbs as Clarence Stein and Henry Wright's Radburn, New Jersey (1928) consists of the progressive adaptation of the principles of large-scale landscaping in the picturesque style to the changing needs and tastes of the suburb.

The beginning of this assimilation occurred as early as the mid eighteenth century, when London merchants replanted the grounds of their weekend villas in the new style. Their model was surely Pope's garden at Twickenham, a marvel of miniaturization, which included all the basic elements of the picturesque (not even sparing the grotto).[24] From such examples as Pope's the picturesque spread to the mansions of the merchant elite and then inevitably to the more modest tradesmen and their boxes. Sir Thrifty's garden, satirized in the poem quoted earlier, boasts its "angles, curves, and zig-zag lines," and in 1750 the connoisseur Horace Walpole could complain, "There is not a citizen who doesn't take more pains to torture his acre and a half into irregularities than he formerly would have employed to make it as regular as his cravat."[25] Once again, the middle class were appropriating the style innovations of their betters, seizing a hitherto aristocratic environment and making it their own. The process that began at Twickenham was to end in Levittown.

By the second half of the eighteenth century all the elements were in place for the creation of the modern suburb. The bourgeoisie had successfully won a place in the countryside outside of London. Their wealth had given them access not only to land but to the basic elements of suburban design: substantial free-standing houses, elegant grounds, the cultural heritage of both the aristocratic country house and the villa based on classical models. Yet something more was needed to complete the *bricolage*: a new determination to make these villas something more than pleasant weekend retreats or ways for a greatly enriched class to display its wealth.

This new determination came from the increasing conflict I have already described between the bourgeois family and city life. The deep reaction against the metropolis as a proper setting for family life led some of the bourgeois elite—especially, as we shall see, those most profoundly affected by the Evangelical movement—to rethink the relation between their weekend villas and their urban townhouses. This new outlook meant, in the end, overturning the traditional concept of the house and its relation to work and to the city. These weekend villas outside London provided a ready-made alternative to the metropolitan core. So they became the setting for the more serious minded members of the bourgeoisie to create their own world of family centered values. Here they would build the bourgeois utopia.

Clapham, a Proper Paradise

In order to show more clearly the emergence of a true suburbia from the weekend houses of the London bourgeoisie, I will concentrate now on a single locale, the village of Clapham in Surrey, south of the Thames. Only five miles by a relatively good road to London Bridge and the City, it was nevertheless still open country in the mid eighteenth century, with one of the few commons left in the countryside near London and fine prospects of the Thames and the metropolis from nearby hills. It was near Clapham that Daniel Defoe stood in 1724 to get his sight of the metropolis, and even then he noted the presence of numerous opulent merchants' villas all around him.[26]

If Clapham was typical of the former agricultural villages that became the favored sites of middle class estates in the eighteenth century, it also had one notable feature that recommends it to our attention. It became the favored home of the most prosperous and most prominent leaders of the Evangelical movement; not only William Wilberforce but so many of his closest colleagues made their home here that the movement was often known as the "Clapham Sect." In Clapham we can follow the influence of Evangelical domestic ideology on the new domestic suburban architecture as it was actually built and lived in by these bourgeois "saints" of the movement. Both in its design and in its ideology, this modest village was to have a profound influence on the Anglo-American middle class.

The connection between Clapham and the Evangelicals arose from a large estate that the Thornton family purchased overlooking Clapham Common in 1735. The Thorntons exemplified that "big bourgeoisie" which would champion both the Evangelical movement and suburbia. Bankers and merchants in the trade with Russia, with close family connections to the textile merchants of Yorkshire, they were also known for their philanthropy. John Thornton (1720–90) was not only a director of the Bank of England but the patron of the favorite Evangelical poet, William Cowper. John's son Henry Thornton (1760–1815), one of the wealthiest bankers in London, was also one of the most religious. When in the 1790s he settled into his own mansion, Battersea Rise, at Clapham, he built next door a substantial house for his close friend, colleague in Parliament, and fellow Evangelical, William Wilberforce.[27]

The Thornton–Wilberforce connection attracted other leading Evangelicals from the same class. John Shore (Baron Teignmouth), president of the Bible Society and former governor-general of India, lived next door. John Grant, chairman of the directors of the East India Company, was another neighbor. Across the common lived the merchant and antislavery activist Zachary Macaulay, father of the historian Thomas Babington Macaulay, who grew up in Clapham. James Stephen, another Clapham Evangelical, was the patriarch of the Stephen family, whose members included Leslie Stephen in the nineteenth century and Virginia Stephen (Virginia Woolf) in the twentieth. Although Hannah More maintained a school with her sister in the countryside outside Bristol, she was a frequent visitor to the village.[28]

The presence of these prominent leaders attracted lesser known but equally pious and prosperous London merchants to Clapham. A map of 1800 depicts seventy-two "gentlemen's seats" around the common, all with substantial houses on grounds of at least ten acres.[29] All these gentlemen whom I have been able to trace through directories had second addresses in the City of London, for example, "John Brogden, Merchant, 143 Leadenhall St., officer in the Russia company."[30]

Because these merchants clearly retained their City town-houses (or similar premises) for business purposes after they had settled in Clapham, it is difficult to establish the exact moment they made their country residence their true abode on weekdays and weekends, and used the City establishment only as an office. Nevertheless, the evidence from letters, diaries, and other sources clearly indicates that as early as the 1790s Clapham had become a true suburb in my sense.[31] Families settled there throughout the week, the men maintaining that all-important direct tie to London by commuting each working day by private carriage. A new style of life had been established.

As the Clapham Evangelicals such as Wilberforce, More, and their colleagues were the very moralists who were loudest in their condemnation of the city and its vices, there can be little doubt that this final break with the merchant's traditional residence in the urban core was motivated by their rejection of the urban social mores, especially as they applied to women. A location like Clapham gave them the ability to take the family out of London without taking leave of the family business. Equally importantly, it provided a whole community of people who shared their values. Unlike the City of London, this community did not have to be shared with the urban poor; neither was its design restricted by urban crowding or by the high price of urban land. Around Clapham Common the Evangelicals could create their serious-minded paradise.

The design of this prototypical suburban community might be described as the union of the country house, the villa, and the picturesque traditions, reinforced by the particular concerns of the Evangelical movement. The Evangelicals never tired of repeating that, if all urban social life must be rejected, the truly godly recreations were family life and direct contact with nature. As William Cowper expressed it, in some of his most famous lines,

Domestic happiness, thou only bliss
Of Paradise that hast survived the fall!
. . .

God made the country and man made the town.
What wonder then that health and virtue, gifts
That can alone make sweet the bitter draught
That life holds out to all, should most abound
And least be threaten'd in the fields and groves
Possess ye, therefore, . . . your element.[32]

Hence it followed that Clapham must resemble as little as possible London, where, again in Cowper's words, ". . . works of man are cluster'd close around, / And works of God are hardly to be found"; and that it should preserve, in spite of its newfound popularity, as much of the countryside as possible.

In practice this goal meant rejecting the temptation to build connected rows of houses, squares, or any other urban forms and creating instead at least the picturesque illusion of the family in direct contact with nature. But, as villas clustered around the common, even the illusion became difficult to sustain. Remember that, even in the most favored locations, the earliest eighteenth century villas had never been numerous enough to define the landscape. They were scattered throughout the fields or perched on the edge of the old villages. Their charm and seclusion came in large part from their relative isolation. At Clapham, however, a new kind of landscape was forming out of the concentration of villas: the villa neighborhood. How to preserve Cowper's "fields and groves" in such a setting?

The solution to this problem not only served to create a true suburban style but also illustrates the idea of suburbia as a collective creation of the bourgeoisie. No form-giver arose to provide an instant answer; instead, the solution evolved through the first decade of the nineteenth century. First, the wealthy landowners who controlled the land around the common used that control to maintain an open setting. As land values rose to over £500 per acre, they did sell off some of their holdings, but only in units large enough to maintain the villa standard.[33]

The common provided another convenient way of maintaining the balance between houses and open space. At the end of the eighteenth century it was still "unimproved," and, in typical eighteenth century fashion, was filled at spots with "heaps of dung, ashes, building rubbish and other things of the like nature."[34] At the beginning of the nineteenth century the residents raised a subscription and commissioned a villa owner, Christopher Baldwin, to turn the "barren sweep" into a "delightful pleasure-ground," by planting it with trees, shrubs, flowers—all in the best naturalistic style. (Baldwin was rewarded when he sold some of his land that bordered the common at a premium price.)[35]

The other residents continued the style of the common on their own property. Contemporary drawings show wide tree shaded lawns sweeping up from the common to Palladian houses behind which large gardens and orchards were planted. Each house added its own well maintained greenery to the whole. What emerged was a collective environment extending not only to the common but to the villa grounds as well. The Evangelical village became an all encompassing park, an Edenic garden that surrounded the houses and made sweet the life of the families within them.

In the traditional country house or villa, the grounds related only to the centrally located house of the owner, who gazed out at his personal prospect. The true suburban landscape, as seen at Clapham, is a balance of the public and the private. Each property is private, but each contributes to the total landscape of *houses in a park*.

The houses at Clapham were formal and geometrical in contrast to the English gardens that surrounded them. The era of Romantic domestic design had not yet arrived. Nevertheless, the Palladian design was modified to provide for the Evangelical ideals of family life and contact with nature. This adaptation is most clearly visible in the Thornton residence, Battersea Rise, where a new room called the library was added, to be the real center of the sprawling house. This large oval room, well lit by French doors that opened onto the rear garden, had only a few bookshelves and was in fact what we would call the family room. All the Thorntons—men, women, and children—gathered here from early morning to late in the evening.[36] The library and the garden outside it were the Evangelical substitute for all the plays, balls, visits, and coffee houses of London. Here the closed domesticated nuclear family became a reality. The social activities of London did not suddenly cease. Instead, the social graces were directed inward, toward the mutual education and moral betterment of the family itself.

One could call the library and similar rooms throughout Clapham a "woman centered" environment, but—accurate as that description is—it would miss the point that these families knew very little of that segregation by sex and age which was to mark the Victorian Age later in the nineteenth century. One is struck at Clapham with how much of their lives these families spent together; not only are men and women constantly in each other's company, but children are equally included in the adult world. Nevertheless, the woman's presence is the constant one. Here wives and daughters fulfilled their mission of elevating the moral and religious tone of those nearest to them. Their erudition or musical talents were never mere displaying as long as they were reserved for the family.

The family rooms at Clapham were therefore taken up with knitting, crocheting, and other "improving" fancywork; with singing and playing at the omnipresent pianoforte; but above all with serious conversation tending toward moral betterment. When Henry Thornton praised his wife Marianne in his private journal, he could find no higher compliment than to say, "Her conversation is on subjects of Importance. I think I have known no woman whose topics are better chosen and more suitably chosen."[37]

The library at Battersea Rise was presided over by Marianne Thornton. She also had the important function of supervising the management of the house—there were always at least ten full-time servants—and keeping the books for household expenses. Marianne came from the same elite merchant class as her husband Henry—her family were merchants in the Russian trade at Hull—and she was a fervent Evangelical even before her marriage in 1796 at the age of twenty-one. After marriage she had nine children, seven of whom lived to maturity. Like other Evangelical wives she disdained the aristocratic custom of sending the children out to a wet nurse, and she breast-fed them all herself. With ample assistance from servants and a nanny, she then devoted herself to the raising and education of the children to the highest Evangelical standards.[38]

But the most solemn moment in the Thornton family room was presided over by Henry: the twice daily family prayers. The Evangelicals reintroduced this custom into English society, and they took it with utmost seriousness. Henry in fact compiled a collection of prayers, published posthumously as *Family Prayers*, the use of which became an identifying sign of the Evangelicals.[39] E. M. Forster, a direct descendant of the Thorntons who has written of them with great understanding, remarked that "Battersea Library with the united family kneeling seemed more sacred to them than any consecrated edifice."[40] Outside the reciprocal support of an Evangelical family they saw little hope for salvation. "May God bless you for all your kindness to me," wrote Henry to Marianne after sixteen years of marriage, "and above all for giving me your helping hand on the way to Heaven."[41]

If Clapham shows the origins of suburbia as a family centered environment, it also shows the crucial importance of providing for children within the domestic setting. As Lawrence Stone has emphasized, a defining feature of the closed domesticated nuclear family was the increasing affection bestowed by both parents on the children. The eighteenth century did not invent love between children and parents, but it flourished then (at least among the bourgeoisie and gentry) as never before. Where children had been ignored, harshly punished, or treated as small adults, the eighteenth century English bourgeoisie saw childhood as a specific stage in life that requires special protection and love.

For the Evangelicals, it was at least as important to remove children from the corrupting influences of the city as it was to remove women. Parents who wished to safeguard the moral purity of their children could not hope to insulate them from the dangers, cruelties, bad language, suffering, and immorality that filled the crowded London streets. And Evangelical parents felt a special responsibility, as Hannah More put it, "for the eternal happiness of these beloved creatures whom Providence has especially committed to [their] trust. . . . What parent, I say, can by his own rash negligence, or false indulgence, risk the happiness of such a soul, not for a few days or years, but for a period compared to which the whole duration of time is but a point?"[42] Such exhortations might seem to point to harsh discipline within the family circle, but the Evangelicals were fortunately so much a part of the Enlightenment movement toward loving care of children that any fears of what More called "ill-judging fondness" were overcome by the spontaneous affection that characterized these homes at their best. It was, after all, the beginning of what J. H. Plumb has called "the new world of children in the eighteenth century," with its innovations in young people's clothes, toys, books, sports, music, and art especially designed for the first time to suit children's interests and to promote their happiness.[43] To this list of child oriented innovations one might add the modern suburb.

Clapham was a child centered environment in the sense that, unlike the city, it was truly open to children without danger both inside the home and outside. It was also set up to provide frequent contact between parents and children and plenty of opportunity for play. A large house like the Thornton's Battersea Rise had its nursery on the top floor with a full-time nanny, but the children were not required to remain there. In contrast to later Victorian ways, the children had surprisingly free run of the house. They were welcome at almost all times in the library, where they joined in the singing and listened to the conversation. If William Wilberforce was present (as he frequently was), he liked to interrupt the grave discussions by taking the children outside to throw a ball or to run a race on the lawn "to warm his feet." All the adults, even the Clapham saints, were not too proud to join their children in games like charades or masquerades.[44]

The major concern of Clapham parents was the early education of their children. There were day schools in Clapham for girls and boys from ages eight to twelve—after twelve the boys went to boarding school—but the earliest education was at home, and not only for such prodigies as Thomas Babington Macaulay. "Tom" was the best known product of Clapham home training: he could read difficult volumes at age three and astounded adults by his erudition at five.[45] More revealing is the education of the oldest Thornton daughter, named Marianne after her mother. She was taught to read and write at age five by her mother, who believed in practical methods of education. Her first practice in arithmetic came from adding up the household accounts in her mother's expense books, and later she progressed to more complicated calculations of household expenditures.[46]

But her father also took an active role in her education. She learned penmanship by copying out his manuscripts and writing his invitations. "Half the naughtiness of little children arises from want of employment," was his motto; so, in addition to book learning, she was taught (in proper Rousseauist fashion) such tasks as churning butter.[47] Later, he taught her the current issues being debated in Parliament, and even tried to instruct her on the paper credit and bullion question, his own parliamentary specialty. This financial education had its effect, for in 1825, when her brother Henry's bank nearly failed, Marianne's letters to Hannah More describing the crisis showed a clear comprehension of the complex banking procedures. Women in Clapham were removed from the business world, but not ignorant of it.[48]

In spite of this serious education, there was always time for play with the other children from the other houses around the common. "Our houses and grounds were almost common property," Marianne later recalled.[49] The common itself—"that delightful wilderness of gore bushes, and poplar groves, and gravel-pits, and ponds great and small"[50]—was their playground; the gardens behind each house had also been specially laid out for children's games and amusements.

No doubt certain features of Evangelical training darkened

the lives of the children, most notably the emphasis on sin and mortality. As was the Evangelical custom, young Marianne and her siblings were taken to see the body of their minister, John Venn, just before the funeral and were given the stern admonition by their father, "This is your first experience that death has entered into the world, may you learn from it how unsafe it is to rest in it for all our happiness."[51] But this dark side was offset by the very real pleasure that members of these families found in one another and in the equally real beauty of the Clapham landscape. "He used to go into ecstacies especially about flowers," young Marianne said of Wilberforce, the sternest of the Clapham saints.[52]

Indeed, the "saints" had created in Clapham something close to their ideal of the Family in the Garden. Here the divine institution of the family could find its proper setting *in God's own nature*—suitably improved by human landscaping. Clapham had that combination of picturesque beauty, deeply felt family ties, and material prosperity that continued to inspire all subsequent suburbias. To be sure, this paradise in earnest—like the Evangelical heaven itself—was only for the few. Only the elite of the bourgeoisie could aspire to share in the benefits, and the Clapham saints felt no guilt about their privilege, only a fear that it might lead to the ungodly ostentation they deplored in the aristocracy. As E. M. Forster describes the Clapham attitude, "Prayers before Plenty. But Plenty!"[53] Henry Thornton aptly summed up the social philosophy of the sect in one of his *Family Prayers* when he besought God to "give to the poor contentment with their lot, and to the rich a spirit of compassion and benevolence."[54]

Clapham, nevertheless, was not a retreat that excluded an active role in the world. On such issues as slavery and child labor the sect really embodied the compassion and benevolence they preached. When Wilberforce was not going into ecstasies over flowers he was a canny and resourceful politician. It was in Thornton's library and Wilberforce's drawing room that the great antislavery crusade was planned; here among the children's play and beautiful gardens the antislavery tracts were written; public meetings were organized; and parliamentary forces were mustered for the bitter battle that resulted in the great 1807 bill that banned the slave trade in the British Empire. For the men, at least, Clapham was one pole of their existence, the other being the hard work of political and business commitments in London.

The new suburban environment cannot be fully understood without keeping in mind that continuing involvement in London which was constantly the counterpoint to the Clapham world of nature and family life. Henry Thornton, it is relevant to note, was the author not only of *Family Prayers* but also of *An Enquiry into the Nature and Effects of the Paper Credit of Great Britain*, a tome that E. M. Forster, with admirable family loyalty, claims is still of use to modern economists. These two books aptly symbolize the poles of the men's lives. If Evangelicalism was a religion of family and emotion, it also emphasized the virtues and rewards of work. For Wilberforce, "industry, sobriety, punctuality, temperance, health, regularity" were what he called "necessary" virtues.[55] By emphasizing the two poles simultaneously, Evangelicalism led almost inevitably to their functional and then physical separation.

We must see Clapham as one half of that specialization in bourgeois life which split in two the family enterprise that had been united physically in the London townhouse. Just as the family home now became a specialized and intensified center of emotion with its own suitable environment, so too did the former townhouse become wholly an office, now dedicated to intensified, unremitting work. The apprentices with their traditional claims as family members came to be replaced by clerks; the old, richly diversified City of London was reduced to a specialized office district. Indeed, it was in 1800 that the City reached its peak of population, only to decline throughout the nineteenth and twentieth centuries as the residences were replaced with modern offices.[56]

The merchant in his coach and four hurrying along the turnpike road from home to office was the fragile link between these two spheres, which from that time proved increasingly polarized and discordant features in modern life. The growth of suburbia was to build into the physical environment that division between the feminine/natural/emotional world of family and the masculine/rational/urban world of work. The Evangelical ideology was crucial to this separation, yet the Evangelicals themselves always tried to hold the two in balance. Nevertheless, it was the family and its home that were the objects of their most creative concerns. For they had no doubt that the family was more than a human institution; that it would survive even death; and they confidently hoped that, after the death of its members, the family would be reunited in a heaven even more beautiful than Clapham Common.

The Suburb as Culture and Commodity

Clapham was perhaps the best developed example of the late eighteenth century bourgeois suburb, but it was not unique. By the beginning of the nineteenth century London was surrounded by a ring of similar suburbs, all located in the open country about three to five miles from the core. From Hampstead, Highgate, Hornsey, and Walthamstow in the north to Dulwich, Walworth, Camberwell, and Clapham in the south, the distinctly modern pattern of a prosperous, residential outer ring was taking shape. Just as important as the transformation of the agricultural villages—Walthamstow, for example, was described as "abound[ing] with the villas of opulent merchants"[57]—was the spread of "ribbon development" along the coach roads. The architect John Nash—who, as will be seen, was a very careful observer of suburban trends—recorded in 1812 that "handsome houses are seen built and building on the sides of all the roads near the Metropolis, wherever there is an open field or a garden to look into."[58]

As always, language lagged behind reality. It was not until the 1840s that the word "suburb" lost its older, primarily plebeian associations and became firmly attached to the middle-class residential neighborhood.[59] One observer in 1810 groped for words when he observed, "The man of business and the Merchant generally sleep in the *country*, or if you please—*near London*, and come to town after breakfast."[60] Behind these linguistic hesitations was the deeper problem of coming to terms with an urban form of life that contravened all established distinctions of town and country, center and periphery.

Suburbia had come into existence without overall planning or formal conceptions. The wealthy elite who created the new landscape had the resources and the patience to reshape their environment to meet their needs. Large landowners like the Thorntons did not scruple to profit by subdividing their holdings, but such merchants and bankers were not "developers" in the usual sense. They proceeded slowly, taking care to safeguard their own holdings and the overall character of the area. In this way they overthrew the fundamental rules of eighteenth century planning without conscious revolutionary intent. They simply knew what they liked.

Such methods sufficed if suburbia were to be restricted to a small elite. But once the demand for suburban residences spread more widely, a more deliberate approach was necessary. John Nash discerned this problem in his discussion of the building of Sloane Street, in what is now fashionable Knightsbridge but was in the eighteenth century a site "attended with many disadvantages, such as distance from town, the unfinished state of the street, the loneliness of the situation." Nevertheless, the sites along Sloane Street sold quickly, to be covered with houses that "had an open field or a garden to look into, and . . . were ranged at distances from each other"—in other words, suburbia. Unfortunately, the popularity of the district meant that the neighboring fields were soon developed, the gaps between the houses filled in, and the "open space, free air, the scenery of nature" that Nash claimed attracted people to the street were lost.[61]

Behind this vignette and the many others like it can be seen a developing convergence of interest between aspiring suburbanites and owners of agricultural land in what would be redefined as the suburban belt around the city. As the suburban style spread from the elite to the rest of the middle class, a demand arose for large numbers of suburban building sites that would retain their distinctively suburban character even after the area around them had been developed. At the same time, landowners around the metropolis saw in the new suburbia an opportunity to sell land that was well beyond the developed edge of the city at relatively high residential prices. This very remoteness could be turned into instant profit if the land's continuing low density and abundant open space could be assured. The problem, therefore, was consciously to design a true suburbia.

The difficulties of this task are well illustrated by the earliest surviving record of such a plan, the Eyre Estate plan usually attributed to John Shaw for the development of St. John's Wood, at what was then the northwest corner of London.[62] The plan, which was exhibited but never carried out, vividly shows the difficulty that designers whose notion of advanced planning came from Bath or the New Town of Edinburgh had in dealing with the open, informal, seemingly unplanned suburban idea. For the design is an awkward mixture of eighteenth century formality and suburban space. As at Bath, uniform houses line long, straight streets or such geometrical showplaces as a square, a crescent, and a grand circus (circle). With one exception we are still in the world of John Gwynn and his "improvements" to keep merchants in the city. The crucial difference is that the houses are semidetached, that is, each free standing unit comprises two houses joined by a party wall. Long, narrow gardens of one to three acres stand to the side of and behind each house. The solid urban row or terrace of houses is thus broken up to give a semisuburban sense of greenery and openness.

The suburban semidetached house proved to be one of the main vehicles of English (though not American) suburbanization. The Shaw plan shows clearly that buyers seeking to live at what was then the rural edge of the city wanted something different from the solid streets and squares of the West End;

already the suburban idea had taken hold. But it also shows clearly that the radical implications of Clapham and the other spontaneous suburbs had not yet been fully understood.

The first architect to grasp these principles and to translate them into a workable plan for a true suburban development was John Nash in his Park Village, built at the northeastern edge of Regent's Park in the 1820s. At first glance, Nash seems an unlikely proponent of suburbia. He was best known for his elegant, aristocratic, and supremely urbanistic designs such as Regent Street or the Regent's Park terraces. As a well known dandy and friend of the Prince Regent himself, he moved in circles far removed from the serious-minded merchants of Clapham.

Yet Nash had an inspired facility with the varied architectural styles of his time. As the fantastic cupolas and interiors he designed for the Royal Pavilion at Brighton demonstrate, he was not constrained by eighteenth century classicism. Borrowing eclectically from the full range of styles available (and inventing a few of his own), he could translate the dreams of his clients— whether decadent royalty or Evangelical bankers—into convincing three dimensional embodiments. All these talents went into his design for an archetypal suburb.

Typically enough, Park Village was a kind of afterthought in Nash's grandiose plans for the development of a 500 acre tract in northwest London (bordering the Eyre Estate), which is now Regent's Park. In the early nineteenth century the administrators of royal property, the crown commissioners, had resolved to develop the estate (still empty fields) to gain revenue. Nash originally proposed to turn the land into a kind of aristocratic suburb, what he called "the apex of the metropolis." Most of these plans never came to fruition, but they are worth summarizing both as a contrast to Park Village and as a sign that even Nash was confused about the future of the urban periphery.

In these original plans the center of the park would be given over to opulent villas for the aristocracy, each with up to twenty acres of grounds. Also in the center was a grand double circus of large connected houses, one circle facing inward to landscaped grounds, the other outward to the park. Around the periphery of the park he designed massive terraces of row houses, each with elaborate ornamentation, which did get built and still overlook the park today. Yet all these grand structures did not, as at Clapham, add up to a community. As he remarks, each should appear to exist alone in its own world of greenery. The park would be planted so that "no villa should see any other, but should appear to possess the whole of the park; and . . . the streets of houses which overlook the park should not see the villas, nor one street of houses overlook those of another street."[63] This attempt at aristocratic seclusion proved impossible. Only eight villas were built and the rest of the land was instead opened to the public; the very grandiosity of the long terraces proved uncongenial to the aristocracy and gentry, who preferred the understated elegance of the more traditional squares that Thomas Cubitt was constructing in Belgravia.

Tucked away from this splendor in the northeast corner of the park was a private speculative development of middle-class houses that Nash undertook on the land not required for his villas or terraces. In the shadow of the great terraces he built a village for the bourgeoisie following design principles that finally solved the problem of turning empty fields into suburbia.

The name Park Village has become a favorite cliché, but for Nash it had a precise meaning in delineating the two major influences that went into the design. It was a synthesis of the picturesque landscaped park with the picturesque village. Nash had grasped the basic idea of Clapham and the other early suburbs: they were houses in a park. As his first (and most original) drawing for Park Village shows, he completely avoided the formal language of eighteenth century urban design. Instead, the houses are set within a picturesque landscape with its characteristic curving paths, scattered plantings, and even ornamental water conveniently provided by the Regent's Canal, which wound around the edge of the park.[64]

Such designs came naturally to Nash, for he had worked as a partner with Humphry Repton, the leading landscape designer of his time. But Nash understood how to create a picturesque

landscape out of individual house lots. He paid particular attention to the use of trees and shrubs both to define the private
property around each house and to contribute to the total park
effect. "The plantations," he writes, "are to screen the more
offensive parts of the cottages, separate them from each other
and give intricacy to the scenery; the division between the
ground of the several cottages are to be live hedges and ironware
fences."[65] Natural "intricacy," not formal clarity, had become
the basic design principle.

As John Summerson was the first to point out, Nash's Park
Village design owes much to his previous work at Blaise Hamlet
near Bristol; not only the landscape but the house design can
be best understood in comparison with Blaise. For at Blaise
Hamlet Nash not only designed the ultimate picturesque village
but also came in direct contact with the Evangelical movement.
The hamlet was commissioned in 1811 by a wealthy Bristol
banker, John S. Harford, who was a friend and later a biographer
of William Wilberforce.[66] Harford wanted to build a retreat for
"aged persons who had moved in respectable walks of life, but
had fallen under misfortunes, preserving little, or nothing, in
the shock of adversity, but unblemished character."[67]

To embody Harford's wish that the buildings appear to be
"humble places of voluntary retirement," Nash dug deep into
his repertoire of images to create a group of ten detached traditional English cottages grouped around a green. Nash's work
reflects the views of design writers like Uvedale Price, who had
begun to see a positive value in the irregularity of the traditional
village. The village, wrote Price, summons to mind pleasing
suggestions of

> long established habitation. . . . The characteristic beauties of a vil-
> lage, as distinct from a city, are intricacy, variety, and play of out-
> line. . . . The houses should therefore be disposed with that view,
> and should differ as much in their disposition from those of a reg-
> ularly built city, as the trees which are meant to have the character
> of natural groups, should differ from those of an avenue.[68]

When we turn from Blaise Hamlet to Park Village, it is clear that

Nash has made the "characteristic beauties" of the picturesque village those of his suburb, and used "intricacy, variety, and play of outline" to establish the essential design contrast between city and suburb.

This contrast is especially evident in Nash's designs for the houses of Park Village. Nash breaks with the classic Palladianism of Clapham to create picturesque adaptations of traditional English cottage architecture, rendered here more substantial than at Blaise Hamlet so that they might be called Elizabethan or Tudor in style. To them Nash did not hesitate to add Gothic or even Italianate influences, the latter most notably in the round tower on one of the cottages. And, as at Blaise, each cottage was self-consciously different from its neighbors.

Because suburbia was to become the characteristic terrain for such eclectic mixtures of period architecture, we must pause here to explore the origins and the meaning of Nash's historicism. As with the landscaping of Park Village, Nash encapsulated a long development. As soon as the picturesque English garden had been established as the norm of landscaping in the mid eighteenth century, a conflict arose between the formal classicism of the Palladian house and the more informal principles of the ground around it. A search had begun for architectural styles that would respond directly to the landscape and incorporate the same emotions into the house itself.

Appropriately enough, the villa belt outside London was the locale for the most influential experiments in new form. These experiments were guided by a principle known as associationism, after Sir Joshua Reynolds's pronouncement in 1786 that architecture affects "the imagination by means of association of ideas. Thus, we have naturally a veneration for antiquity; whatever building brings to our remembrance ancient customs and manners, such as the castles of the barons of ancient Chivalry, is sure to give this delight."[69] Sir Joshua might well have been thinking of Horace Walpole's villa, Strawberry Hill, near Twickenham, which Walpole gothicized between 1750 and 1770 precisely to give delight through the extravagantly intricate ornamentation and "charming" historical associations.

To Gothic was soon added another historicist style, the Italianate. This style came originally directly from the canvases of Claude Lorrain, whose Arcadian landscapes often showed rural farmhouses of irregular shape surmounted by square battlements or round towers. These irregularities were intended to represent both a natural response to the picturesque landscape and the growth of the house over time. The asymmetrical outline and mixture of classical, Romanesque, and Gothic elements expressed a building rooted in the landscape, which had taken a unique shape over the centuries. To Englishmen enchanted by the picturesque landscape, it seemed natural to build in its midst the kind of structure that Claude had painted. Nash himself designed a very influential Italianate villa at Cronkhill for a wealthy lawyer.[70]

Finally, there is the "Old English" cottage, the most obvious stylistic influence on Park Village. In the associationist vocabulary, it stood above all for stability, simplicity, domesticity, and retreat from worldly cares. Thomas Malton, in his *Essay on Architecture*, defines the cottage as "a small house in the country; of odd, irregular form, with various harmonious coloring, the effect of weather, time, and accident; the whole environed with smiling verdure, having a contented, cheerful, inviting aspect."[71] To recreate this "aspect" (at a bourgeois standard of size and comfort) became the aim of many villa owners around the metropolis. Woodland Cottage, near Clapham—built to enable its owner to "relax from the fatigues of professional employment"—was described as a thatch-covered "elegant little cottage" in modern Gothic: "in the dining parlor, the same [Gothic] style is pursued; the tables, chairs, wainscoting, and sideboard resemble, in miniature, the ancient appearance of the hall of an old castle, to which the stained glass windows give a somber finish."[72] That a little cottage would contain, even in miniature, the furnishings of a castle shows how little the realities of the medieval world impinged upon the play of associations. What counted was to create that "contented, cheerful, inviting" appearance, an appearance that Nash applied first to the charity cottages at Blaise and then (with appropriate social adjustments) to Park Village.

Historicism in this sense was to prove triumphant in all areas of nineteenth century architecture, but it has a peculiar relevance to suburbia. When the country house or villa was still an emblem of its owner's culture and standing, the restrained and patrician Palladian style held sway. But when the new suburban house became a specialized home for the emotional life of the family and a self-conscious retreat from the world of power and economics, architects and clients turned inevitably to those historical styles which most forcibly suggested those emotions.

In this picturesque world of associationism the old criteria of formal unity and consistency no longer applied. Gothic, Italianate, or Old English all signified the much the same emotional message of retreat, contentment, and duration over time; hence there was no real inconsistency in mixing them together on the same street or in the same house. Indeed, as Nash clearly realized, such eclectic mixtures promoted that variety which was necessary to separate the suburban environment from the urban.

Thus Park Village not only foreshadows, in Pevsner's phrase, that "fancy dress ball of architecture"[73] which would soon be under way throughout suburbia but it points to the deeper links between suburbia and both picturesque landscape and historicist design that still define the suburb. In Park Village Nash brought together all of the varied elements of the suburban style that had existed only in scattered form and turned them into a convincing unity. He thus created a basic formula that could be followed to turn any piece of empty land around a city into a middle-class residential community. He transformed suburbia into a commodity, a product that could be reproduced indefinitely.

What is perhaps most remarkable about Nash's formula is that it was proved remarkably flexible. An urban square, for example, is a design game played according to very precise rules. Suburbia, however, is tolerant. Straight streets could be substituted for curved ones; unplanned diversity for aesthetic eclecticism; even consistency can work; the only thing necessary is to preserve the basic contrast with urban forms expressed in the idea of "houses in a park." Park Village thus prepared the way for that rapid, uncoordinated spread of suburbanization which will be the subject of the rest of this book.

But before we turn to the specific social and economic forces that transformed suburbia from an elite privilege to a mass-produced product available to the whole middle class, we might pause to reflect on the strange nature of this commodity: "The bourgeoisie has subjected the country to the rule of the towns. . . . It has put an end to all feudal, patriarchal, idyllic relationships. . . . It has drowned the most heavenly ecstacies of . . . sentimentalism in the icy water of egotistical calculation. . . . The bourgeoisie has torn away from the family its sentimental veil."[74] These words from the *Communist Manifesto* suggest the paradox of Park Village. For in suburbia the conquering bourgeoisie has chosen to re-create an invented version of the "feudal, patriarchal, idyllic" village environment it was destroying. These masters of rationality at the workplace were not only preserving but intensifying the "most heavenly ecstacies of . . . sentimentalism" at home. At the same time that bourgeois economic initiatives were swelling the metropolis and undermining the traditional balance between man and nature, this class was creating a private retreat that expressed tradition, domesticity, and union with nature.

Perhaps, as Marx suggests in *The Eighteenth Brumaire of Louis Napoleon*, no revolutionary class can face its own actions except in disguise; in suburbia the bourgeoisie could pretend to be happy villagers. Yet the paradox of suburbia is also a direct expression of that division of middle-class life encountered in the Clapham Evangelicals. Rationality and sentimentality coexist, but they are strictly separated into work and family realms. Nash carried this division even further than the Clapham saints. To their concepts of God-given country for the family versus the manmade city for business, Nash added his own complex symbolism of the picturesque suburban village versus the formalist city, incorporating these moral and aesthetic divisions into the modern concept of suburbia.

Charles Dickens gives us the best image of this deep dissociation in middle-class sensibility. In *Great Expectations* (published 1861 but set in the 1830s) he depicts Mr. Jagger's hard faced legal clerk Wemmick, who lunches on dry biscuits and has a mouth like a post office slot. But Wemmick is also the proud owner of a Gothic cottage at Walworth (near Clapham), which he has ornamented with a miniature pond, mock battlements, and a tiny cannon that goes off every night at nine.

Dickens shows Wemmick softening every evening as he leaves the City and hardening in the morning when he returns. When Pip asks his opinion on a personal matter, Wemmick replies that his answer depends on whether he is at Walworth or the office. "Walworth is one place and this office is another. . . . They must not be confounded together. My Walworth sentiments must be taken at Walworth; none but my official sentiments can be taken in this office."[75] If suburbia began as the chosen refuge for a small elite of London merchants, its message was so deeply ingrained in bourgeois culture that it almost inevitably became the dominant domestic form for middle-class Britain. Where change was most rapid, as in the new industrial centers of northern England, the great suburban divide was soon to reshape the basic structure of the modern city.

CHAPTER 3

The Suburb and the Industrial City: Manchester

IF SUBURBIA originated in London, its importance there throughout the nineteenth century was as one element in a complex urban mosaic that resisted rapid change or simplification. Only when the London suburb was transplanted to Manchester and the other early industrial cities of northern England did suburbia demonstrate its revolutionary power to dominate middle-class residential patterns and to transform urban structure.

London, it should be remembered, experienced very little industrialization before the late nineteenth century. Its economy remained based on the eighteenth century elements of world trade and finance, government, and the provision of luxuries to the upper classes. To these activities were added a great mass of "sweated" trades producing clothing, furniture, and household goods in the small, crowded workshops of the East End.

Compared to a city like Manchester, London was resolutely retrogressive in its economy, even undergoing a deindustrialization as formerly important industries like shipbuilding moved north.[1]

London, therefore, retained a preindustrial complexity both in its class relations and in its urban structure. The middle class did pursue the separation of residence and workplace begun by the Clapham bankers, but when a genteel family left their dwelling above the shop they often retained the old house and rented single rooms in the upper stories to workers and even families engaged in the sweated trades. This practice produced to the east of the core a dense preindustrial mix of commerce, residence, and work, often within the same house.[2]

Moreover, the middle-class families leaving the core did not necessarily go all the way to suburbia. For the upper class had remained loyal to the fashionable squares of the West End, and substantial portions of the bourgeoisie imitated them by settling in the large townhouses of South Kensington and Bayswater.[3] Suburbs on the model of Clapham and Park Village thus competed with these more traditional urban dwellings for the loyalty of the London middle class. Although the London suburbs grew even faster than the city as a whole—by the end of the century more than a million commuters were entering the City of London each day[4]—it was not until the 1870s that middle-class London shifted decisively to the peripheral suburb as the model of bourgeois residence.[5]

London residential patterns therefore showed both continuity and complexity, two qualities rarely associated with nineteenth century Manchester. Middle-class suburbanization began later in Manchester than in London, but its impact was far more decisive. As late as 1830 the Manchester bourgeoisie was still firmly established in townhouses near the urban core. But in a single decade—1835 to 1845—Manchester achieved a higher degree of suburbanization than London did in the whole century from 1770 to 1870. Long before the automobile or even the commuter railroad, with no more sophisticated transportation systems than the private carriage and the horse drawn omnibus,

Manchester established the pattern of middle-class suburban-ization in the industrial city. It brought to almost total completion that tendency toward class segregation and the separation of bourgeois work and residence which had first been seen in eighteenth century London.

When Friedrich Engels wrote *The Condition of the Working Class in England* in 1844 he depicted Manchester as a modern industrial city that had already achieved its classic form: a central business district now almost devoid of residents; a factory zone surrounding the core densely packed with industry and worker's housing; and a peripheral suburban zone for the villas of the bourgeoisie.[6] Lest Engels be accused of exaggerating the degree of suburban flight and class segregation in mid nineteenth century Manchester, I shall quote at length from an 1857 visitor's guide to the city, which gives as clear a description of the classic form of the industrial city as do the celebrated Chicago School diagrams of the 1920s.

The guide presents a picture of three concentric rings, with the central point—fittingly enough—the Royal Exchange, the heart of the capitalist system where the price of cotton goods was set each working day. The area around the exchange is

> the heart of Manchester, which embraces, within a comparatively small circle, a large portion of the principal buildings and commercial transactions of the city. This is the district which sends life and vigor through every street and alley, and which moves the vast machinery, and myriads of spindles, through the entire district. It is the neighborhood of warehouses, counting-rooms, banks, offices, commission houses, and agencies.

This central business district is contrasted with the urban periphery, the "encircling . . . outskirts or suburbs," which consist of

> long vistas of enchanting villas, in the most attractive architecture, ornamented in front with spacious gardens, grass plots, and shrubberies exquisitely laid out. Here resort our merchants, those who can bear the expense of residence beyond the region of smoke. These suburbs of Manchester resemble so many Edens, and you

wonder such loveliness can exist so near the brown masses of chimney and streets in the city.

Finally, it depicts the intermediate factory zone:

> Between these two regions, the region of warehouses, banks and offices, and the region of crescents, gardens, parterres—the residence of the Manchester aristocracy—lives the mass of the laboring, sweltering, spinners and weavers of Manchester. The forest of chimneys mainly rise out of this inward belt, and underneath them dwell in crowded alleys of two-story houses, which run in innumerable labyrinths, those men, women, and children, who fill our factories and mills, and make calicoes, silks, and prints, for every portion of the civilized world.

"Manchester," the guidebook concludes, "is emphatically a place of business."[7]

Besides its clarity, this description has the virtue of reminding us that suburbia can never be understood simply as a beautiful artifact in itself—"so many Edens," in the guidebook's phrase— but must always be juxtaposed with its opposite, the "crowded alleys" and "innumerable labyrinths" of the industrial working class. It was the increasing sharpness of class divisions in this first industrial city that gave suburbanization in Manchester its meaning and its urgency.

One might call suburbia in its original London setting a preadaptation, a term biologists use to designate a feature of an organism that has only limited utility for the organism in its native environment; but, when the environment changes, the preadaptation suddenly assumes a crucial importance. In the relatively fluid and complex social setting of London—still dominated by small scale production and a preindustrial sense of multiple castes inhabiting the same social space—suburbia remained the choice of only one section of the middle class. In the far harsher and more deeply divided environment of Manchester, suburbia became the universal remedy.

Suburbanization in Manchester was not simply a flight from the industrial city. The decision of the middle class to break with their tradition of living in the urban core decisively altered the form of the whole city. Indeed, the classic form of the industrial city as depicted from Engels to the Chicago School was not, I would argue, the necessary result of industrialization itself. Continental cities industrialized quite successfully on a very different pattern, and even Manchester itself stuck to its preindustrial pattern for the first three decades of its intensive industrialization.

It was, rather, middle-class suburbanization itself that created the structure of the classic Anglo-American industrial city. Not only the suburban belt but the factory zone and the central business district all attained their modern form as a result of the bourgeois choice to seize the rural land at the periphery of the city for their own residential use. To understand the crucial role of suburbanization in defining the modern city we must therefore look closely at the evolution of the first industrial metropolis.

Creating the Divided Environment

If late eighteenth century London had already established the pattern of the whirlpool city, drawing people and resources irresistibly toward it, early nineteenth century Manchester intensified that whirlpool effect through the new stimulus of industrialization. From a quiet country town of perhaps 17,000 people in 1750, Manchester grew to 70,000 by 1801 and reached 303,000 in 1851. In the decade of the 1820s alone the population increased by 45 percent.[8]

Such growth created the classic conditions for middle-class suburbanization: economic forces that concentrate opportunities within an urban core while at the same time making that core increasingly expensive and uninhabitable. In retrospect, bourgeois flight from the center seems inevitable; "nothing," wrote J. H. Clapham and M. M. Clapham in 1934 of Manchester suburbanization, "is more easily explained."⁹

Nevertheless, the people who actually created nineteenth century Manchester did not consciously create the pattern of growth that developed. Through the mid 1830s, in fact, they tried to preserve a very different pattern, one in which the "bourgeois aristocracy" maintained their residences near the core in close proximity to the busy warehouses that were their business headquarters. The social and cultural changes that caused them to abandon this structure reveal the forces that were actually shaping both suburbia and the industrial city.

The ultimate force behind the expansion of Manchester was, of course, the cotton industry. Manchester had been traditionally a center for textile merchants who supplied home workers in the agricultural districts of Lancashire with materials for spinning and weaving and then collected the yarn or cloth, finished it, and sold it. The new popularity of cotton goods in the mid eighteenth century vastly increased the volume of business for these merchants; and the mechanization of spinning put Manchester at the heart of the world's first industrial region.

Yet the factory system did not come to Manchester until the 1790s, when the steam engine made it possible to move the factories from their original power source—fast running rural streams—into the cities. Even after Manchester became a great center of spinning and then weaving factories, it was always much more than an overgrown factory town. It was, rather, the capital of the whole Lancashire cotton district. Cotton goods from factories throughout Lancashire were brought to Manchester for specialized finishing; buyers throughout the world came to the city to see the goods; factories produced and serviced machines for factories throughout the region; bankers, brokers, and traders clustered around the Royal Exchange to set the prices that determined the fate of the whole industry.¹⁰

Manchester was thus—like the City of London—an information society in which access to the face-to-face network of expertise that gathered at its core was crucial to the broker seeking the lowest price for cotton; the merchant accumulating stock from factories scattered around the city and the region; the buyer seeking the widest choices of the latest fashions; the toolmaker struggling with constantly changing technology. The growth of the cotton industry in Lancashire thus inevitably created a dense urban core—Manchester as "Cottonopolis"—and there the merchants congregated, along with the producers, for whom access to the latest information on orders and fashions compensated for the high costs of land.

Manchester thus attracted a wide range of workers and their families: would-be factory operatives fleeing the overpopulation of the countryside; unskilled Irish immigrants fleeing an even more brutal poverty in their homeland; but also ambitious young men from the middle class who came from small towns or the back rooms of London counting houses to seek their fortune.

Yet as Manchester expanded in the early nineteenth century it kept its original form. Mid eighteenth century Manchester was a tight network of narrow streets where merchants (as in London) lived in houses that were also their places of business. Such manufacturing stages as bleaching or dyeing cloth took place in small shops on the outskirts near the open fields, which were, in any case, no more than a five minute walk from any place within the city.[11]

The vast expansion of Manchester soon made this arrangement obsolete, and the older streets either were converted to offices or degenerated into slums. Yet the basic principle was retained. Just beyond the traditional urban core the Manchester elite built a new central district intended both for their homes and for their places of business. The homes of the leading Manchester merchants and manufacturers lined Mosley Street, a fashionable avenue just four blocks from the new Royal Exchange. Even these houses could no longer accommodate the goods that merchants had formerly stored under their own roofs, so warehouses were constructed on the narrower back streets just behind their owner's homes to keep and display the stock.

The leading merchants and their families thus intentionally

reconstructed the core as a kind of patrician quarter, but one that maintained their intimate contact with their business and with the whole world of Manchester production. One author described this elite neighborhood, the home of "some of the most opulent characters [in] the United Kingdom," as "one mass of congregated commerce." Behind the elegant townhouses, he wrote, "the back streets, avenues, entries, courts, and cellars, are thronged with the inferior tradesmen and country chapmen. On market-days, all is one moving mass of merchants, traders, chapmen, commission-dealers, porters, draymen, warehousemen, and wares."[12] Clearly, the Manchester elite still had no idea of a rigid separation of work and residence or of leaving the center.

If the wealthy kept to the core, the factories of Manchester were pushed to the outskirts of the town. They clustered especially around the canals and small rivers with which Manchester was abundantly endowed. Surrounded by newly built, closely-packed housing for the workers, these factories formed "industrial villages" in a setting that still seemed more rural than urban. One worker recalls that as late as the 1820s it was still possible to walk a complete circuit of Manchester on rural pathways that were no more than a two mile radius from the exchange.[13]

The Manchester merchants thus had a collective strategy for the city that involved creating a central patrician district which would be both home and place of business for the elite. Here elegant townhouses would be steps away from the busy warehouses and family life never out of touch with the world of commerce. Many workers too would be close by, living literally in the backyards of the elite in the back streets of the core. The bulk of the workers would live in relatively open settlements at the fringes of the town, where, ironically, they would enjoy a greater proximity to the rural surroundings than the elite. This structure as a whole preserved much of the traditional urban form—the elite at the center, the poor at the outskirts—and it did so through the most expansive decade of Manchester's growth.

Yet this structure was to change suddenly and radically in the 1830s. In the local histories this change is invariably associated with a single initiative, that of Samuel Brooks in 1834. A native of Scotland, Brooks made himself into the archetypal Manchester man: a wealthy merchant and factory owner, a compulsive worker who decorated his home with quotations from *Poor Richard's Almanac*, one of the most prominent of the Mosley Street merchants. Yet in 1834 Brooks bought from the aristocratic Egerton family a tract of farmland, which he renamed Whalley Range after the Scottish district of his birth. There he built a suburban villa for himself and his family, and soon subdivided the land to sell to other merchants. Moreover, on moving to Whalley Range he converted his Mosley Street townhouse into his warehouse.[14]

After recovering from the shock of seeing a warehouse breach the sacred precincts of Manchester's most prestigious residential street, Brooks's fellow civic leaders soon followed his example. Within five years of Brooks's move, almost all the townhouses on Mosley Street had been converted to warehouses.[15] And their former residents built suburban villas on one of the "breezy heights" surrounding the city.

This decision to suburbanize had two great consequences, both of which are clearly seen as early as Engels's account of Manchester in 1844. First, the core emptied of residents as the middle class left and workers were pushed out by the conversion of their rooms in the back streets to offices. Not only warehouses—now splendidly decorated in Gothic or Venetian styles—but banks and elegant stores replaced the old residences. Visitors were surprised to find an urban core that was totally quiet and empty after business hours. The central business district was born.[16]

Meanwhile, the once peripheral factories were now enclosed by a suburban belt, which separated them from the now distant rural fields. The grounds of the suburban villas were enclosed by walls, and even the tree lined streets on which they stood were often forbidden except to the residents and their guests. One group of workers attempted to keep open a once rural footpath that now ran through the grounds of a factory owner's suburban villa. They "walked across the grounds directly in front of and close to Mr. Jones's newly-created mansion, making their way through the lately laid-out shrubberies and flower parterres." Mr. Jones responded with iron gates and ditches.[17]

As workers and their factories were thus confined, the modern factory zone came into being. Once the "breezy heights" were firmly in the possession of the middle class, factories and their workers were increasingly crowded into the zone between the high land values of the core and the privileged residential zones at the outskirts.

So fundamental a shift in urban structure clearly had fundamental causes. For me, the most significant was the issue of class relations. The older urban form involved the frequent and intimate contact of the middle and working classes. This closeness was precisely what the Manchester bourgeoisie had come to fear. They sought the most complete separation possible while maintaining the all-important contact with the information sources at the core. Suburbia as it had already developed in London provided a remarkably useful form—a preadaptation— which exactly answered the needs for class segregation. All that was necessary for suburbanization to occur was, first, the increasing familiarity with this new urban structure and the economic conditions that made the move from core to suburb both pleasant and highly profitable. Both of these conditions came together in the 1830s and 1840s.

Even in eighteenth century London, the impetus for suburbanization had contained a large element of class fear, the desire to isolate oneself and one's family from the turbulent lower orders of the urban core. Yet the London merchants and their families still lived within a preindustrial order in which small scale production and traditional patterns of deference still obtained. In Manchester the bourgeoisie found themselves captains of industry, employers of large numbers of workers but lacking in the older trappings of aristocratic authority. As George Saintsbury put it in his perceptive comment on Elizabeth Gaskell's Manchester novel, *Mary Barton*: "The main subject and motive of the book—the contrast of great wealth and of poverty, conscious that it has helped to make that wealth, and that the actual possessors of it have in many cases risen from the very class which they now employ—is the central problem of the life of all great manufacturing towns, and especially of Manchester."[18] To this central problem was added the inherent instability of the cotton trade, the periodic depressions and strikes, which led to frequent unrest. In 1829, for example, there was a series of riots that even troops were unable to control, and the agitation for the Reform Act of the 1830s prolonged the unrest.[19]

Lacking legitimacy, the bourgeoisie tended to withdraw from all contact with the working class beyond what was necessary to economic life. Indeed, as Asa Briggs emphasizes, the very language of separate classes engaged in a "class struggle" comes directly from the Manchester urban experience. Briggs quotes at length from the observations of Thomas Parkinson made during the height of middle-class flight and, I believe, highly relevant to explaining it: "there is no town in the world where the distance between the rich and the poor is so great, or the barrier between them is difficult to be crossed. . . . There is far less *personal* communication between the master cotton-spinner and his workmen . . . than there is between the Duke of Wellington and the humblest laborer on his estate."[20] Parkinson was referring to a social distance between classes and to personal barriers; but in suburbanization both the distance and the barriers became physical facts which regulated and defined the urban environment.

Elizabeth Gaskell gives a vivid example of this gulf in *Mary Barton* when she shows the worker Jem setting out from his squalid cellar dwelling to "beg an Infirmary order" for a sick friend from his employer Mr. Carson:

> Wilson had about two miles to walk before he reached Mr. Carson's house, which was almost in the country. . . . Mr. Carson's house

was a good house, and furnished with disregard to expense. But, in addition to lavish expenditure, there was much taste shown, and many articles chosen for their beauty and elegance adorned his rooms. As Wilson passed a window which a housemaid had thrown open, he saw pictures and gilding, at which he was tempted to stop and look; but then he thought it would not be respectful.[21]

Suburbia was one solution to the problem that Saintsbury had identified in Manchester of the relations between rich and poor. Where an aristocracy had surrounded themselves with the lower orders as a sign of their privilege and status, the keynote of the bourgeois city was to be separation and willful blindness. Suburbia accomplished both. In one of Engels's most celebrated observations he shows that the streets that the middle class took from their suburban homes into the center concealed rather than revealed the true nature of the factory zone: for these main streets were, naturally, lined with shops and other structures which their owners kept clean and neat. The real squalor was concealed behind these relatively well kept fronts. Thus, the middle class could traverse the distance from their suburban "Edens" to the now beautified urban core without having to be confronted by the true nature of the urban society in which they lived.[22]

Yet suburbanization arose out of more than the cultural contradictions of the middle class. If it expressed bourgeois fears and values, it was also a good investment. The rush to suburbanize could never have occurred without a structure of land speculation and building that permitted and encouraged it. We must now turn explicitly to the economics of suburbanization.

Speculation and Suburbia

When Samuel Brooks converted his townhouse on Mosley Street into a warehouse, bought a field that he renamed Whalley Range, built a suburban villa there for himself, and then subdivided the rest of the land for others, he neatly encapsulated the whole process of suburban development and speculation.

The first element was the move from a core area of relatively high land values to a periphery of relatively low values. The great boom of the 1820s and early 1830s had caused land values in central Manchester—especially property on Mosley Street—to increase greatly in value. At the same time, the fields beyond the town remained at or close to their low valuation as agricultural land. Thus, Brooks was holding extremely valuable property, in his original home, which he could profitably exchange for substantial acreage at the periphery. He merely fulfilled the imperative of all Manchester merchants: to sell in a dear market and buy in a cheap one.

The second stage came when, by settling in Whalley Range himself, he was able to isolate that area of the Manchester periphery as fashionable and hence suitable for suburban building. Thus he was able to sell off the remainder of his land as building plots and reap the benefits of the conversion of land values from agricultural to residential levels.[23]

In a wider sense Brooks and all the subsequent suburban speculators were capturing for themselves the higher land values created by the growth of Manchester. Because the cotton industry boomed, values of property in the urban core shot up, and those who owned property there reaped what the American land reformer Henry George would call the "unearned increment" due ultimately to the growth of the whole community. Brooks used this "unearned increment" to purchase his suburban holdings and then further increased his profits through suburban development.

None of it would have been possible if the Manchester merchant aristocracy had remained stubbornly loyal to their residences in the core. A true urban patrician class might have done so, but the Manchester elite were often outsiders with no sentimental associations with central Manchester. At the same time, the London form of the middle-class suburb showed the way for a prestigious residence outside the core. The combination of a suburban residence and a substantial profit proved irresistible. Thus, for the Mosley Street elite who initiated the process, suburbanization was virtually self-financing.

This process did not exhaust itself with the Manchester elite but soon spread to include virtually the whole of the middle class. Such speedy and total reversal of previous habits would have been impossible without the enthusiastic participation of another group not yet specifically examined: the speculative builders. Using borrowed money, a speculative builder erects homes for the market, not to order for specific commissions. The methods and limitations of the nineteenth century English speculative builders fitted the conditions of suburbia much better than they did those of the central city. For that reason, the Manchester suburbs always had a good supply of houses on the market.

The speculative builders favored suburbia because the building industry was itself highly decentralized. Developers and builders were able to tap a remarkable number of different sources of capital, but an individual could rarely get very much capital at any one time. So even in boom years building was scattered and haphazard. This lack of organization made residential development at the urban core especially hazardous, for middle-class buyers had begun to demand a relatively homogeneous neighborhood. J. C. Loudon, the most influential writer on middle-class domestic architecture and landscaping of the 1830s, advised his readers to always "choose a neighborhood where houses and inhabitants are all, or chiefly, of the same description and class as the house we intend to inhabit, and as ourselves." Otherwise, "we are likely to be isolated, either from an appearance of greater pretensions, or from actually having inferior means to those around us."[24]

To create such a neighborhood required either a single builder with great resources, such as Thomas Cubitt who built the fashionable squares of Belgravia in London, or the close cooperation of many small builders. But if a large effort fails or cooperation falters urban land is always subject to invasion, usually by less desirable neighbors or uses.

Suburbia, in contrast, was remarkably open to small scale,

piecemeal development. Suburban districts could grow slowly, almost haphazardly, without endangering their middle-class status. Almost by definition, a desirable area for villa construction was sufficiently far from the core and the factory zone to be beyond the reach of the urban poor. Distance alone prevented any such invasion, while the cost of a private carriage or omnibus fares virtually guaranteed class segregation. Aesthetically, an urban district under construction is almost invariably ugly, but a suburban district retains its rural or village environment while filling up with houses. In this sense, scattered development worked in suburbia as it did not in the city.

This tolerance for the small builder or investor vastly enlarged the range of developers who could work successfully in suburbia. The process of speculative building usually started with a landowner who undertook to subdivide his land into building plots. Subdivision was itself a haphazard operation, for no certain formula existed for knowing when a particular district was ready for suburban development; landowners acted haphazardly, some starting too early, others waiting too long.

A good suburban location was close enough to the central business district to provide easy access while far enough outside the factory district to ensure that smoke and the proletariat could not follow. One writer advised that "the neighborhood of manufactories and mills should be avoided, not only on account of the dense clouds of smoke constantly pouring forth, nor of the continual noise, nor the vapors, nor smells; but of the class of people usually employed; they are unpleasant and sometimes dangerous neighbors."[25] In Manchester the factory district extended only two or three miles from the core, beyond which there was abundant unspoiled land along the many roads that led out of the city. For those without private carriages, transportation was provided by an efficient system of horse-drawn omnibuses whose relatively high fares made them a middle-class preserve. With names like "Industry" and "Jenny Lind" these Manchester omnibuses were "large and roomy vehicles, drawn by three horses harnessed abreast . . . continually moving between the suburbs and the center of the city, from eight in the morning till nine at night."[26] Their proprietors claimed to provide frequent service at thirty-minute or even fifteen-minute intervals.[27]

The network of omnibus routes defined a peripheral zone of suburban development which included a generous supply of land that exceeded demand and kept land prices low. Developers controlled the pace and locale of subdivision, but subdivision required heavy short-term borrowing to meet the immediate expenses in surveying and laying out streets and sewers. Once a developer had converted agricultural land to building plots, he rarely attempted to build houses on the plots himself. Instead, he disposed of the land as quickly as possible, ideally to wealthy individuals who could pay cash for land on which to erect their own homes. More commonly, the plots were taken up by speculative builders who deferred payment to the developer until their houses had been constructed and sold.

By necessity, the builder also borrowed heavily—sometimes fifteen or twenty times his capital—in order to construct the houses. The source of funds was usually solicitors who lent out their clients' money in "building mortgages" at 5 percent interest. The aim was to get enough money to construct a few houses in a development and then sell them quickly and profitably enough to repay the mortgage within a year and earn enough to begin the process the next year with more capital and on a larger scale of building and borrowing.[28]

A typical mortgage now preserved in the Manchester Archives was drawn up in 1854 between "Elizabeth Rushton, widow" and the speculative builders William Clarke and Joseph Jones for £3,600 to buy land and build four houses. As was the custom, the money was not paid out at once but according to the progress of the construction. The mortgage specified £1,200 to be lent at once, £400 when the first floor of the four houses were laid, £400 more when the second floor was completed, £200 when the houses were completed except for papering and grates, and £800 when they were entirely finished.[29]

Such mortgages implied many unhappy experiences with

houses left unfinished. Too often builders started small and increased the scale of their operations in good years until a bust left them hopelessly overextended. Uncompleted houses went back to the lender, whose solicitor then sought another builder who could complete them. Some houses went through as many as three builders from start to completion, each of whom worked in a different style.[30]

Land developers were subject to similar contingencies. Some, like Brooks, were wealthy men who had plenty of capital to see their projects through. Others borrowed heavily to begin laying streets on just one part of their land, hoping that quick sales would enable them to complete the task. Bankruptcy usually meant a forced sale to another developer, who often completed the street network in a different pattern from the original design.

Such uncertainties would have been fatal to any middle-class residential area within the city. But suburbia was sheltered by its location from the worst consequences of failure, while the great urban virtues of regularity and efficiency counted little in the suburban landscape. The houses on any particular street might reflect an anarchic variety of taste derived from the many speculators who built them; the street map might disclose a crazy quilt of juxtaposed crescents, circles, and grid plans, a whole archaeology of speculations; but as long as the houses are substantial and the streets quiet and tree lined, it is all the "suburban style."

Developers generally aimed for the highest level of the bourgeoisie by laying out multi-acre lots intended for large houses; but, if the lots failed to sell, they were further subdivided for small suburban houses to be erected quickly by speculative builders. Even highly successful developments had areas of small houses at their fringes.[31] Thus, a place was made in suburbia for less affluent members of the middle class. As early as the 1830s J. C. Loudon was specifically recommending the "suburbs of town" to his lower middle-class readers as "alone calculated to afford a maximum of comfort and enjoyment for a minimum of expense. . . . A suburban residence, with a very small portion of land attached, will contain all that is essential to happiness."[32]

In reality, such small houses were often as cramped as their urban counterparts and as poorly built. One Manchester clerk described the sitting room of his suburban mini-villa as "one in which, you might, without moving from your position, stir the fire, ring the bell, close the door and open the window."[33] One architectural writer described the common experience of moving to a new house in a new neighborhood that is "a little farther off" and "more airy—there is a nice field to look on—vain delusion! The house is just finished, it is clean—the floors are level—the staircase does not give way—the ceilings are unstained; there are no cracks in them—the walls have not yet settled; but in a short time this delightful residence is out of repair and delapidated, and closely hemmed in by countless houses."[34]

These small houses were usually rented rather than owned by their occupants, but many of the grandest bourgeois villas were also investment properties leased for one to five years. The long-term, fixed-rate mortgage which enabled a buyer to purchase a house with only a small initial payment was virtually unknown. Even among the wealthier members of the middle class, home ownership was associated with only one part of a typical bourgeois life cycle for investments. A young businessman was usually required to put whatever capital he possessed into the firm or partnership in which he worked. Even if his income was high, his savings went back into the firm and were not available for investment in a family home. Only after many years could he begin to withdraw his capital for other uses. At that point he might purchase the home he had been leasing. Indeed, if he wished to withdraw both his energies and his capital from his business, he had few options more suitable than purchasing houses for lease.[35]

Thus a single bourgeois suburbanite might be a renter for most of his life but wind up an owner not only of his own home but of several others in the neighborhood as well. This pattern is well illustrated in the life of Richard Cobden, perhaps the best known of all of Manchester's business elite for his political leadership. Cobden was born in a small village in Sussex where his father was a farmer and a small trader. After working as a clerk in London and then as a commercial traveler, he was attracted to Manchester in 1831 by the opportunity to invest in a calico printing works. This investment tied up what little capital he possessed, but the works prospered so quickly that by 1837 he was able to invest in the development of Victoria Park, a new suburb near Whalley Range, to build a large house for himself there and to act as a speculative builder in constructing two more houses as investments.[36]

Cobden's real estate activities help to explain why the suburbanization of Manchester survived the end of the cotton boom in 1836 and the difficult years of the "Hungry Forties." Once the growth in the cotton industry slowed, entrepreneurs could no longer automatically reinvest their earnings in firms that were no longer expanding. Because almost all firms were privately held partnerships, passive investors had to choose between low yielding government bonds or highly speculative railroad shares. By comparison, a real estate investment in a locality one knew well appeared highly attractive. Investment in Manchester's suburbanization was therefore countercyclical. It took on strength as the cotton boom cooled, and it reshaped the first industrial city just when the industries that caused the boom had passed their first explosive peak.

Victoria Park: An Exclusive Victorian Paradise

In 1837 a group of Manchester's business and political leaders formed a company to purchase 140 acres some two miles south of the Royal Exchange and to develop the land as a model suburb. They planned to build their own homes along the curving, tree lined streets that their architect, Richard Lane, was laying out; and, once their own residences had established the new development as the city's best suburb, they hoped to sell the remaining lots at a large profit. As always, the cultural ideal and the profit motive were inextricably linked. They named the new development Victoria Park after the young princess who was about to ascend the throne.[37]

The troubled business conditions of the late 1830s deprived the partners, of whom Richard Cobden was the most prominent, of the windfall profits for which they had hoped. But, for reasons already described, suburbia was highly tolerant of temporary failure. Many of the original partners did build in the Victoria Park, not just for themselves but also speculatively. Indeed, by the mid 1840s, the development had become a symbol of bourgeois suburbia, the equivalent for the mid nineteenth century industrial city of what Clapham had been for London a few generations before.

Yet, if Victoria Park had become a kind of symbol of Manchester—recommended for visits by the tourist guides—another 1840s development less than a half mile away was also receiving visitors of another kind. This area was Little Ireland, one of the worst slums of the district. A local health officer in 1848 described the River Medlock, which passed through the slum, as receiving

> every possible abomination (night-soil, dead dogs, dead cats, offal, etc.) [in addition to industrial pollution] . . . until every natural watercourse may be termed a lengthened and gigantic cesspool. . . . During the dry weather of summer, fermentation takes place to an extent that the refuse may be seen, not merely bubbling with the escape of gases, but literally boiling, foaming, throwing up a thick and foul scum like an immense cauldron; millions of cubic feet of unwholesome gases are thus generated; much of which must be passed into the adjoining houses, mills and workshops.[38]

Engels had visited Little Ireland four years earlier and described it as composed of

> two groups of about two hundred cottages, most of which were built on the back-to-back principle. . . . The cottages are very small,

old and dirty, while the streets are uneven, partly unpaved, not properly drained and full of ruts. Heaps of refuse, offal, and sickening filth are everywhere interspersed with pools of stagnant liquid. The atmosphere is polluted by the stench and is darkened by the thick smoke of a dozen factory chimneys. A horde of ragged women and children swarm about on the streets. . . . The creatures who inhabit these dwellings and even their dark, wet cellars, and who live confined amidst all this filth and foul air—which cannot be dissipated because of the surrounding lofty buildings—must surely have sunk to the lowest level of humanity.[39]

Little Ireland might seem remote from a history of suburbia, but Victoria Park cannot be properly understood without considering its opposite. Little Ireland was part of the world that the bourgeoisie did not want to see, but its presence can be felt in every shady corner of Victoria Park.

The design principles of Victoria Park are essentially those which John Nash had put forward for Park Village in London some twenty years earlier; but they take on a new point in the context of the industrial city. The green world of suburbia is not just the natural world of godliness and morality it was for the Clapham sect; it is also a world of class privilege. Access to clean air and water must be bought and is available only to a few. The natural environment of Victoria Park is as direct an assertion of bourgeois privilege as the fur lined cloaks and rich brocades of the medieval bourgeoisie had been in a city in which the poor wore tatters.

But if middle-class suburbia was defined in part by its contrast to the environment of the poor, it also gained meaning through its relation to the estates of the old aristocracy. Clapham had borrowed many elements from the rural gentry and nobility, but the London merchants "knew their place" and never challenged the aristocracy directly. Victoria Park carried a much heavier load of anxiety and assertion. Remember that many of the founders of Victoria Park were also among the founders of the Anti-Corn Law League, a direct challenge to the right of aristocratic landowners to a tariff that kept grain prices (and thus their own incomes) high. Richard Cobden, calico printer, league leader, and secretary of the Victoria Park company, assailed the present occupants of the aristocratic country houses as little different from their "barbarous ancestors" who "used to make excursions from their strongholds to plunder, oppress, and ravage, with fire and sword, the peaceable and industrious inhabitants of the towns."[40]

Yet, while the commercial leaders of Manchester and the other industrial cities were organizing against the political power of the aristocracy, this rising new class was also appropriating the architectural symbolism of the old. The designation "Park" referred unmistakably to the country estates of the aristocracy. In case the point was missed, the whole development was surrounded by walls similar to those which ringed a country estate and could be entered only via a gatehouse, where a watchman refused entrance to all but residents and their guests.

Once inside, the curving streets and ornamental plantings were borrowed directly from the picturesque landscaping of the country house as translated through Nash's influence. More strikingly, the architecture of the industrialists' villas resembled nothing more than smaller versions of those baronial castles which Cobden had deplored.

Although Nash and others had already suburbanized the Gothic as a suitable style for a middle-class villa, these early Gothic residences were more playful than serious, using the Gothic as a source of fanciful cottage ornamentation. The Gothic villas of Victoria Park, however, represent a quantum leap in size and pretension. From the dark slate roofs to the bulging irregularity of the plans, this new Gothic style was intended to connote individuality, character, force, and endurance over time. Victoria Park Gothic is heavy with authority.

By the 1840s, moreover, Gothic had become the principal style for the expression of domestic emotions. It had won the approbation not only of a theorist like John Ruskin but of the publicist J. C. Loudon, who wrote of Gothic architecture that

Towers, battlements, buttresses, pointed windows, mullions, and porches have been, from infancy, before the eyes of everyone who has been in the habit of attending his parish church; and whenever they occur in other buildings they recall a thousand images connected with the place of our birth, the scenes of our youth, the home of our parents, and the abodes of our friends. In this frame of mind, how easy it is to be pleased.[41]

This appropriation of aristocratic symbolism by the industrial bourgeoisie is not surprising if one considers that suburbia was not "a retreat from urban society and its problems" but a new way of expressing dominance within that society. Suburbia proved to be the perfect setting in which the older symbolism of aristocratic power could be appropriated by the middle classes. Insecure in its new status, the bourgeoisie grasped eagerly at the well established symbolism of the traditional power elite.

One crucial ambiguity in the layout of the plan is the conflict between the self-sufficiency of each house and the environment of the whole. The layout called for a relatively open design, with the lawns and gardens of each house contributing to a unified effect. This openness, however, conflicted with the tradition of a wall around each house. As might have been predicted, individualism won out. The streets were thus lined with high walls, which cut off most views of the gardens behind. At most one glimpsed an imposing roof line above the wall.

Yet this diminution of the streetscape expressed the basic idea of the villa, which, as Loudon put it, was "in favor of exclusive enjoyment; and the general object, whether in small villas or extensive ones, has been to shut out everything belonging to the neighborhood which would indicate that there was any other proprietor in residence in the vicinity." Especially worthy of being shut out, according to Loudon, were objects that "serve to recall the idea of a town, or of manufactories."[42]

This concept of the villa gave special importance to the garden. Not coincidentally, Loudon himself began as a landscape gardener and devoted most of his attention to defining what he called "the gardenesque," in other words, the adaptation of picturesque principles to the more limited sphere of the suburban garden. For Loudon, the main values of such a garden are "variety and intricacy," especially when they make it possible "to give the place credit for a greater extent than it really possesses."[43]

So Loudon, echoing his clients, did not hesitate to use design to increase the apparent size of a house and its property. He recommended that the entrances to a semidetached pair of houses be so placed that the two appear as one large house. In discussing the appropriate size of doorways, he indignantly dismissed the suggestion that a doorway should be no larger than was appropriate to the size of the house itself. "[W]e feel that the source of all improvement has its origins in the desire of individuals to better their condition," he announced.[44]

If the garden reflected the isolation of the villa, this isolation and the larger urban segregation were carried inside to the plan of the house itself. As we saw in eighteenth century Clapham, the social activity of eighteenth century London suburbs took place within the family's drawing room, which served as a kind of theater of sociability for the whole family and their friends. But in Victoria Park and its era of Victorian housing, the segregation that had become the norm for the city became the basis for the internal organization of the house.

This change is most evident in the attention devoted by Victorian architects to the segregation of servants from the family they served. A complicated network of back stairways and specialized cooking and cleaning rooms reduced contact to the minimum required for direct supervision. One might say that the suburban house itself mirrored the complex routes of segregation that had been imposed on urban space.

Equally striking was the increased segregation of ages and sexes. Far more than at Clapham, the children of a proper Victorian household were restricted to a children's wing, supervised by a nurse and nanny. Moreover, houses tended to divide into men's and women's spaces. This separation was accomplished by multiplying the number of rooms. Adjoining the bedroom were the man's dressing room and the woman's boudoir. Downstairs the drawing room for mixed company was supplemented by the library, study, or billiard room for men and by the parlor or sitting room for women. Such segregation between the sexes was an odd contradiction within the Victorian ideal of domesticity.[45]

Indeed, we must now turn to this domestic ideal itself, and especially to the position of women in the Victorian bourgeois suburb. As in so many other respects, a suburb like Victoria Park represented a culmination of the Clapham Evangelical ideal but also a sharpening and intensification of it. By the mid nineteenth century the ideals of William Wilberforce, Hannah More, and the other Clapham saints had come to provide the common discourse of Victorianism for expressing the proper role of respectable women within society and the family.

Ironically, the very same economic forces that made working-class women an integral part of the factory system completed the separation (which the Evangelicals had urged) of middle-class women from the "demoralizing" sphere of work. The factories could not run profitably without a constant supply of working-class women (and their children) to tend the machines, but these same factories had no place for middle-class women. During the early years of the factory system in Manchester the traditional close ties between the middle-class home and work had been so strong that a few millowners actually located their homes next to their factories or even within its yard. But this relationship soon went the way of townhouses with warehouses behind them, yielding to a complete separation of middle-class Manchester women from both the factory and the countinghouse.

That women were suited by God and nature to the task of elevating the moral and religious state of men and of raising children to be God-fearing Christians—this doctrine was one that the Manchester millowners were as eager to accept as the Evangelical bankers. The strength of bourgeois domestic sentiments can be seen in the "personal narrative" that George Hadfield—a successful lawyer, member of Parliament, and resident of Victoria Park—drew up at the close of his life and which is preserved in manuscript at the Manchester Central Library Archives. The most deeply felt portion of Hadfield's narrative is devoted to praise of his deceased wife, Lydia. "To her I am deeply indebted for success at home and for any usefulness abroad. We had eleven children and she nursed them all."[46]

As Hadfield describes her, Lydia seems more a cultural ideal than an actual woman, but one senses in every line the sincerity with which the ideal was held. "She was an excellent house-keeper and had a sound judgment and good sense. She appreciated my circumstances; and by her excellent management at home liberated me from care, and enabled me to give exclusive attention to business and works of usefulness in the Church and the world."[47] And, if the good wife liberated the husband from household cares, she also elevated that household beyond what the husband alone could ever accomplish. "Her zeal and industry were shown, not only in the promotion of [the family's] health and intellect, but likewise in their moral and religious training. Our children may recall to their recollection the hours she spent with them and the counsel she gave them. Fruit abounded and will abound."[48] In the end Hadfield presents Lydia as a kind of martyr to the Victorian religious ideal of a wife and mother, not surprising in view of the physical burden of bearing eleven children in the first seventeen years after their marriage. "Her devotedness and anxiety brought down her noble constitution, and she suffered much in later life but we had a happy married life and she will have her reward."[49]

A more prosaic but perhaps equally revealing picture of the ideal Victorian suburban wife can be gleaned from the manuals of "domestic economy" and household management that proliferated in that era. Not surprisingly, they emphasize the wife as manager—supervisor of servants, master of the household accounts, educator of the children—a domestic counterpart to the husband in his work. The picture of bustle and efficiency that they present is no doubt as much idealized as Hadfield's portrayal of Lydia's virtues, but it is significant in the same way as a cultural ideal.

Alexis Soyer's *The Modern Housewife* of 1850 instructs its readers through a fictionalized portrait of "the B.s" of "Bifron's villa." Mr. B. praises his wife as an "accomplished woman" in terms that derive directly from Hannah More's strictures. Mrs.

B., her husband boasts, "speaks two or three languages tolerably well, and, as an amateur is rather proficient in music, but her parents, very wisely considering household knowledge to be of greater importance, made her first acquainted with the keys of the storeroom before those of the piano." Mr. B. concludes, "I always say, give me a domesticated wife."[50]

Mrs. B. is soon allowed to speak for herself. We are led to understand that the B.s have come up in the world, for their breakfasts once included "the three young men in the shop"— apprentices who lived with the family when the family itself lived "above the shop." No more. The B.s now possess their own suburban villa and their own carriage in which Mr. B. leaves for the city every morning at twenty minutes after nine and returns every evening at twenty minutes to five.

In the interim, Mrs. B. supervises the running of the house, which she does—as she does everything—in an exemplary manner. After breakfast she confers at ten o'clock with the cook about the day's menu. Then, "If I go out or not, I always get my toilet finished by 12 o'clock. I thus have an hour to write notes, or see tradesmen or my dressmaker, and Monday mornings check and pay my tradesmen's accounts." If Mrs. B. goes out to shop or to visit, she takes the brougham—her husband has obligingly taken the omnibus that day. "If I stop at home, I amuse myself by reading, or going to see the children in the nursery [the B.s have three children], or sometimes go again into the kitchen and assist the cook on some new receipt or preparation."[51] Meanwhile, the two maids are cleaning the house or doing the laundry.

The pace of the household quickens in the late afternoon in preparation for Mr. B.'s return and the evening meal. "The servants dine at one, and have tea at quarter to five, by which time the cook has everything ready, all but to take it from the fire, and the maids the dining room ready." Mr. and Mrs. B. then dine at half past five, served by the maids without the assistance (as appears to have been the custom in other households) of the coachman. "I would never allow the coachman to defile our carpets with his stable shoes," she affirms. "The duties of the stable are incompatible with those of the table."[52]

Contact with the children is also carefully limited. The children eat separately with their governess in the nursery. "After dinner, should we be alone, we have the children and the governess down; if we have company we do not see them; they go to bed at quarter to eight." After the children have been put to bed the governess is allowed to join Mr. and Mrs. B. in the drawing room. "Eleven is our usual hour of retiring, before which Mr. B. likes his glass of negus, a biscuit or a sandwich which is brought to him upon a tray." The servants are to be up promptly the next morning at seven and everything made ready for breakfast at eight thirty.[53]

The Modern Housewife represents the mundane element in the Evangelical tradition of womanhood, Clapham ideals as filtered through Victorian materialism. A far different interpretation of the suburban woman was offered by John Ruskin, who came to Manchester in 1864 to deliver a series of lectures that were published the next year under the title *Sesame and Lilies.* One of the lectures was delivered in the Rusholme Town Hall, the township that included both Little Ireland and Victoria Park. His address to women, titled "Of Queens' Gardens," was delivered in the Town Hall of Manchester itself.

Ruskin's address represents both a summation of the Evangelical tradition of womanhood and an attempt to reorient it. Ruskin could speak with authority on this tradition. He grew up in the south London suburb of Herne Hill, close to Clapham both physically and intellectually through the Evangelical moralism and Bible training inculcated in him by his mother.[54] "Of Queens' Gardens" mixes the imagery of medieval romance with that of Loudon's *Suburban Gardener* to produce an image of the suburban housewife as a "queen" of a "sacred place."

Ruskin's tribute to the "true wife" is perhaps the most eloquent statement of the Evangelical ideal of the home and womanhood that began with Wilberforce. The true wife, Ruskin proclaims, "by her office and place" is protected from all danger and temptation. The man, in his rough work in the open world, must encounter all peril and trial: —to him, therefore, must be the failure, the offense, the inevitable error: often he must be wounded or subdued; often misled; and *always* hardened. But he guards the woman from all this; within his house, as ruled by her, unless she herself has sought it, need enter no danger, no temptation, no cause of error or offense. This is the true nature of home—it is the place of Peace; the shelter, not only from all injury, but from all terror, doubt, and division. In so far as it is not this, it is not home; so far as the anxieties of the outer life penetrate into it, and the inconsistently-minded, unknown, unloved, or hostile society of the outside world is allowed by either husband or wife to cross the threshold, it ceases to be home. . . . But so far as it is a sacred place, a vestal temple . . . so far it vindicates the name, and fulfills the praise, of Home.[55]

Yet Ruskin's point is not to vindicate the complacency of a Mrs. B. or even to praise a Lydia Hadfield, who stays at home to liberate her husband to perform good works in the world. He turns the Clapham tradition on its head by affirming the Evangelical ideal of womanhood and the home in the strongest possible terms, and then asserting that the Evangelical woman has a role in the outside world at least equal to a man's.

Ruskin compares England to a suburban garden threatened by coal shafts dug in the middle of the lawn and heaps of coke among the roses. "The whole country is but a little garden, not more than enough for your children to run on the lawns of, if you would let them *all* run there. And this little garden you will turn into a furnace ground."[56] If a woman's duty is to protect her home against depredation and ugliness—to secure, as Ruskin puts it, the home's "order, comfort, and loveliness"—so her duty "as a member of the commonwealth is to assist in the ordering, in the comforting, and in the beautiful adornment of the state."[57]

These are no small functions. For Ruskin virtually the whole of what we have come to call the welfare state lies within women's sphere of public action, and her absence from these functions accounts for continued suffering. Men, he proclaims, are "feeble in sympathy, and contracted in hope." Only women "can feel the depths of pain, and conceive the way of its healing. Instead of trying to do this, you turn away from it; you shut yourself within your park walls and garden gates; and you are content to know that there is beyond them a whole world in wilderness—a world of secrets which you dare not penetrate, and of suffering which you dare not conceive."[58] He demands of Manchester's middle-class women, "Will you not . . . be no more housewives, but queens?"[59]

As Ruskin understood, the Evangelical virtues of bourgeois suburbia—a sanctified family life in union with nature—had in the context of the industrial city turned into an escape and an evasion. Because middle-class women and their families were safely placed behind the walls of Victoria Park, the rest of Manchester could indeed be turned into a "furnace ground." Because the bourgeois Eden had been realized in suburbia, human beings a short distance away could be left to sink, in Engels's phrase, "to the lowest level of humanity." Like Engels, Ruskin indicts the sheer blindness of this class-divided society, the inability to look beyond the garden gates.

Ruskin's solution is perhaps no more utopian than Engels's: to use Evangelical idealism to bring the values of bourgeois suburbia to the whole society. A beautiful and natural environment is no longer to be a class privilege but the right of everyone. The same care that had gone into saving Victoria Park and the other exclusive suburbs from the horrors of industrialization should now be lavished on the whole society. In time many women were indeed to become "queens" in Ruskin's sense, and their contributions have left a deep impression on what is best in the British environment. But in Ruskin's own time the gulf between Victoria Park and Little Ireland was too deep for Evangelical enthusiasm to bridge. For all their solid comforts and gardenesque beauties, the suburbs of the new industrial metropolis were built upon a divided environment that continues to deform our cities.

CHAPTER 4

Urbanity versus
Suburbanity: France
and the United States

> ... already, there are to be found [in suburbia] ... the most
> attractive, the most refined and the most soundly wholesome
> forms of domestic life, and the best application of the arts of
> civilization to which mankind has yet attained.
> —FREDERICK LAW OLMSTED, 1868[1]

IN the early 1850s two visitors came separately to England
with a particular interest in suburbs. César Daly was already
France's best known architectural writer and editor of the *Revue
générale de l'architecture*. Once a follower of the utopian socialist
Charles Fourier, Daly still retained his interest in designing the
perfect dwelling for the modern age. Outside London he un-
expectedly discovered a new solution: the suburban villa. He
saw at once its origins in middle-class aspirations to domesticity;
its aesthetic possibilities as the marriage of urban and rural architecture; its financial possibilities as the residence of choice
for an increasingly prosperous and powerful bourgeoisie. Daly

was convinced that suburbanization was inevitable for the middle class, not only in England but also in France.[2]

Frederick Law Olmsted, the other visitor, arrived from New York in 1850 in more modest circumstances. Twenty-eight years old, a gentleman farmer on Staten Island with literary aspirations, Olmsted had not yet found the vocation as a landscape architect and planner that would make him famous. While touring England making notes for a book, he saw Birkenhead Park near Liverpool; and, though he could not have realized it at the time, he encountered there the prototypes for his later work both as a park designer and as a suburban planner.[3]

Birkenhead Park was designed by Joseph Paxton, who began his career as a gardener and wound up creating the Crystal Palace for the Great Exposition of 1851. In 1844 Paxton laid out a public park of picturesque design that became a model for New York's Central Park, designed by Olmsted and Calvert Vaux. More importantly for our purposes, Paxton surrounded the park with a picturesque suburb. The curving roads and artful plantings, the substantial villas on separate lots recall not only Manchester's Victoria Park of 1837 but also John Nash's Park Village of twenty years before. The suburb that Olmsted saw in 1850 not only summed up the tradition of English suburban design; it also embodied the principles that Olmsted was to apply so widely and so successfully in the United States.[4]

Olmsted's advocacy of suburbia developed more slowly than Daly's, but both men came to share a common faith that, in Olmsted's words, "no great town can long exist without great suburbs."[5] Indeed, the 1850s and the 1860s seemed to be the ideal time to advocate and to profit from the mass suburbanization of the middle class both in France and in the United States. In both countries the middle class still tended to occupy the crowded center of the cities. A Parisian bourgeois family of 1850 lived much as their London counterparts had done a century before: in townhouses that combined work and residence, located in neighborhoods even more crowded than those of the City of London.[6] A New York, Philadelphia, or Boston merchant of the same period occupied premises that resembled those of the Manchester middle class *before* the suburbanization of the 1830s and 1840s: townhouses virtually next door to warehouses, with artisans and casual laborers crammed into alleyways just behind the most substantial residences.[7]

Yet the French and the American middle class had come to share precisely those cultural preferences which, in England, had led to suburbanization. The Victorian emphasis on domesticity was by no means confined to those territories where the Queen herself actually ruled. In French and American publications one can find the same stress on the primacy of the family and the emotional ties that bind it; the necessity of privacy and isolation of the family unit; and the consequent need to separate the domestic sphere from the world of work. One also finds the same desire for class separation: the growing uneasiness at close contact between classes; the rejection of neighborhoods that make such contacts inevitable; and the search for class-segregated bourgeois residential neighborhoods, which the older city could not provide.

At the time that these cultural preferences took hold, namely, the 1850s and 1860s, French and American cities were beginning to experience that explosive growth which, in England, had made the restructuring of middle-class housing patterns not only necessary but profitable. In France urban growth had lagged behind that of England. Only in the late 1840s, when a national rail network centered on Paris was begun, did the conditions exist for extensive urban redevelopment.[8] American cities had always grown rapidly but from a relatively small base. Lacking the gigantism of an imperial capital like London or the accelerating growth of the northern English industrial cities, the American cities retained the form of the eighteenth century mercantile city well into the nineteenth century.

French and American cities thus reached a stage of rapid change and inevitable transformation precisely when English models were most influential.[9] The Great Exposition of 1851 carried the implicit message that the English had invented the form of the modern age. It seemed only natural that French and American entrepreneurs who were rushing to adopt the technological innovations of the English bourgeoisie would also adopt their invention in the field of housing, the middle-class residential suburb. Both Daly and Olmsted were ardent nationalists, but in championing suburbia they gratefully accepted England's example.

The 1850s and 1860s did see the beginning of the great rehousing of the middle class in France and America, but only in the United States did this transformation take the suburban form that Daly and Olmsted anticipated. Olmsted not only witnessed the emergence of the "great suburbs" he had predicted; he himself participated in planning suburbs of a scale and design that surpassed their English models. In this same period, by contrast, Daly saw his beloved suburban villa relegated to a position of minor and eccentric use among the French middle class, who overwhelmingly preferred the form of housing the English most despised: an apartment in a large building located on a busy boulevard near the center of the city. In Paris it was the well-to-do who maintained their hold on the inner city, while industry and workers were pushed toward peripheral "suburbs" known primarily for their poverty and dreariness.

The history of a city like Paris thus lies outside the history of suburbia as it is defined in this book. This chapter will nevertheless examine the Parisian experience, because only by understanding how and why a modern city rejects suburbia can we fully understand why other cities embrace it. The Parisian middle classes were as bourgeois as their Anglo-American counterparts; they shared many of the same assumptions about family and urban life; they had reached a comparable level of economic development; yet they rejected suburbia. Thus, suburbia proved to be neither a universal middle-class phenomenon, nor a localized English housing type. It was instead an Anglo-American phenomenon, with some influence in northern and central European cities but very little in those European or Latin American cities which took their lead from Paris. A closer look at Paris will help to explain this resistance to suburbia. Similarly, a comparison of Anglo-American cities with Paris will help to explain why middle-class housing choices not only created different kinds of residential areas but ultimately also created different kinds of cities.

Paris in 1850 — more densely crowded than London

Paris had wall around city

Its residents called it "the capital of the universe," but anyone who knew its narrow, dark, fetid, and overcrowded streets could well understand why Daly predicted the imminent suburban flight of the middle class. Although the city walls had ceased to provide any real barrier to urban expansion, the vast majority of the city's 1.054 million people still lived within the boundaries established by the seventeenth century walls. In the business district of the Right Bank, where most of the city's middle class both lived and worked, population densities were more than double even the most crowded London district of the same period; indeed, they exceeded the densities of New York's Lower East Side in the 1930s.[10]

Under these circumstances, middle-class families rarely had even a complete row house to themselves. The old three and four story structures generally had a merchant's shop on the ground floor, a sitting room behind the shop, his family's dining room, kitchen, and bedrooms crowded onto the second and third floors, with any space above rented to poor artisans who were forced to put both their workshops and their families into a single garret room. Frequently these artisans did piecework for the merchant who lived below, so a whole mercantile establishment—owners, workers, and their families—was crowded into a single small house.[11]

Although this system was well adapted to the needs of small scale luxury trades, which were the heart of the Parisian economy, it took a terrible human toll, as is perhaps best symbolized by the recurrent cholera epidemics. (The most recent, that of 1848–49, claimed more than 19,000 lives.)[12] The impenetrable maze of streets, virtually unrelieved by any open space, not only bred disease in its open sewers and gutters; it also made any kind of direct travel between the different districts of the city impossible. Yet the close physical contact between rich and poor in these isolated "urban villages" did not create any measure of class harmony. On the contrary: it bred the ferocious class hatred of the June Days of the Revolution of 1848, in which more than 3,000 workers died defending their barricades against the rifles and artillery of the army.[13]

Yet less than a mile from this region of overcrowding, disease, and class conflict lay open fields and quiet villages. Beyond the central zone defined by the line of the seventeenth century fortifications could be found an intermediate zone enclosed by the eighteenth century customs wall, which marked the legal limits of the city in 1850. A mile beyond the customs wall was a nineteenth century line of fortifications, which in 1860 became the new boundary of the enlarged city. The outer area between the customs wall and the new fortifications was still virtually rural. Already the Parisian middle class had begun to erect summer villas there, just as their London counterparts had done outside London a century before. Daly, who printed the plans and elevations of many of these villas in his architectural journal, hailed them as the French forerunners of a comparable great movement of Parisian suburbanization.[14]

Nevertheless, by 1850 only a few of the French bourgeoisie had taken the crucial step and converted their summer and weekend villas into full-time residences. The lack of enthusiasm for suburbanization was not due to inadequate transportation between the rural outskirts and the center. On the contrary, Paris had a surprisingly efficient horse drawn omnibus system— the London system was, in fact, established by French entrepreneurs who copied the Parisian model—and there were even steam railroads that made the trip in less than half an hour.[15]

During the 1840s the most prosperous French merchants and bankers—the counterparts of the English group that had estab-

lished Clapham—did leave the crowded center, but not for suburban villas. Instead, they created a new urban district, called
the Chaussée d'Antin after its principal street. Located on the
Right Bank at what was then the northwest edge of the city,
the Chaussée d'Antin embodied the "suburban" principles of
domesticity, privacy, and class segregation, but in an urban setting. The Chaussée d'Antin presented a solid front of luxurious
structures that proclaimed their affiliation with the city and not
the countryside.[16]

The characteristic building type of the Chaussée was the
apartment house, but these grand edifices had nothing in common with the haphazardly divided row houses of the older
districts. Their real design affiliation was with the aristocratic
palais, most notably the eighteenth century Palais Royal, the
archetypal upper-class apartment dwelling that the duke of Or-
léans had built as a profitable speculation behind his own palace.
The apartment houses of the Chaussée were urban palaces for
the upper middle class, their imposing five and six story facades
copied from the classical forms of the Palais Royal or from other
eighteenth century aristocratic urban mansions.[17] Behind these
facades lay not a jumble of workspace and family space but
elegant suites of rooms, each apartment generally occupying a
whole floor.[18]

The new apartments were very much residential space. Offices and salesrooms remained in the urban core, which—like
the City of London and the center of Manchester—was changing
into a nonresidential business district. They were also class segregated spaces. Although rents decreased as one ascended the
stairs, all apartments were designed for the well-to-do, and those
garret spaces which remained under the roof were used for
servants from the apartments below.[19]

The apartment houses of the Chaussée d'Antin were to be as
influential for the French bourgeoisie as the suburban villas of
Clapham or Victoria Park had been for the English. They established a model of affluent domesticity toward which the middle
class could aspire. In England the Evangelical movement had
united defense of the family with a strong antiurbanism. Not

over →

only must the family be separated from the world of work; it must leave the corrupting city completely for the natural world of the countryside. The French bourgeoisie also felt strongly the ideal of domesticity, but, lacking the Puritan tradition of the Evangelicals, they saw no contradiction between family life and the pleasures of urban culture. On the contrary, their ideal combined a bourgeois concern for family isolation and privacy with a ready access to the theaters, balls, cafés, and restaurants of Paris that had previously been the privilege of the upper class. The urban apartment house—at once aristocratic in its facade and thoroughly bourgeois in its domestic arrangements—exactly expressed this ideal.[20]

By a curious paradox, the English Evangelicals, though extravagantly loyal to the established political order, rejected aristocratic tastes in urban culture as dangerous and dissolute. Their French counterparts, who violently rejected aristocratic political leadership, nonetheless were extravagantly loyal to the aristocratic urban ideal. As Louis Bergeron writes, the fundamental conquest of the Great Revolution in France was "the 'democratization' of an aristocratic style of life which in previous ages had been both a source of envy and a source of oppression."[21] Bergeron's phrase, "the 'democratization' of an aristocratic style of life" describes exactly the dominant impulse behind the great middle-class Parisian innovation in urban housing, the large apartment house.

If the apartment house provided an ideal for middle-class life, we might nevertheless wonder whether this ideal was attainable for anyone but the elite of the bourgeoisie who inhabited the Chaussée d'Antin. In the 1840s the relatively undeveloped Parisian housing industry was poorly equipped to cope with the special demands of large apartment houses. First, locating a suitable site was a major problem; most streets were too narrow for such high buildings, and even property along the principal streets was divided into small parcels jealously guarded by their owners. Capital for undertaking a large building was equally difficult to obtain. The French notaries, who performed the same function of placing mortgages as the English solicitors, were even less able to provide large lump sums for a major construction project.[22]

In view of these limitations, it seemed unlikely that apartment houses would ever be built in sufficient numbers to satisfy the pent up demand of the middle class in the central districts for a new form of domestic living. A few might be erected in an area of special privilege to serve as a symbol for the elite; but that the majority of the middle class could be housed in such *beaux quartiers* seemed as unlikely as the local draper being invited to dine with the Rothschilds.

In this context Daly's prediction of middle-class suburbanization made sense. The suburban villa might not be the first choice of the French middle class, but it admirably suited both the strengths and the weaknesses of the French housing trade. No great concentration of capital was needed; villas could be built one by one on whatever cheap land at the outskirts was most readily available. Piece by piece, using only the small, scattered sums that the notaries were able to provide, a suburban belt outside Paris could take shape. As in England, where villas clustered around particularly favored spots, a suburban style would be established that would draw the mass of the French middle class out of the city.

This predictable result never took place. Instead, a massive government intervention into the French housing market totally changed the rules of the game and made possible the construction of apartment houses near the center of Paris on a scale that no one could have foreseen.

Baron Haussmann
and the Rebuilding of Paris

This government intervention was Louis Napoleon's and Eugène-Georges Haussmann's reconstruction of Paris. Napoleon III wished to transform Paris into a grand imperial capital, and to this end he gave virtually dictatorial powers to the prefect of Paris, Baron Haussmann. Haussmann's plan was to cut wide, straight boulevards through the maze of narrow streets, buying up and demolishing any buildings that stood in the way. These boulevards were to provide the crucial means of communication that would finally unite Paris into a great city.[23]

But opening new routes of communication was far from Haussmann's only concern. He wished to make the new boulevards truly monumental, which required that they be lined with massive, luxurious buildings. He settled on the new apartment houses of the Chaussée d'Antin as the building type that best suited his needs. These elegantly designed structures, uniform in height and sumptuous in decoration, would provide the glorious architectural borders to complement the width of the boulevards. Socially, the new apartment houses would make the boulevards the center of life and fashion. Politically, these elaborate and prestigious dwellings would reward the bourgeoisie and symbolize their adherence to the Napoleonic regime.[24]

Haussmann therefore set to work to ensure that apartment houses along the boulevards be built quickly, in sufficient numbers, and to his specifications. His goal, he proclaimed, was to make sure that a new boulevard was "completely lined with finished houses the moment it was opened to traffic."[25] The basic financial and administrative techniques were first tried in the frantic efforts to complete the buildings on the extension of the Rue de Rivoli in time for the World's Fair of 1855. By the end of the 1850s these techniques had been perfected.

Haussmann controlled the most valuable prize from his massive demolitions: the prime land that bordered the new boulevards. Suddenly a wealth of prime sites opened in the heart of Paris, and Haussmann reserved this land for builders committed to erecting apartment houses according to his plans. These favored builders often got the land for less than its market value.[26]

Moreover, the government made it possible for developers to escape the limitations of the traditional mortgage market and to receive as much credit as they required from a government sponsored mortgage bank. The Crédit foncier, as it was called, raised money by selling shares to small investors throughout France. It then combined these investments into large sums, which it loaned—at Haussmann's direction—to Parisian apartment house developers. These developers were thus assured of almost unlimited capital with which to erect apartment houses and long term mortgages when the apartment houses were complete.[27]

Finally, the largest developers formed joint stock companies, which also raised money from small investors. These companies permitted them to operate on an even larger scale and thus respond to the unprecedented opportunities created by the continuing construction of boulevards throughout the Second Empire. They were, in effect, industrial scale operations employing permanent staffs of architects, engineers, craftsmen, and foremen on projects throughout the city. The most prominent such company was the Société Immobilière de Paris, founded by the Pereire brothers. Needless to say, such companies enjoyed a special relationship with Haussmann and with the Crédit foncier.[28]

Haussmann's reliance on state power and state supported banks and corporations reflects the philosophy derived by Henri de Saint-Simon that the underdeveloped French economy must be organized in order to undertake the large scale task of modernization. Haussmann mobilized the Parisian building industry to accomplish what private enterprise unaided could never have attempted. With power and profit both committed to the task of middle-class housing, the boulevards were soon lined with the apartment houses of Haussmann's vision.

This governmental initiative suddenly made the middle-class cultural ideal of the luxury apartment house attainable. The massive boom promoted the rapid improvement in apartment house design and standards of construction, an improvement furthered—ironically—by César Daly's publishing the most notable innovations in his journal. These structures presented an elaborate and expensive carved stone facade to the street. A classical ordering of half-columns or pilasters provided the basic discipline, which was relieved by exuberant sculptured detail—lions' heads, maidens' bodies, cornucopia—around windows, over doorways, or wherever it could be fitted. Wrought iron balconies provided the necessary horizontal accent.[29]

Most apartment houses had shops on the ground floor, grouped around a large central entrance where the residents entered and through which carriages could pass to an inner courtyard. The shops not only provided income to the building's owners but also helped to ensure that the boulevard itself would have a lively street life. Nevertheless, to ensure privacy the shops did not connect with the residences. Servants and tradesmen used the back stairs, while only the residents and their guests used the main stairway.[30]

The apartments were usually decorated with parquet floors, elaborate plastering, marble fireplaces topped with gilt framed mirrors, and other luxuries that proclaimed the occupant's (spiritual) kinship with the aristocracy. Even within the apartment the distinction was maintained between the family rooms—living room, dining room, parlor, and bedrooms, usually arranged as a suite of interconnecting rooms facing the street—and the servants' space (including the kitchen) facing the interior courtyard.[31] At night the servants slept in the garrets under the roof. The French thus introduced into the heart of the city the same domestic isolation that the English had achieved by fleeing to suburbia.

Not surprisingly, the Parisian middle class moved en masse to the apartments of the boulevards and the *beaux quartiers*; and their loyalty to the large apartment house has never wavered. The consequences of Haussmannization have further ensured that the suburban ideal would make few converts among the Parisian bourgeoisie. First, Haussmann's financial arrangements choked off the supply of small investments that might have supported gradual suburbanization. The savings of small French investors, which in England and the United States found their way into the hands of small suburban builders, were instead attracted to the shares of the Crédit foncier or the joint stock development companies that financed the apartment houses that Haussmann desired. In England the network of small investors and small builders had guaranteed a constant supply of suburban houses for the market. In France, that supply network never developed, while the government sponsored apartment house network flourished.

At the same time, Haussmann's activities drastically altered the social geography of the city. The poor, who received none of the largess that Haussmann bestowed on the favored bourgeoisie, found their neighborhoods demolished and were forced by government policy to move to the outskirts. Industry too was forced to the periphery, and a working-class industrial belt was formed in precisely those picturesque areas which might have attracted middle-class villas.[32]

The industrialization of Paris in the mid nineteenth century thus had the opposite effect it had in Manchester. It hastened the movement of the working class to the outskirts, and the growing industrial belt at the periphery confirmed the middle class in their loyalty of the central areas. "Suburbanization" in the French sense has thus come to refer almost exclusively to a working-class or lower middle-class movement to the periphery.

Haussmann was forced to resign in 1870 after conservative bankers raised serious questions about his financial procedures, and the regime itself collapsed in the defeat of the Franco-Prussian War later that year. Nevertheless, the Third Republic confirmed the work of the Second Empire, acknowledging that in the twenty years of Haussmannization, Paris had achieved its classic form.[33] And this form exercised a deep fascination on other western European cities, starting with Lyons and Marseilles.[34] In the late 1860s Vienna began its Ringstrasse development, another government sponsored effort to create a zone of privilege in the urban core based on monumental apartment houses whose facades imitated Baroque palaces and whose apartments housed the bourgeoisie. From Vienna the form spread through central and eastern Europe.[35]

The example of Paris proves that middle-class suburbanization was never the inevitable fate of the bourgeoisie. With bourgeois commitment to a distinctly urban culture, the central city could be rebuilt to suit their values. But this rebuilding was impossible without a government willing to intervene massively both in the housing market and in the urban fabric. In the nineteenth century, suburbia represented the path of small scale enterprise and laissez-faire. The great Parisian boulevards lined with rows of apartment houses expressed the union of middle-class values with authoritarian planning.

Suburbia Comes to the United States

wasn't it Oscar Wilde?

Although, as Mark Twain claimed, good Americans when they die may go to Paris, living Americans have sought a very different kind of city. In the very years that Paris was rejecting the bourgeois residential suburb, American cities made it an integral part of their structure. The roots of this acceptance go deep in the culture and economy of the American middle class, so deep that even the most careful students of American suburbia have assumed that suburbanization was "made in the U.S.A." Nevertheless, the comparison of English and American cities shows not only the priority of English suburban designs but also a surprising loyalty on the part of the American bourgeoisie to the urban row house and mixed neighborhood, long after the English bourgeoisie had opted for the detached or semidetached suburban villa.

Kenneth Jackson's definitive history, *Crabgrass Frontier: The Suburbanization of the United States*, presents the most comprehensive argument for the indigenous origins of American suburbia. He demonstrates effectively that the first half of the nineteenth century saw a significant separation of work and residence in American cities—a vital prerequisite for suburbanization—and also that the middle class tended to move their

The Ideal of the Villa. Alexander Pope's villa (1720s) on the Thames at Twickenham, ten miles southwest of London. Photo copyright and reproduced by permission of Guildhall Library, London.

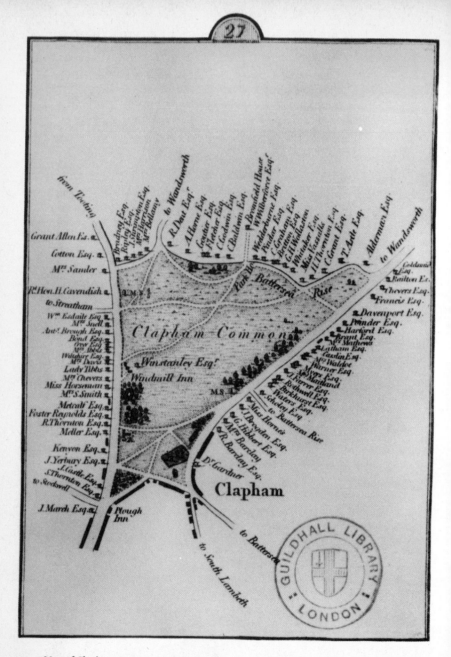

ABOVE: Map of Clapham Common (1800) shows the spontaneous clustering of villas to form a suburban neighborhood (from *Smith's Actual Survey of the Roads from London to Brighthelmston* [1800]). OPPOSITE: This anonymous watercolor in the Guildhall Library depicts Clapham Common circa 1820 with its suburban landscape of large detached villas on lawns sloping down to the Common. Photos copyright and reproduced by permission of Guildhall Library, London.

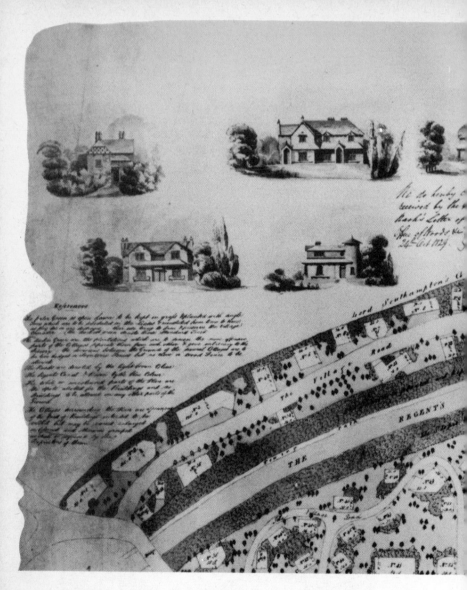

John Nash's original plan for Park Village in Regent's Park, London (1823). With his combination of picturesque landscaping and eclectic, historicist architecture, Nash here defines the essential language of suburban design. Photo copyright and reproduced by permission of the Public Record Office, London.

INSET OPPOSITE: Park Village East as it was actually built in the 1820s and 1830s by John Nash and James Pennethorne. Photo copyright and reproduced by permission of Guildhall Library, London.

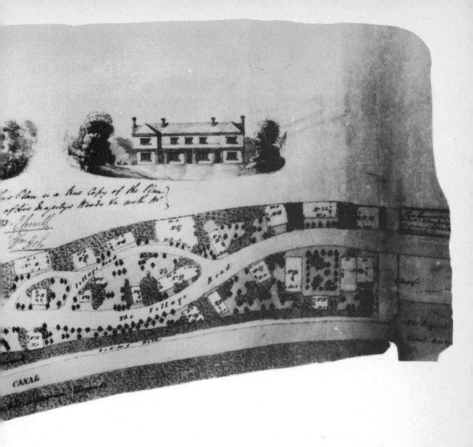

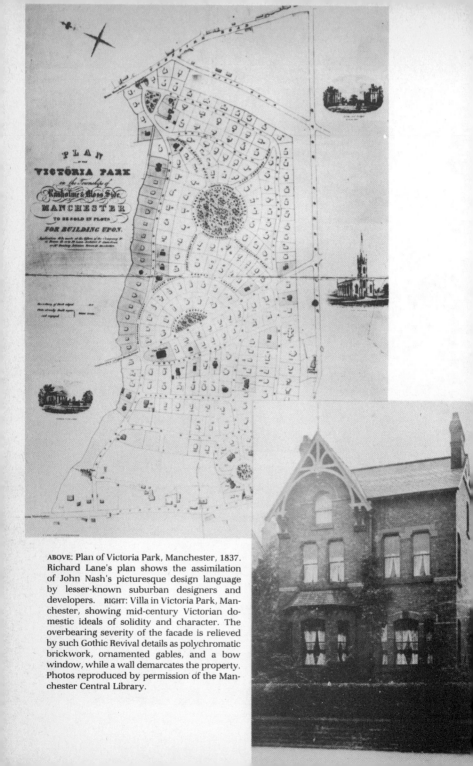

ABOVE: Plan of Victoria Park, Manchester, 1837. Richard Lane's plan shows the assimilation of John Nash's picturesque design language by lesser-known suburban designers and developers. RIGHT: Villa in Victoria Park, Manchester, showing mid-century Victorian domestic ideals of solidity and character. The overbearing severity of the facade is relieved by such Gothic Revival details as polychromatic brickwork, ornamented gables, and a bow window, while a wall demarcates the property. Photos reproduced by permission of the Manchester Central Library.

houses, which cut straight through the dense fabric of the older city. Intersection of the Boulevard Richard-Lenoir (*center*), with the Boulevard Beaumarchais (*left*), looking north from the Place de la Bastille (from Adolphe Alphand, *Les promenades de Paris* [1867]). Photo reproduced by permission of the Fine Arts Library, University of Pennsylvania.

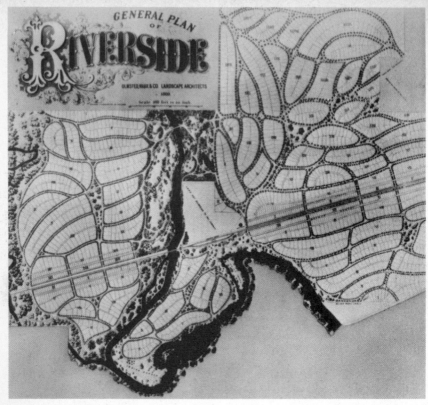

ABOVE: The suburban vision for the United States. Olmsted, Vaux & Company, plan of Riverside, Illinois, 1869. The plan specifies not only extensive tree planting along the curving roads but also a landscaped "public park" along the banks of the Des Plaines River. Photo reproduced by permission of Frederick Law Olmsted National Historic Site, National Park Service.   BELOW: Building suburbia. Subdivision of the Carpenter Estate, Germantown section of Philadelphia, 1880s. The semidetached houses appear especially massive in still-rural surroundings. Photo reproduced by permission of the Library Company of Philadelphia.

ABOVE: W. T. Harris House (1886), Bala, Pennsylvania. G. W. Hewitt, architect. A model Philadelphia suburban villa, proudly eclectic. The massive verticality of the steeply pitched gable, turreted dormer, and chimneys is set off by the horizontal lines of the porch. Photo reproduced by permission of the Historical Society of Pennsylvania, Philadelphia. BELOW: Edgar H. Butler House (1914), Chestnut Hill, Pennsylvania. Charles H. Willing, architect. A horizontal style for the twentieth-century suburb based on regional eighteenth-century Colonial prototypes and local traditions of stonework. Photo reproduced by permission of the Fine Arts Library, University of Pennsylvania.

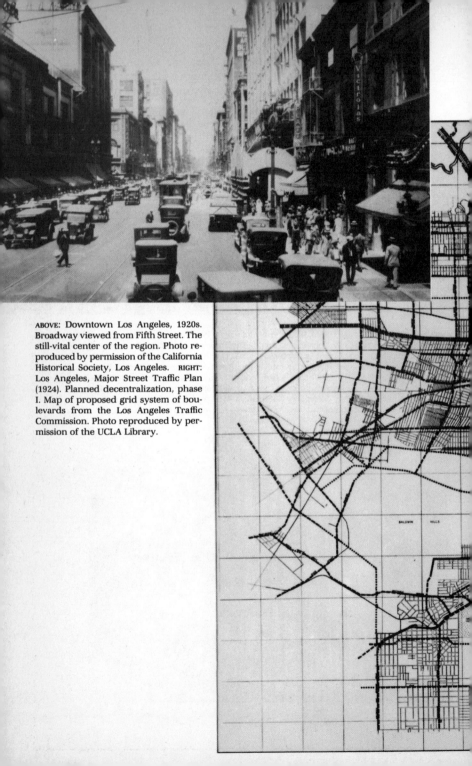

ABOVE: Downtown Los Angeles, 1920s. Broadway viewed from Fifth Street. The still-vital center of the region. Photo reproduced by permission of the California Historical Society, Los Angeles. RIGHT: Los Angeles, Major Street Traffic Plan (1924). Planned decentralization, phase I. Map of proposed grid system of boulevards from the Los Angeles Traffic Commission. Photo reproduced by permission of the UCLA Library.

Aerial view of Los Angeles (1930s). Landscape of decentralization. Looking north from Manchester Avenue on Figueroa Street, showing growth along the grid plan of major streets built in the 1920s. The closeup of the corner of Manchester Avenue and Central Avenue shows the results of haphazard subdivision and development. Photos reproduced by permission of the Department of Geography, UCLA.

Los Angeles, Traffic Survey (1937). Planned decentralization, phase II. Original freeway plan from 1937 advanced by the Automobile Club of Southern California whose proposals have been the basis of all subsequent Los Angeles freeways. Photo reproduced by permission of the UCLA Library. INSET: Tract development, Westchester section of Los Angeles, 1940. Simplified ranch house design, mass-production construction techniques, federally-guaranteed mortgages, and a decentralized system of automobile transportation combined to create mass suburbia. Photo reproduced by permission of the Henry E. Huntington Library and Art Gallery, San Marino, California.

Technoburb, USA. Cherry Hill, New Jersey and other surrounding communities, formerly residential suburbs of Philadelphia, now show a complex mix of offices; shopping malls; industrial parks; and single-family tract houses, cluster housing, and even high-rise apartments. Organized along a network of highways, this region has become a new kind of decentralized city. Photo courtesy of Stephenson Air Photos and reproduced by permission of Seltzer Development Corporation.

homes from the core to increasingly prestigious areas of peripheral residence. He even identifies what he calls "the first commuter suburb," Brooklyn Heights, across the harbor from lower Manhattan, in "the early decades of the nineteenth century." (The commuters traveled by ferry.)[36]

A true suburb, however, is more than the edge of a city inhabited largely by the middle class. It must embody in its design a "marriage of town and country," a distinct zone set apart both from the solid rows of city streets and from rural fields. This design is more than a cosmetic feature. It protects and defines the villa community even after it has been surrounded by subsequent growth, and it sets the pattern for low density development. As we have seen, Clapham and other suburbs outside London had attained this true suburban design in the late eighteenth century, well before the first ferry service linked Manhattan and Brooklyn Heights in 1814.

What is notable, not only in Brooklyn Heights but in other "fringe areas" of early nineteenth century American cities, is that the American bourgeoisie—though tending toward the peripheries—still resolutely favored the urban row house. To be sure, the richest merchants, imitating their London counterparts, had as early as the mid eighteenth century constructed beautiful villas in the fields beyond the settled areas of New York, Philadelphia, and Boston.[37] But these villas remained summer or retirement homes and never coalesced into genuine communities as in London. Still less was there an American John Nash to turn these tendencies into community design.

In Brooklyn Heights, as Jackson notes, an early developer did propose in 1823 to sell large lots for an "association" of detached villas there. But when development actually came over the next twenty years, it took the form of conventional urban row houses similar to those being constructed in Manhattan.[38] That was the pattern not only in New York City and Brooklyn but in the other large cities as well. The march of brick and then brownstone townhouses up Manhattan Island remained the great symbol of urban growth in antebellum America. They advanced as a solid mass, pushed from below by the continuous conversion of houses in lower Manhattan to commercial uses. In turn, this expansion pushed farther to the outskirts a disorderly mass of noisome enterprises and squatters, which continually threatened to engulf the few merchants' villas that stood in the countryside outside the solid streets.

This process was echoed in the stately advance of Philadelphia's elite from Society Hill west toward Rittenhouse Square and in the movement of the Boston bourgeoisie out from Beacon Hill to the most impressive row house development of the nineteenth century, the Back Bay. Begun in the 1840s, the Back Bay reached its peak of townhouse construction only in the 1860s and 1870s.[39]

The absence of a true suburban style in the United States is hardly surprising. American cities lacked the sheer bulk of London, which had more than a million residents in 1800, compared to 60,000 in New York.[40] London's size not only suggested the need to escape but also provided the critical mass of bourgeois necessary to define an alternative style. No large American city in the period, moreover, had the industrial importance of Manchester, so their mercantile offices and workshops did not generate either the intense pollution or the intense class conflict of that city. One also senses that the American bourgeois elite did not feel the same pressing need to isolate themselves in walled retreats like Manchester's Victoria Park; neither did they seek out the individual display of a free standing, highly ornamented villa. As one New York writer put it in the 1880s, "The brownstone front is a democratic institution; it being the most elegant and fashionable style of house, millionaires have been satisfied to show their splendor rather by interior decoration, pictures, and statuary, than by fine architecture or external magnificence."[41] No doubt "patrician" is a better word than the writer's "democratic" to describe such houses. They represent a collective self-confidence in their owners' ability to dominate the urban scene, regardless of the poverty and commercialism constantly pressing in around them.

What, then, caused the suburban form to supplant the townhouse among the American bourgeoisie after the mid nineteenth century? The answer is clearly related to the loss of that self-confidence which had sustained residence in a disorderly, democratic city. No doubt the most familiar reasons are still the most valid: mass immigration, industrialization, and machine politics. Underlying all of them is the great impetus that operated at Manchester: the desire for class segregation.

For all but the wealthiest, an urban townhouse district represented a considerable economic and social risk. The wealthy could afford to move their residences as the dictates of fashion changed, or even to ignore these dictates as they chose. Many New York dowagers remained loyal to the posh districts of their youth even when they had been converted to warehouses, vowing like Edith Wharton's mother to be moved "only by the undertaker."[42] At the other extreme, Andrew Carnegie could build his mansion at Fifth Avenue and 91st Street in 1889 when the site was surrounded by squatters' hovels. He was confident that he would eventually be surrounded by more suitable neighbors. In the interim he remained Andrew Carnegie.

The less secure members of the middle class had much more to lose if they were caught in a rapidly changing urban neighborhood engulfed by commercialism or the poor. As late as the 1860s Philadelphia gentlemen built alley cottages to rent to poor families behind their new row houses, which fronted on the main street.[43] Such intentional mingling of rich and poor, comparable to that which obtained in Manchester thirty years earlier, no longer was desirable once the ideal of single-class neighborhoods took hold in the United States as it had in England.

Once again, the choice was essentially simple. Either develop some coordinated political and economic construction program to "reclaim" the center for the middle class, or turn to the periphery where distance alone sufficed to isolate the bourgeoisie and enable piecemeal development to work effectively. In the absence of Napoleon III and the autocratic French state, there could be no American Haussmann. At most, an exceptionally fortunate urban row house district like Boston's Back Bay might, through excellent planning and strictly enforced land use controls, achieve stability and identity in the heart of the city. But, as American cities swelled with a new immigrant population, the single-class elite residential district seemed incompatible with the urban core.

At the same time, the example of English suburbia provided a ready-made, pretested model of a stable, peripheral community with which to direct the anarchic forces of land speculation and development. Such a model was especially important because, before 1850, an isolated, detached villa residence beyond the city—however elegant—was at least as great a financial risk as any urban dwelling. In a letter of 1860 Olmsted gives a vivid picture of the financial difficulties to which the owners of detached villas in still rural sections of Manhattan were subjected:

> Yet where five years ago there was nothing but elegance and fashion, you now see unmistakable signs of the advance guard of squalor, an anxiety to sell out on the part of the owners of the finest villas, no sales except for public houses, and an absolute deterioration in value of property. Look again at the Brooklyn suburbs. Jersey City. See the process repeated at Philadelphia and Boston.[44]

Olmsted's analysis of the problem was essentially the same as John Nash's in London fifty years earlier. As was the case in northwestern London in the 1810s, villas built haphazardly along the roads leading out of New York City were exceptionally vulnerable to "nuisances" as the city expanded. The isolated villas were soon joined by workshops seeking a convenient location along the highway, and workshops brought workers seeking "cheap tenements and boarding houses." So, Olmsted concludes, "gradually from a quiet and secluded neighborhood, it is growing to be a noisy, dusty, smoking, shouting, rattling, and stinking one."[45]

As Olmsted realized, distance from the city alone could not prevent this suburban decay. If true suburbs were to be built, what was needed was "to offer some assurance to those who wish to build villas that these districts shall not be bye and bye invaded by the desolation which thus far has invariably advanced before the progress of the town."[46] The American suburb could expect none of the implicit deference that had protected Victoria Park, Manchester from decay even during the years of its bankruptcy. Olmsted observes that unsold villas on the edge of Manhattan were soon occupied by the shanties and pigsties of Irish squatters, who kept their goats on the untended lawns and stole the timber.[47]

Like Nash, Olmsted saw the solution in a conscious process of planning and design that would isolate a tract of undeveloped land from all "undesirable" uses and define that land as a suburb suitable only for middle-class dwellings. Suburban design must become a recognized commodity, but it required a relatively wide understanding of the suburban ideal among developers, builders, and home buyers.

This ideal did spread, even more rapidly than Olmsted could have predicted. It did not, I believe, emerge from an indigenous Jeffersonian tradition of domestic architecture and antiurbanism that had somehow lain dormant in the American urban soul. The success of the suburban ideal in mid nineteenth century America came from a group of publicists who successfully presented—one might say marketed—the English suburban villa as the ideal American dwelling.

The Americanization of Suburban Style

Kenneth Jackson has identified the three authors between 1840 and 1875 who were "the most important voices in shaping new American attitudes toward housing and residential space" as Catharine Beecher, Andrew Jackson Downing, and Calvert Vaux.[48] I would add that the most salient characteristic of all three was their debt to the English sources of the suburban style: Evangelical domestic ideology and the picturesque tradition of design. Indeed, the more often they proclaimed their truly American character, the more deeply they borrowed from

English precedents. Nevertheless, they succeeded in American-izing the English detached villa and in putting forward the sub-urban style as an attractive alternative to the urban row house, which still dominated bourgeois aspirations. With a truly spir-itual fervor they preached the virtues of the detached villa in a picturesque landscaped setting as the ideal environment for American domesticity.

Catharine Beecher, whose *Treatise on Domestic Economy* (1841) became the definitive statement of American domestic ideology, was formed both intellectually and emotionally by the doctrines of the Clapham sect. Her father, Lyman Beecher, was the most influential exponent of Evangelical theology among the American clergy. Her sister, Harriet Beecher Stowe, produced in *Uncle Tom's Cabin* the great antislavery novel that added popular appeal to Wilberforce's doctrines. And Catharine herself was a true daughter of Clapham, convinced of woman's higher religious role and aptitude, intent on establishing a woman's sphere in an unspiritual man's world, and sure that domesticity was the means by which woman's spirituality would play its part in uplifting American life.[49]

Beecher's great success was in embodying these ideas in a manual of domestic economy the clarity, organization, and good sense of which made it the definitive handbook of the American home. Yet throughout her carefully elaborated instructions on, for example, the layout of a kitchen or the feeding of infants, there was implicit the great Evangelical theme that the home was the best source of Christian morality. As such, it must be separated from the profane concerns of the city. Women must see the importance of their role as homemakers and reject the temptations of urban life. Homemakers, she wrote, were "agents in accomplishing the greatest work that was ever committed to human responsibility. It is the building of a glorious temple, whose base shall be coextensive with the bounds of the earth."[50]

Beecher was never a publicist for suburbia as such, but her *Treatise* was crucial in spreading the Evangelical idea of the sanctified home, which, as in England, led directly to suburbia in America. There was nothing in her writing of which Wilberforce or Hannah More could not approve, except for her constant emphasis on the special role to which providence had called the United States. This view led to a vision of the importance of the home that even Ruskin could not equal. The United States, she believed, was the hope of the world, but that hope could only be realized through the beneficent influence of women, to whom "is committed the exalted privilege of extending over the world those blessed influences, which are to renovate degraded man."[51] But this "renovation" could only take place in the context of a truly spiritualized American home.

Andrew Jackson Downing, whose *Cottage Residences* was published the year after Beecher's *Treatise*, was her necessary counterpart in the field of domestic architecture. If Beecher Americanized the doctrines of Wilberforce, More, and the other Evangelicals, Downing Americanized the designs of John Nash and the picturesque movement. Like Beecher, he believed "above all things under heaven, in the power and influence of the *Individual Home*."[52] His constant concern was to demonstrate that only the picturesque villa or cottage, "whose humble roof, whose shady porch, whose verdant lawn and smiling flowers all breathe forth to us, in true earnest tones, a domestic feeling that at once purifies the heart and binds us closer to our fellow beings"—only the picturesque could truly embody Beecher's vision of a sacred home.[53]

Downing thereby amalgamated the picturesque aesthetic with Evangelical piety to produce the same suburban synthesis of design and moralism that had inspired the English. He began his career as a landscape gardener for the affluent estates that lined the Hudson River, but his real education came from his immersion in the forms of the English picturesque. His influence derived from the success with which he compiled and popularized the dominant styles of English villa architecture for consumption in the United States. He was especially indebted (to put it politely) to J. C. Loudon, the architect and journalist who, as we have seen, was a dominant influence in England.[54]

In view of Downing's sources of inspiration, it is hardly surprising that his ideal American house was "An Irregular Cottage in the Old English Style," a design based on fantasies of medieval England set in a miniaturized version of an eighteenth century landed estate. This type of cottage would fit very nicely into Nash's Park Village, from which, indeed, it was indirectly derived (via Loudon). Downing had well absorbed Nash's essential lesson: that picturesque architecture is not an authentic revival of the past—true authenticity is irrelevant—but an emotional style, the association of which "strengthens and invigorates our best and holiest affections."[55] What count are the feelings inspired by architecture, the capacity to make "the place dearest to our hearts a sunny spot where social sympathies take shelter securely under the shadowy eaves, or glow and entwine trustfully with the tall trees or wreathed vines that cluster around, as if striving to shut out whatever bitterness or strife may be found in the open highways of the world."[56] Only the picturesque—preferably the Gothic—could embody the irregular, spontaneous, and irrational quality that made the home an emotional refuge from the marketplace. And only a natural setting could protect the home against the city, that "arid desert of business and dissipation." In 1850 he published a plan for his ideal "country village," in which detached houses on tree lined streets surround a landscaped public park—an American Birkenhead Park.[57] Through Downing, the design philosophy of English suburbia entered into the mainstream of American domestic architecture.

Calvert Vaux, the third of Kenneth Jackson's important American voices, was born and trained in England. Downing met him in Paris in 1850 and brought him back to the United States. This background is clearly reflected in Vaux's *Villas and Cottages* (1857), though he too emphasizes the uniquely American character of his designs in terms borrowed directly from the English Evangelicals and the European picturesque architects.[58] His most important contributions came, however, as a partner first of Downing and then, after Downing's untimely death in 1852, of Olmsted.

Perhaps the culmination of this phase of English suburbia's assimilation by America came in Llewellyn Park, New Jersey (1857), an elaborately landscaped villa development in the foothills of the Orange Mountains. Named for its principal developer, Llewellyn S. Haskell, and designed by him and the architect Alexander Jackson Davis, Llewellyn Park was conceived as a picturesque assemblage of villas on curving roads surrounding a fifty acre shared park, the Ramble. Kenneth Jackson calls it "the world's first picturesque suburb"; but, as John Archer has recently demonstrated, Llewellyn Park comes directly out of the half-century-old English tradition of picturesque suburban development, starting of course with Park Village but also including Calverley Park, Tunbridge Wells (Decimus Burton, 1827–28), Prince's Park, Liverpool (Joseph Paxton and James Pennethorp, 1842) and Victoria Park, Manchester.[59]

Yet, if Llewellyn Park borrows heavily from these English precedents, it also embodies a relationship to the landscape that does seem distinctly American. Its dramatic mountainside site, with views extending down to Manhattan some twelve miles away, has little in common with the level, placid settings of English suburbs. There is an intensity in the attempt to retain the natural setting unknown in England. With lots matched carefully to the sloping ground, careful landscaping to accentuate the terrain, a prohibition of fences to divide the property, and the expanse of the Ramble, the large villas of Llewellyn Park seem almost swallowed up in nature.[60]

As Walter Creese has pointed out, Llewellyn Park owes much to the country estates of the Hudson Valley where Davis, Downing, and others attempted to find a style to match the grandeur of the scenery.[61] If the suburb is the meeting place of the city and nature, then the American suburb must attempt to match the greater dimensions of the American landscape. Most suburbs after Llewellyn Park have shirked this challenge, but the design tradition begun there later gave rise, as will be seen, to the houses poised dramatically on the Santa Monica Mountains, the Hollywood Hills, and the Palos Verdes Peninsula overlooking Los Angeles and the Pacific Ocean.

Olmsted and Riverside

As Llewellyn Park shows, the English origin of American sub-urbia does not mean that American planners and architects were doomed forever to imitate English models. The career of Frederick Law Olmsted is the clearest proof that an American steeped in the English landscape tradition could use this tra-dition creatively to formulate a suburban vision for the United States.

Even before Olmsted visited England and Birkenhead Park in 1850, he had already studied with great care the major works of English picturesque design. While still a student in his native Hartford, Connecticut, he found and read in the public library the most important works of the English picturesque: Uvedale Price's *An Essay on the Picturesque*, the source for the idea of the "picturesque village"; and William Gilpin's *Picturesque Tours*, which described admiringly the early suburban devel-opment around London. At the end of his career, Olmsted was still recommending Price and Gilpin, which he described as "books of the last century, but which I esteem so much more than any published since, as stimulating the exercise of judg-ment in matters of my art, that I put them into the hands of my pupils as soon as they come into our office, saying, 'You are to read these as seriously, as a student of Law would read Black-stone.' "[62] He also found in the Hartford Public Library the works of Humphry Repton, Nash's sometime partner and principal practitioner of picturesque landscaping; and the pastoral poet William Shenstone, a contemporary of Cowper and an advocate of the picturesque aesthetic.[63]

Having learned the theory from these works, Olmsted was able to appreciate the practice of the suburban style when he saw it in England in 1850. He was then an unknown writer struggling to make a living as a gentleman farmer on Staten Island. In 1857, while still a part-time farmer and author, he was chosen as superintendent of New York's Central Park, which was then a dreary, undeveloped wasteland. The competition for the design of the park brought him into partnership with Calvert Vaux and gave him his first opportunity to practice his ideas of the picturesque. The winning design established Olmsted, Vaux and Company as the nation's leading landscape architects and as the heirs of Downing's aesthetic leadership.[64]

Despite—or perhaps because of—Olmsted's intensive urban experience while working on Central Park, he had come by the 1860s to advocate the suburb as the "most attractive, the most refined, the most soundly wholesome" form of domestic life.[65] This attitude was not due to any slavish imitation of English ways; neither could the creator of one of the greatest urban parks be called antiurban. It proceeded from a careful analysis of the problems of the modern city and of nineteenth century America.

As Olmsted asserted in 1868, "the most prominent characteristic of the present period of civilization has been the strong tendency of people to flock together in great towns."[66] He saw this trend as essentially positive, leading not only to the "unprecedented movement of invention, energy, and skill" in the modern age, but also to the diffusion among the mass of city dwellers of comforts, luxuries, and culture that had once been available only to an elite. Yet this flocking together has its negative aspects in the psychological strains of living in crowded areas, the "peculiarly hard sort of selfishness" which inevitably takes hold in cities where conditions "compel us to walk circumspectly, watchfully, jealously," and to "look closely upon others without sympathy."[67] Such strains could lead to nervous breakdowns among the elite or to vice, crime, and intemperance among the masses.[68]

For Olmsted, as for the Evangelicals, nature was the great remedy against the evils of the city. Only if urban dwellers can experience a daily "change both of scene and air" will their physical, psychological, and moral health be maintained, and the full benefits of the city for civilization preserved. Olmsted promoted the urban park for the same reason he promoted suburbia, as "strongly counteractive to the special enervating conditions of the town."[69] Indeed, he conceived the park as a kind of in-town suburb, accessible to rich and poor. The dominating aim of park design must be "to completely shut out the city from our landscapes."[70]

But Olmsted's confidence in the healing power of urban parks diminished in the 1860s, and he grew especially critical of the urban row house—even one close to a park—as a proper home. The New York brownstone, he wrote, was "really a confession that it is impossible to build a convenient and tasteful residence in New York, adapted to the civilized requirements of a single family, except at a cost which even rich men find prohibitive."[71] At the same time, he came to believe that a villa in a properly planned suburb could, at much less cost, provide both easy access to all the benefits of urban civilization and far better opportunities for contact with nature.

The suburb, he argued, did not betoken an ebbing of the nineteenth century flood tide of urbanization but "a higher rise of the same flood"; it was "not a sacrifice of urban conveniences but their combination with the special charms and substantial advantages of rural conditions of life."[72] As he put it in a letter to Edward Everett Hale, the suburb meant "elbow room about a house without going into the country, without sacrifice of butchers, bakers, & theatres."[73] Unlike the Clapham Evangelicals, Olmsted did not see suburbanization as a withdrawal from urban culture. He emphasized that not only jobs would be accessible but the whole range of advantages only obtainable in the city. Villa residents, he stated, want and will find "the advantages of society, of compact society, of the use of professional talent in teachers, and artists and physicians. . . . They want to be served in a regular, exact, punctual, and timely manner with superior comestibles, and whatever else it is desirable to have supplied to a family, freshly, frequently, or quickly on demand."[74] In thus combining town and country, the suburb was indeed "the best application of the arts of civilization to which mankind has yet obtained."[75]

The suburb was therefore the perfected form of city dwelling, and Olmsted hoped that it would soon be available not only to the rich but to all. "I never lose an opportunity," he wrote to Hale, to urge the

> ruralizing of *all* our urban population and the urbanizing of our rustic population. For I regard it as doubtful which of two slants toward savage condition is most to be deplored and struggled with, that which we see in the dense poor quarters of our great cities and manufacturing firms or that which is impending over the scattered agricultural population of more especially the sterile parts of the great West.[76]

These ideals were very much in Olmsted's mind when, at the request of a businessman named E. E. Childs, he undertook in 1868 to plan the suburb of Riverside, Illinois. It was not, however, a suburb for "all." As Olmsted confessed, "the laws of supply and demand compel me to *work* chiefly for the rich and to study rich men's wants, fashions, and prejudices."[77] But Olmstead brought to this project not only his deep knowledge of English sources and his own genius for design, but also his ideal of what an American suburb could be. His plan represents both a summation of previous Anglo-American suburban design and a highly personal statement of Olmsted's vision of a community in harmony with nature. If there is a single plan that expresses the idea of the bourgeois utopia, it is Olmsted's Riverside.

Childs had acquired a featureless 1,600 acre tract of Midwest prairie—"low, flat, miry, and forelorn," Olmsted called it[78]—relieved only by the Des Plaines River and by the tracks of the Chicago, Burlington, and Quincy Railroad, which ran to Chicago some nine miles away. As with Central Park, Olmsted had no ready-made picturesque features to work with. Design alone had to create both the landscape and the community.[79]

The plan aimed for the balance of man and nature that had defined suburbia since Clapham—the community of houses in a park. It relied on the same picturesque design language that Nash employed at Park Village: tree lined roads that contrast with the "ordinary directness" of the city streets through their "gracefully-curved lines, generous spaces, and the absence of sharp corners, the idea being to suggest and imply leisure, contemplativeness, and happy tranquility."[80]

But Olmsted carried through this idea not only on a scale ten times as great as Park Village but with a far greater attention to the crucial interplay of public and private spaces. The developers provided the basic landscape through extensive plantings of trees and shrubs along the curving roads and in the public "greens." The plan called for 7,000 evergreens, 32,000 deciduous trees, and 47,000 shrubs.[81]

In addition, Olmsted prescribed that each house be set back at least thirty feet from the road and that "each householder shall maintain one or two living trees between his house and his highway-line."[82] Here Olmsted was reacting against the English practice seen at Victoria Park of each villa owner surrounding his property with a wall—"high dead-walls," Olmsted called them, "as of a series of private madhouses."[83] In Riverside, the tree shaded front lawns of the houses continue the effect of parkland in from the roadsides. So the homeowners on their own property were to contribute to and enhance the theme of the "community in the park."

Yet Olmsted did not wish to merge all the individual lots into a single undifferentiated landscape; that, he thought, was the great fault of Llewellyn Park. "In the present shape of civilization people are not in a healthy way who do not want to make the line between their own families and family belongings and others, a rather sharp—at least a well-defined one," he advised.[84] The aim, again, was balance between the family and the community. "The essential qualification of a suburb is domesticity, and to the emphasizing of the idea of habitation, all that favors movement should be subordinated."[85] He desired a setting of "pleasant openings and outlooks, with suggestions of refined domestic life, secluded, but not far removed from the life of the community."[86]

The "life of the community" was provided for in the extensive public spaces: more than 700 of the 1,600 acres were for common use.[87] Olmsted specified that, in addition to the private domestic needs of each family, a suburb must engender "the

harmonious association and co-operation of men in a community, and the intimate relationship and constant intercourse,
and inter-dependence between families."[88] To this end he specified an arcadian array of pleasure grounds: village greens,
playgrounds, croquet and ball grounds, sheltered resting spots
along the roads. The river would be dammed to form a lake for
boating and ice skating, and the lake surrounded by public
walks and "pretty boat landings, terraces, balconies overhanging
the water, and pavilions at points desirable for observing re-
gattas, mainly of rustic character, and to be half overgrown
with vines."[89]

Olmsted further recommended that land for a wide, landscaped pleasure drive be purchased to connect Riverside with
the outskirts of Chicago. Lined with fashionable villas, this drive
would not only provide a pleasant route between suburb and
city; its constant traffic of elegant carriages and riders would
also make the drive a center of social activity.[90] Olmsted once
recalled the great pleasure he derived from being on the
Champs Elysées and watching the fashionable crowd that
promenaded there. A community, he held, must gratify "the
gregarious inclination," the desire to "see congregated human
life."[91] Riverside would provide even this archetypically urban
delight with an American suburban counterpart to Haussmann's
Parisian boulevards.

Yet, in evaluating the pleasures of the Riverside environment,
we should not forget one important contrast with similar amen-
ities that Olmsted included in his plans for urban parks. In writing about Central Park Olmsted was particularly proud of the
mixture of classes who enjoyed it, the "vast number of persons
brought closely together, poor and rich, young and old, Jew
and Gentile."[92] Riverside, however, was a paradise for the few.
And if, in Catharine Beecher's phrase, the creation of an American community of homes was "the building of a glorious temple," then that temple was built on land speculation.

In fact, the Riverside plan existed only in the context of a
speculative enterprise to sell lots, and to sell them at a price
sufficiently above the cost of the original agricultural land and

of the subsequent improvements that the investors could enjoy a substantial profit. These lots could command such elevated prices only if, as Olmsted realized, they offered "very decided and permanent advantages for suburban residence."[93] "Permanence" in this context meant essentially the long term capacity to exclude. Lurking in the wonderful elaboration of the plan was Olmsted's memory of the Manhattan villas overrun by the "Dutch boarding houses and groggeries" and occupied by Irish squatters who kept pigs and stole the timber. Olmsted's picturesque aesthetic and his attempt to envision a truly civilized community cannot be disentangled from his equally pressing aim of creating a tightly knit, exclusive society that would enjoy forever the unique benefits of its affluence.

It is somehow fitting that this ultimate bourgeois utopia should be the product not just of land speculation—that was inevitable—but of a particularly egregious form of financial legerdemain. Olmsted admitted that the Riverside Improvement Company was a "regular flyaway speculation," managed "on Gold Exchange and Erie [Railroad] principles [two notorious financial scandals of the period]."[94] When in the early 1870s lots sold more slowly than had been anticipated, one of the promoters who was also City Treasurer of Chicago pilfered more than $500,000 from city accounts to cover cost overruns at Riverside.[95] Even this illegal transfusion of funds did not save the project from the consequences of the Panic of 1873 and the subsequent depression. By 1874 the Company was bankrupt.[96]

The bankruptcy did not destroy Riverside; as with Manchester's Victoria Park and its financial difficulties, the best planned suburbs seem to have both an inherent propensity to bankruptcy and also a remarkable ability to survive it. But financial distress did mean the curtailment of many of the finer features of Olmsted's plan, most notably the grand pleasure drive. The suburb developed slowly over the next thirty years and, as will be seen in the next chapter, took on many of the general characteristics of the "railroad suburbs" that flourished at the turn of the century. In his admirable analysis of Riverside, Walter Creese acknowledges that "Olmsted never quite reached the effect he wished," but Creese still calls Riverside "The Greatest American Suburb."[97]

The bankruptcy, however, does emphasize that the whole "green world" of community, family life, and union with nature that Olmsted strove to create in Riverside rested ultimately on a frighteningly unstable economic base. The bourgeois utopia depended for its survival on market forces that even the bourgeoisie could not control.

CHAPTER 5

The Classic Suburb:
The Railroad Suburbs
of Philadelphia

I N the history of the middle-class residential suburb, the late nineteenth century railroad suburb represents the classic form, the era in which suburbia most closely approached the bourgeois monument and the bourgeois utopia. It exemplified the central meaning and contradiction of suburbia: a natural world of greenery and family life that appeared to be wholly separate from the great city yet was in fact wholly dependent on it.

Inevitably, this classic stage of suburbia coincided with the classic stage of the industrial metropolis itself. At the close of the nineteenth century great cities reached their most dominant phase in the world economy. They were, in H. G. Wells's word, whirlpools whose vortices sucked in both population and industry from farms and from smaller regions. Not only was the agrarian population of Europe and North America drawn with tremendous force out of the countryside and into great cities—

often crossing the Atlantic in their migrations—but the most advanced industries deserted the countryside and the small towns to find in the booming inner city that surrounded the metropolitan core the most profitable location for growth.

Finally, the great cities were the inevitable setting for large scale organizations: the public and private bureaucracies that were coming to dominate the modern world. And the large cities saw the largest growth in the "service" sector of the economy. The consumer culture of the late nineteenth century was almost entirely an urban phenomenon; only in the great cities did the bright lights shine. The unprecedented crowding of humanity in these cities, far from limiting their appeal, seemed to double it, drawing more and more people and industries.

In this context the middle-class suburb was at once the conquering outer edge of urban expansion and a kind of protest against that expansion. Suburbia expressed both the increasing concentration of people and resources in the inhumanely crowded, man-made world of the great cities and kept alive an alternative image of the relationship of man and nature. If suburbia was the bourgeois utopia, it existed in an inevitable tension with the bourgeois hell—the teeming world of the urban slum—from which suburbia could never wholly escape because the crowded city was the source of its prosperity.

If the classic suburb of the late nineteenth century was built ultimately on these general contradictions in bourgeois civilization, its actual form depended on a highly specific piece of industrial technology: the railroad. Although to the late twentieth century mind suburbia is inevitably associated with the automobile, this association is a mistake. The automobile, when it came, helped to destroy the basic conditions for classic suburbanization; the true suburban means of transportation has been the commuter rail line.

We tend to think of transportation and suburbanization in terms of access: a transportation system makes suburbanization possible by providing convenient access from the center to the periphery. Yet, in the history of suburbia, inaccessibility has usually been at least as important as accessibility. The relatively cheap land at the urban outskirts inevitably draws poor people and noisome industries unless that land is relatively hard to reach. This difficulty confines the bulk of people and factories to the core, while only the well-to-do have the time and resources to take the trouble to reach the outskirts.

Thus relatively inconvenient transportation facilities characterized suburbs until the late nineteenth century. Both London and Manchester suburbs made do with slow and expensive omnibus lines (or private carriages). Often new roads were resisted, as were attempts by the early railroad lines that ran through suburban areas to place their stations in such fashionable areas as Hampstead near London. Such accessibility, it was feared, would lower the tone of an area.[1]

Only in the second half of the nineteenth century did developers and residents grasp the potential of rail lines for suburbanization. For the rail system—especially the steam railroad—combined to a unique degree accessibility and inaccessibility. It provided remarkably rapid access to the center, yet its relatively high cost insulated the bourgeois peripheries from lower-class invasion. The structure of the rail system in a late nineteenth century metropolis—or rail systems, because they soon included not only steam railroads but electric trolleys, streetcars, elevated lines, and subways—came to resemble a diagram of the class structure. Each income group was distributed along the system according to how far it could afford to travel from the center and which line it could afford to take.[2]

The rail system limited accessibility in another important way. Development necessarily proceeded along the rail lines; in the usual rule of thumb, commuters could rarely live more than a fifteen minute walk from the rail station, so development was drawn into certain coherent nodes organized around the station. It inevitably created a kind of railroad village—a community with its own identity, limited in space, and surrounded by open countryside—and gave a unity of design even to railroad suburbs that had been developed piecemeal. Not every suburb was designed as a coherent whole as Olmsted's Riverside had been, but the natural unity of the railroad suburb did provide the necessary context in which Olmsted's design innovations could be assimilated on a wide scale. Finally, the rail system was almost always a radial one. Its many lines were organized as spokes from a hub, focusing the many suburban communities on a single "downtown" center.

"Suburbanites," wrote Agnes Repplier in the 1920s, "are traitors to the city."[3] This statement is at best a half truth with regard to the railroad suburbs. Precisely because they excluded so much of the city in their quest to escape from it, they remained wholly dependent on it. Downtown was a daily destination for men and an almost equally frequent destination for women. There could be found not only the jobs that supported the suburban economy, but also those urban monuments of consumption: department stores, concert halls, clubs, restaurants, theaters, and cultural centers.

Suburbanization in the railroad era thus strengthened the city, especially the downtown area. Every suburban house meant greater demand for office space, stores, and other facilities patronized by the middle class. Indeed, the urban core was the only possible place for those central institutions like the department store or the teaching hospital, which drew their clientele from all the peripheral locations. This functional unity of city and suburb was more important than whether a particular suburb was located within or outside the boundaries of the central city. For a brief moment, the railroad tracks held city and suburb in precarious equilibrium.

Although the railroad suburb existed in both Britain and the United States, it reached its classic form only in the United States. The difference was not due to any growing cultural divergence in the two countries; indeed, the turn of the century represented the greatest convergence of the Anglo-American bourgeoisie over the defense of "Anglo-Saxon" values. It was, rather, a divergence in the urban economies of the two nations.

In 1891, Sidney J. Low, in an article entitled "The Rise of the Suburbs," correctly interpreted the 1890 British census to show that both the countryside and the urban core were losing population, and that the bulk of British population growth from

1880 to 1890 had been in the suburbs. He remarked that if current trends continued, "the majority of people of this island will live in suburbs."[4]

But those trends did not continue, at least not as strongly. British cities still saw extensive suburban building, especially in London, but in the 1890s the British building industry began to slow down. The slower rate of development stemmed from such specific causes as the diversion of capital to overseas investment and then to rearmament leading to World War I, but also from the general climacteric in the British economy. As a result British cities remained relatively frozen in patterns that date back to the 1880s and beyond; only in the 1930s did suburban building again take off in Britain.[5]

In contrast, the 1890s saw American urban expansion, robust in the 1880s, explode into rapid growth that continued through the first three decades of the twentieth century. The American metropolis thus took its basic form during the railroad era, not only in such relatively new cities as Chicago, which went from a town of 30,000 in 1850 to a metropolis of over a million by 1890, but also in older eastern cities like New York and Philadelphia, which were essentially reshaped during these years.

The United States therefore had the resources and the necessity to create the most complete embodiments of the classic suburb. From Isle of the Lakes in Minneapolis to Oak Park outside Chicago, Roland Park in Baltimore, Scarsdale outside New York, and Brookline outside Boston, a common style was taking shape.[6]

I have chosen the suburbs of Philadelphia to exemplify this era in the history of suburbia. Philadelphia not only has an urban heritage that goes back to the seventeenth century; it also became a major industrial power in the course of the nineteenth century. With the dynamism of the post–Civil War American economy, Philadelphia became a textile center rivaling Manchester, a shipbuilding center rivaling the Clydeside shipyards of Glasgow, an iron and steel center rivaling Sheffield, and finally a center of such new industries as electrical goods and food processing. A major railroad terminus, home to both the Pennsylvania Railroad and the Baldwin Locomotive Works, Philadelphia was reshaped by the steam locomotive and the electric trolley. Middle-class suburbanization transformed the wealth created by the enterprises of the inner city into a bourgeois utopia at the outskirts.[7]

Origins of the Philadelphia Railroad Suburbs

Philadelphia began with a kind of suburban vision. When in 1683 William Penn laid out the checkerboard pattern of streets between the Delaware and Schuylkill rivers that still forms the basic pattern of the city, he envisioned Philadelphia as a "green country town." The citizens, he hoped, would spread their dwellings over the whole area of the city, leaving ample space for a city composed of detached dwellings interspersed with yards, fields, and orchards.[8] (Quaker ideals of plainness and aversion to urban amusements were surely among the sources of the English Evangelical attitudes that were to be so influential in creating a suburban style a century later.)

Penn, however, was premature. Even in the vast spaces of the New World, the Old World notion of a city prevailed. People crowded close to the port on the Delaware, and Philadelphia evolved into a city based on the ubiquitous row house with substantial dwellings fronting on the major streets and alley dwellings for the poor crowded in behind. In this space intensive manner, the city advanced slowly as a solid mass from the Delaware to the Schuylkill, advancing from east to west much the way contemporaneous New York City building was advancing from south to north along Manhattan Island. Only in the 1840s did the city reach the "Center Square" that Penn had laid out as the midpoint of his decentralized city of the 1680s.[9]

As early as the 1820s and 1830s the middle class showed some tendencies to separate work and residence, with workplaces remaining close to the older districts near the port and homes moving to the peripheries. Nevertheless, this movement could hardly be called suburban. The bourgeois residence remained a row house on a solid street of houses; most builders even retained the alleyways for the poor as part of their projects. The city maintained its separation from the countryside, advancing in stately rows toward the west.[10]

The one partial exception was the country villa, which the Philadelphia merchant in imitation of his London counterpart had been building since the eighteenth century in picturesque sites outside the city. As in London, these weekend and summer villas were essentially harbingers of a genuine suburbia. But unlike London or even Manchester, Philadelphia in the first half of the nineteenth century never developed a Clapham, in other words, a site in which weekend and summer residence was transformed into a year-round commuters' village.[11]

I speculated on the reasons for the relatively late date of American suburbanization in the previous chapter, and these reasons apply with special force to Philadelphia. Despite its size—Philadelphia in 1776 was larger than Manchester, and its growth kept pace with that of the first industrial city—Philadelphia was essentially a city of workshops and small offices as late as the 1840s, lacking both the exaggerated densities of London and the hard edged class distinctions of Manchester.

The 1840s, however, saw the beginnings of both rapid industrialization and—in the anti-Catholic riots—social conflict. Perhaps not coincidentally, the patrician elite was displaced from its mastery of the city's government during these years, which lessened its attachment to the old center.[12] There was no overnight shift in form. The movement of substantial row houses continued toward the Schuylkill; Philadelphia even developed its own brownstone era like Manhattan's and created in Rittenhouse Square a bastion of bourgeois urbanity. But by the mid nineteenth century the balance had shifted to genuine suburban development.

For the expansion of Philadelphia was no longer the advance of a solid city into the countryside. It was genuinely suburban

in that it sought by design to incorporate natural elements per-
manently into a domestic landscape. At first the models were
all English, or at least English as filtered through the sensibility
of Andrew Jackson Downing. Powelton Village, a suburban West
Philadelphian settlement beloved by the Quaker elite, was identical to the London suburbs built by Evangelicals twenty-five
years earlier.[13]

These first suburbs were located at the old "gateways" of the
city and were easily reached by horse drawn omnibus or tram.
But the incessant growth of the city was forever threatening to
overwhelm them. By the nineteenth century, Philadelphia was
already a low density city based on individual row houses even
for the working class. The Quaker sense of thrift had inspired
the creation of building societies, which put the purchase of a
modest row house within the grasp of most regularly employed
workers. Their houses spread out rapidly from the factory districts just beyond the urban core.

The need to put some distance between bourgeois suburbia
and the expanding industrial city inspired the shift to the railroad suburb. The early attempts to forge a rail connection between Philadelphia and the eastern Pennsylvania coal fields had
by the 1840s led to several lines that ran north from the city
through a hilly area called Germantown. Settled by German
religious refugees in William Penn's time, Germantown was still
a quiet agricultural village only five miles from Independence
Hall. Its picturesque heights had already attracted a number of
bourgeois villas; the railroad connections provided the spur that
turned the area into a true suburb.[14]

The 1850s and the 1860s were the transition years in which
the number of villas multiplied and their functions changed. At
first they were still weekend and summer retreats, useful as a
refuge from the tropical heat and tropical diseases that marked
the Philadelphia summers. But by the 1860s Germantown had
become the locale for permanent dwellings of those who
worked in the central city.[15] It had achieved the three characteristics of suburbia: first, an identity as a middle-class community; second, the exclusion of other classes and nonresiden-

tial functions; and finally, an open design that distinguished it from the city. There were, to be sure, factories and their workers scattered through the Germantown area, but the bourgeois enclaves were sufficiently defined to ensure their identity.[16]

Before we turn to the internal characteristics of these bourgeois utopias, we must recall that—as in Manchester—the suburb's final meaning is determined as much by what it excludes as by what it includes. In Manchester there was the contrast between the millowner's zone and the factory zone; the gates and walls of Victoria Park and the other northern English industrial suburbs were an assertion of authority by a group who had only a tenuous hold on it.

By the 1870s Philadelphia was far more prosperous and diverse than Manchester had been. Nevertheless, there remained the same anxiety that ultimately pervaded the suburb's relation to the city. In addition to the tension between the owners of capital and their employees, one can discern the fear of "native" Americans of being overwhelmed by an immigrant tide that lacked their values.

In this context the late nineteenth century railroad suburb was a kind of Anglo-Saxon preserve, a protected place where the true American family could prosper and reproduce itself and thus hold off the alien invasion. Prejudice along with aesthetics helped to form its leafy streets and comfortable homes. It was not a utopia for everyone, still less a democratic vision. If the railroad suburb was the classic embodiment of the bourgeois dream of property, family life, and union with nature, it was built on a foundation of fear as well as hope.

Chestnut Hill: The Making of a Railroad Suburb

Among the early residents of Germantown was Henry Howard Houston, a prominent executive with the Pennsylvania Railroad. In the late 1870s he conceived the idea of turning some 3,000 acres of hilly farmland just beyond the settled part of German-town into an exclusive suburb. This land, eleven miles northwest of the commercial center of Philadelphia, was part of the village of Chestnut Hill which had been annexed by Philadelphia in 1854 but which in the 1870s still retained its near-rural quiet and isolation. Houston's acres overlooked the picturesque valley of the Wissahickon, so he called his development "Wissahickon Heights." Houston's initiative set the tone for the suburbanization of Chestnut Hill. Because he had far greater resources than the average developer, Chestnut Hill under his direction approached the suburban ideal of his time.

Houston himself was an apt symbol of the American bourgeoisie of his time. He represented the growth of large scale organization: the Pennsylvania Railroad was perhaps the best organized American corporation of its time, and Houston had played a particularly prominent part in creating its nationwide freight service. He thus stood for the American executive who was profiting from the opening up of the national market. Yet he was also an entrepreneur on his own account, speculating successfully in the western Pennsylvania oil fields. And finally he turned to real estate speculation, with an ambitious plan not only to create an ideal for his own class but also to profit enormously from it.[17]

As a railroad executive, he grasped a basic point, which held true not only in the railroad era but also in the highway era that followed it: the ultimate purpose of suburban transportation lines is not to move people; it is to increase the value of the land through which it passes. The best suburban land developer must also be a rail developer, so he can direct his lines through land he already owns, and retain the bulk of the increased value for himself.

Houston did not own the Pennsylvania Railroad, but he was sufficiently influential to persuade the line to build a special branch line with stops along his property ending in the village of Chestnut Hill.[18] Suddenly his land was within thirty minutes of the center of Philadelphia. It was also surrounded by land that remained relatively inconvenient, land that was unlikely to be developed rapidly and which thus remained as an agricultural buffer around his village.

The rail line, however, was not in itself sufficient. There were many lines leading out of Philadelphia, and more land available within commuting distance than there were prosperous families to purchase it. The next step was a street plan for his land in Chestnut Hill that would distinguish it from its rivals. Houston's design for Chestnut Hill, executed through his chosen firm of architects G. W. and W. D. Hewitt, proved serviceable enough, but it lacked the special merits of Olmsted's plan for Riverside. The Chestnut Hill checkerboard showed none of the graceful curves of Olmsted's plan, nor Olmsted's careful provision of public space.[19]

Nevertheless, Houston and the Hewitts had grasped the essentials: the balance of public and private land secured through large houses set well back on substantial landscaped plots ranging from one to three acres. More important than the design, moreover, were the institutions that Houston founded for Chestnut Hill or persuaded to locate there. First came a grand resort hotel, the Wissahickon Inn; then a country club, the Philadelphia Cricket Club; and finally an Episcopal church called St. Martin-in-the-Fields.

The hotel came first because it established immediately the social tone of the community. Its presence points to the close relation between the resort and the suburb in this period. In the 1880s a resort could still be located only eleven miles from the city center; it served as a summer retreat for those still living in townhouses in the urban core. As such it was a natural point of transition between urban living and a suburban residence near the hotel.[20]

The ideal upper middle-class life at this time possessed a surprising amount of mobility. With servants to do the packing, it was possible for a wealthy family to move each spring from a townhouse in Rittenhouse Square to the Wissahickon Inn, then to a New Jersey shore resort in the summer, back to the Wissahickon Inn in the autumn, and finally to Rittenhouse Square for the winter season. This mobility was possible only for the very rich. Houston, however, knew very well the value of capturing them for at least part of their migratory pattern. They might be persuaded to buy lots in the community; but, more importantly, their presence was an incentive for others who could only afford one house.[21]

The country club and the Episcopal church completed the trio of Chestnut Hill institutions founded by Houston. However their earthly purposes may have diverged, socially they stood for the same thing. Physically, the church, designed by the Hewitts in an English Gothic style, adjoined the neo-Georgian cricket club (which, in fact, soon devoted itself to tennis and golf). The membership of these two institutions defined exactly that bourgeois class which Houston was trying to attract.

The extravagantly English tone of both institutions was also significant. It was the sign of an American Protestant elite attempting to detach itself from a metropolis whose Catholic, Jewish, and fundamentalist Protestant populations were rapidly growing. It reveals, moreover, the odd anomaly between these "traditions" and real history. Philadelphia had been established and first settled by men and women who had attempted to escape the oppression of the Anglican church and the English establishment. Just as the Manchester manufacturers had seized upon the trappings of a hated aristocracy to justify their authority, so the Philadelphia gentlemen of the late nineteenth century revived the styles of their ancestors' oppressors in order to buttress their position in the industrial metropolis.

The Landscape of the Classic Suburb

The distinguishing feature of Chestnut Hill and other classic suburbs, however, was not such community institutions as ←
churches or country clubs but the landscape. The pattern of tree shaded streets, broad open lawns, substantial houses set

145

back from the sidewalks was a pattern of prosperity, family life, and union with nature that represents the culmination of the suburban style.

This style is difficult to describe because it could be neither the creation of the original planners nor that of the individual householders. Nor could it be created immediately; it required decades of patience before the foliage and shrubbery could achieve its intended effect. It is, rather, a genuinely communal creation, a style created by the bourgeoisie for itself. The suburban landscape, not the individual house, is the true monument.

Although the roots of this style can be traced directly back to Clapham and to Park Village, its perfection required a long evolution. In England, large plots tended to be walled in imitation of aristocratic country houses, blocking the view from the sidewalks. Olmsted, as we have seen, compared walking on such streets to walking outside the walled precincts of a madhouse.[22] Houses on smaller plots were usually placed very close to the sidewalk, with the front yard a small enclosed area generally densely filled with plants and shrubs. Even if the houses were detached, they were placed so close together on the street that they tended to look as if they were a terraced row. Backyards, moreover, were generally neglected even in the grandest homes.

Olmsted in his Riverside plans was perhaps the first to sketch out a genuine American suburban landscape. To eliminate the "madhouse" effect he prohibited high walls and required that each house be set back a minimum of thirty feet from the sidewalk. At the same time he provided for elaborate tree plantings along both sides of the streets. He thus specified the design conditions for that greatest of American suburban landscape institutions, the front lawn.[23]

The front lawn is not family space, and family members rarely venture out into it except to maintain it. It belongs, rather, to the community. The lawns, in conjunction with the roadside trees, create the illusion of a park. Their greenery transforms an urban street into a country lane. The lawn is the owner's principal contribution to the suburban landscape—the piece of the "park" he keeps up himself. At the same time the lawn is also private space, which no casual sidewalk passerby can make his own. It insulates the house while helping to create the green world of the landscape. Not surprisingly, lawn maintenance is considered a civic duty at least as important as any other form of morality. The lawn thus maintains that balance of the public and the private which is the essence of the mature suburban style.

The lawn is also the scene of what the landscape historian J. B. Jackson has called "the lawn culture," that complex of games and other social activities that took place on the lawns of late nineteenth century suburbia. It was a safe space in which young men and women could properly engage in such games as archery, horseshoes, badminton, and croquet, watched by their elders on the porch. The lawn thus provided a kind of space unavailable to the urban townhouse.[24]

The culmination of the lawn culture was the country club, with its carefully tended golf course. It represents the suburban equivalent of the urban park, the railroad suburb's closest approach to genuine public space. Golf and suburbia have been intimately connected since the late nineteenth century. St. Andrew's, the first American golf club, was founded in 1889 in Yonkers, New York, and the institution spread to all the other bourgeois suburbs.[25] Golf had the right British associations; it was exclusive without the expense or danger of horseback riding; it represented open air exercise with a moderation appropriate to a busy executive. The fairways captured for suburbia the large scale landscaping derived ultimately from Capability Brown and the other English country house designers, which had previously been available only to the very rich. The beautifully planted grounds of the older country clubs may be the most perfect realization of the cultural ideal of the picturesque ever created in the United States.

Yet these institutions were of course *clubs*, institutionalized means to define the social boundaries of suburbia. The result is an apt symbol of "public space" in the railroad suburb. The most impressive spaces are the most strictly private; and "nature" itself (as controlled by the country club) becomes the instrument of social snobbery and of racial and religious prejudice.

Domestic Architecture and the Railroad Suburb

In response to the classic suburban landscape, American architects created the classic suburban house. It was a slow process. When Olmsted designed Riverside, he feared that the houses were unlikely to be worthy of the terrain, and he hoped only that the landscaping would obscure the more inaesthetic examples. His criticism of domestic architecture in his time was encapsulated in his description, "stuck up." He meant both the "uneasy pretentious air" most houses possessed and their unseemly verticality.[26]

Although the suburban villa had escaped from the confines of a small town lot, it still looked squeezed into a narrow verticality. Detached houses were still packed together, giving to a line of separate houses the appearance of a solid urban row. Developers instinctively divided land into lots with a relatively narrow street frontage but a depth three times as great (75 by 225 feet was a common dimension). Even when a house was placed on a wider lot, it retained this narrow look; the Italianate style, with its insistently vertical windows and ornamental tower, best embodied Olmsted's "stuck up" appearance.[27]

Such houses did sit uneasily in the suburban landscape. The great achievement of American domestic architecture in the years before World War I was to recapture the horizontal for the suburban house. Just as importantly, they minimized the narrow divisions within the house, eliminating the boxy rooms of the typical Victorian dwelling to create a relatively open plan that flowed from room to room in duplication of the openness of the suburban landscape.

In architectural history these developments are inevitably associated with Frank Lloyd Wright and especially the houses he built for Oak Park and other Chicago suburbs between 1894 and 1911. Yet Wright and the other members of the Prairie School were, in this respect, part of a larger movement of suburban architecture. In the Philadelphia suburbs architects working with more traditional forms achieved the same horizontality and openness. The names of the architects and their firms—Hazelhurst and Huckel; Duhring, Okie, and Ziegler; and Horace Trumbauer—are less known because they expressed their innovations within the context of reviving two important regional forms: the Georgian or Colonial Revival villa and the Pennsylvania stone farmhouse.[28]

There were important formal reasons why these forms should attract renewed attention from architects and their clients in the late nineteenth century. Colonial Revival betokened a new concern for simplicity, while the farmhouses possessed not only simplicity but the horizontality so much to be prized. Both were marked by a relatively open plan. In addition to these formal matters, there were also the all-important historical associations. Colonial Revival identified its owners with the colonial settlers who had preceded the immigrant hordes. It was the perfect setting for the evidence of ancestral roots (real or hastily purchased) to be displayed.

The stone farmhouses were even more "native." In the mid nineteenth century the rough stonework of the farmhouse had stood for the hardships of rural life from which so much of the middle class had fled, and which few wished to recall. The Gothic or Italianate villa, by contrast, had represented culture and affluence. Now, however, with more recent Europeans pressing in, European associations seemed less important than a closer identification with the native virtues of the yeoman farmer.

The suburban Philadelphia house thus evolved into that expansive center hall Colonial which, in its smaller, post-1945 form, still influences American domestic architecture as Wright's forms never did. In its 1900 American incarnation the

Georgian villa lost its boxy geometry and careful separation from its environment. It assumed the longer, lower horizontal lines of the farmhouse, along with the roughstone walls or clapboard.

For the interior space, the Georgian floor plan provided an excellent alternative to the Victorian division of space. As in the eighteenth century villas around Philadelphia, the central space was an open hall and stairway, generously lit by a fanlight over the entrance door, windows on each landing, and sometimes a skylight. The ground floor was divided into just a few large rooms: a den or library, dining room, and kitchen on one side of the hall, and one very large "living room" on the other.

Above, all recollection of the Victorian "upstairs parlor" had been lost. There was in the new plan a complete division between a ground floor that was semipublic space, open at a glance to the visitor and completely available to him, and a second floor that was for the family only. Servants, however, remained carefully segregated in the Victorian mode, with backstairs connecting the back door, kitchen, and servants' apartments.[29]

The motivation behind this new openness was the same as in Wright's contemporary Oak Park houses: a greater degree of togetherness for the family. No longer are there rigidly segregated men's, women's, and children's spaces within the family. Even in the largest houses, the male "smoking room," the female parlor, and the children's wing became things of the past. Instead there was a common downstairs area, where all family members gathered when not in their own rooms, an open space that found its focus—as in Wright's designs—in a central fireplace that symbolized the unity of the home.[30]

If this intensified domesticity looks ahead to the "togetherness" of the twentieth century, it also looks back to the openness of the first suburbanites. The Clapham villas had also championed an open plan, the free association of all members of the family in a specially-designated family room. With the overcoming of the Victorian pattern of interior segregation, the suburban house reclaimed the domestic openness which was its true legacy.

150

The Classic Suburb in the Changing City

If segregation within the suburban house was overcome, the railroad suburb itself remained an increasingly defensive enclave. Even as the city expanded, its lavish use of space set it off from the working class and (more pertinently) from the aspiring members of the lower middle class. Surprisingly close to Germantown and Chestnut Hill were the spinning mills and other industries from which many of the most prosperous suburbanites derived their incomes. A subtle but deep division kept the factory workers' row houses from straying too close to the bourgeois utopia. This division did not correspond to any political boundary; it reflected instead the power of property, as reflected in the restrictive covenants that prohibited division of lots for smaller houses or their use for multifamily dwellings. The typical covenant set a minimum value for a house; prohibited any commercial or industrial use; and frequently barred Jews and blacks.[31]

A different kind of segregation kept out the lower middle class. The steam railroads carried the bourgeoisie to their suburban retreats. The trolley lines of the 1890s and 1900s brought the rest of the middle class to different destinations. "Streetcar magnates" such as Peter A. B. Widener and William Elkins followed Henry Howard Houston's lead in joining transportation and real estate speculation. Their new lines carefully followed the map of their property holdings. On each new tract opened up to trolley commutation they built solid blocks of row houses, substantial structures with large back yards, all built essentially to the same plan. Land was too expensive to attempt to imitate the detached houses of bourgeois suburbia.[32]

As the lower middle class pressed in from one direction, a new upper class moved out in the other. Encouraged by the success of the Chestnut Hill line, the Pennsylvania Railroad took the initiative in developing the quiet farm villages that lay ten to fifteen miles outside Philadelphia on its main line to Harrisburg and Pittsburgh. The beautiful countryside attracted the very rich, who built mansions on estates that covered hundreds of acres. The merely affluent soon followed, along with their country clubs and Episcopalian churches.[33]

In the industrial metropolis every social stratum thus grouped itself along the all important rail lines that organized the region. Yet, in spite of all the growth at the periphery, the center still held. Only the historic core, where all the rail lines converged, could offer a prime commercial location. So Wanamaker's Department Store expanded their already massive headquarters across from City Hall into a palazzo to dwarf any that Michelangelo ever saw; skyscrapers vied for space with new theaters and hotels; the downtown area attained its own kind of monumentality.[34]

Similarly, the factory districts adjacent to the core gained what seemed to be an ever increasing advantage over their counterparts in small towns or the countryside. They had not only the best transportation facilities and the largest pool of skilled workers; they also had a virtual monopoly on flexibility and innovation. The multitude of firms closely packed together gave each one the crucial personal contacts that made it possible to profit from each tiny shift in rapidly changing markets. Innovation, too, seemed to be an urban monopoly, as the largest cities gained an advantage in the most advanced techniques.

The metropolis seemed to be an unbreakable growth machine, and the railroad suburb reflected this confidence and prosperity. Its solid houses were built to last, and they have lasted. The factories whose profits built these suburbs have closed or moved; the downtown area has entered a permanent crisis of rebuilding and renewal; the railroads themselves have long been bankrupt. Yet the classic railroad suburb remains a sought-after monument.

It has been suggested that monuments rarely exactly coincide with the high point of confidence of the class that built them. When confidence and power are unshakable, there is no need to build monuments. It is only when confidence begins to wane that people feel the need for the reassurance that a solid embodiment of their beliefs can bring. According to this argument, the cathedrals were less the outward sign of an unquestioned age of faith than a desperate attempt to hold onto faith when inner belief was slipping. The classic suburb is one such ambivalent symbol. Its appearance of solid confidence conceals a deep anxiety over the reality of its values. It stands for the prosperity of a bourgeois elite, yet that elite could not conceal from itself the fragility of the economic system that supported it.

The building of Chestnut Hill exactly coincided with the "long wave" economic depression from 1873 to 1896, the relatively brief upturns of which were counteracted by the Panic of 1873, the depression of 1883–85, the recession of 1890–91, and then the depression of 1893–96. The latter hit Philadelphia particularly hard, because it began with the failure of the Philadelphia & Reading Railroad. Even the boom of 1897–1914 was marred by financial setbacks in 1903, 1907, 1910–11, and 1913–14. Each took its toll on the "solid" middle class.

Similarly, the family had entered into its long period of crisis, which belied the togetherness implied by the classic suburban house. Although these houses might return to the open plan of the Clapham villas, their residents could hardly hope to duplicate the certainty of the eighteenth century Evangelicals, who saw the family as a divine institution and the difference between men and women as divinely ordained, and who sincerely expected to find the family reunited after death in heaven. These certainties had been replaced by feminism, divorce, and disbelief. Not surprisingly, the great suburban theme in serious American fiction was to become the breakup of the family.

The tension closest to the surface was that between the implied confidence that suburbia represented the natural leadership of the city and the nation, and the fear that the city was now under the control of "alien" elements. This fear led to the portrayal of the city as a dumping ground of Europe's refuse, inferior people incapable of understanding the American values, which survived only in suburban isolation. Owen Wister, the patrician Philadelphian who wrote the cowboy story *The Vir-*

ginian to celebrate true Anglo-Saxon virtue against "Poles or Huns or Russian Jews," captured the hysterical tone of these fears when he wrote of America in 1891: "No rood of modern ground is more debased and mongrel with its hordes of encroaching alien vermin, that turn our cities into Babels and our citizenship into a hybrid farce, who degrade our commonwealth from a nation into something half-pawnshop, half broker's office."[35]

As Wister's references to pawnshops and broker's offices imply, the main target of this hysteria was usually the Jews. An anti-Semitism that ranged from the genteel to the vicious was endemic in these suburbs and still has its bastions even today. Yet the habit of mind that distinguished between the pure, American suburb and the "debased and mongrel" city has survived the particular targets of Wister's fears to enter into our national subconscious.

The classic suburb has thus left a dual legacy. It is first a monument to bourgeois civilization at its most prosperous and self-confident, an aesthetic achievement in both landscape and domestic architecture that commands respect; but it is also a testimony to bourgeois anxieties, to deeply buried fears that translate into a contempt or hatred for the "others" who inhabit the city. Both elements have left their mark on American culture in the twentieth century.

CHAPTER 6

Los Angeles:

Suburban Metropolis

> I see California as a deluxe subdivision—a hundred million
> acre project.   —STEPHEN BORNSON,
>   California Real Estate Commissioner, 1931[1]

WITH the emergence of Los Angeles as a great metropolis, the history of suburbia reached its climax. From the earliest suburbs outside eighteenth century London to the elaborate railroad suburbs of the nineteenth century, suburbia had always been a subordinate element in the city. It was a refuge for a privileged minority, and its design stood apart from and in contradiction to the centralized structure of the modern city.

In Los Angeles, however, the single family detached suburban house escaped from the periphery to become, paradoxically, the central element in the structure of the whole city. All other land uses were subordinated to the provision of the maximum number of residential lots. The explosive growth of the city was accompanied by the decay of precisely those urban elements which had previously been the mark of a great city: a unifying, centralized downtown and a viable mass transit system. Suburbia had redefined the modern city in its own image, creating decentralized urban forms that nevertheless served the needs of a vast region. Los Angeles had become the suburban metropolis.

Not surprisingly, this new city was incomprehensible, at least to outsiders. Richard Neutra, the great Los Angeles architect, describes the 1931 International Conference for Modern Building (CIAM) at Brussels, where an attempt was made to provide maps for all the world's great cities, using the same scale and standard symbols for business districts, factory zones, slums, suburbs, and so on. Not only did the Los Angeles map dwarf all the others, virtually monopolizing the available wall space, but the symbols seemed almost inapplicable. "To the puzzled amazement of European students," Neutra recalls, "business zones, for example, seemed to stretch hundreds of miles along endless traffic boulevards which cut through unoccupied or agricultural areas. Cottage suburbs and satellite garden cities . . . seemed to extend amorphously over three hundred square miles on this monster map. Multi-story slums . . . seemed anomalously absent."[2] The Europeans wondered, "Was this metropolis a paradise, or did there exist here a type of blight which fitted none of its classical descriptions?"[3] The question is still hotly debated; my concern here, however, is not to judge Los Angeles but to understand it. For most observers, the explanation of its "monstrous" size and "amorphous" structure could be given in one word: the automobile. The ascendancy of the private car and the creation of a freeway system to support it has been the all-purpose explanation for Los Angeles and for all subsequent cities that resemble it.

I do not wish to deny the importance of the automobile in shaping Los Angeles, only to suggest that the automobile has been essentially a tool in the attainment of a deeper goal that predates the automobile era: the suburban ideal. The Los Angeles Master Plan of 1941 states, "This region can and should remain one in which the single-family dwelling predominates";[4] but the sentiment had been the crucial determinant of the city's growth for more than fifty years. Even in the streetcar era at the turn of the century Los Angeles already possessed many of the "anomalous" features associated with the automobile age city. The single family house was the great constant uniting the early period with the later. To open the region for suburban development, the city created the world's largest mass transit system.[5] When in the 1920s that system appeared to threaten the viability of the single family house, it was ruthlessly sacrificed and a massive automobile system put in its place.

To the quest for the suburban ideal Los Angeles sacrificed not only its mass transit system but also the downtown area, which depended on mass transit. The massive demands for housing land swallowed up the seemingly limitless open spaces of Los Angeles County and led to the loss of that balance between agriculture and housing which had been a characteristic feature of the city before 1940. Los Angeles, which had set out to eliminate the congestion of the older industrial city, wound up creating its own novel form: decentralized congestion.

Throughout these transformations the commitment to the single family house was maintained by an alliance between the mass of recent and would-be homeowners and a civic elite so deeply involved in real estate speculation that any challenge to the single family house would have meant their ruin. For both groups, urban decentralization and the road system to support it meant the universalization of suburbia. Every man a homeowner; every man a potential customer for a building lot, a house, and a mortgage. In the quasi-Mediterranean climate of southern California, the Palladian, aristocratic ideal of the villa was to reach its ultimate expression. No longer for leisured aristocrats or even for a bourgeois elite, the villa home gave to all classes the opportunity for leisure, family life, and union with nature.

In the end, of course, the universalization of the suburban ideal proved to be impossible. Nature was virtually abolished in the endless spread of subdivisions, and not even the hundreds of square miles of California land could prevent the massive rise in land prices in the 1970s that has threatened to restrict the suburban ideal once more to an elite. In the 1980s Los Angeles has finally been forced to confront the contradictions inherent in the idea of a suburban metropolis.

This chapter, however, deals primarily with the period from 1910 to 1950, when the suburban ideal was at its height. The growth of Los Angeles was not only explosively rapid; it was also virtually unhampered by previous traditions and settlements. The city was surrounded by seemingly unlimited land, supported by a massive influx of people and capital, and led by an elite wholly committed to suburban expansion. Under these conditions Los Angeles created a new kind of metropolis.

Origins of the Suburban Metropolis

Like so many other revolutionary movements, the creation of the new city was less a conscious quest for innovation than an attempt to preserve older values under conditions that threatened to destroy them. The boulevards of the 1920s and the freeways of the 1950s both attempted to recreate the sense of space and mobility that Los Angeles had attained seemingly effortlessly at the turn of the century as a sparsely populated regional city based on light rail transportation.

Modern Los Angeles grew out of the Pueblo de Los Angeles, founded in 1781 by Felipe de Neve where the Los Angeles River emerges from the foothills onto the vast, arid plain on which early settlers tried to raise cattle and the few crops that could survive on the meager rainfall. A direct transcontinental railroad connection in the 1880s finally overcame Los Angeles's geographical isolation; and, perhaps more importantly, a simultaneous development in artesian well technology enabled farmers to tap vast sources of water beneath the dry surface of the land. Adequately watered, the land proved to be remarkably fertile, especially for citrus crops, which were still luxuries in the cities of the eastern United States.[6]

As citrus groves and green, irrigated fields began to displace the dry brown of the old cattle ranches, the area's potential to house a great city suddenly became obvious. To the prosperous agricultural base was soon added important oil discoveries. Los Angeles had definitely displaced Santa Barbara and San Diego as the southwestern terminus of the nation's rail system, and an artificial harbor at Long Beach gave the area a major port.

This growth touched off the first of the great Los Angeles land booms in the 1880s and made the southern California city the goal of numerous settlers, especially from the Midwest. From the first, the great migration to Los Angeles was a migration of prosperity, of people with capital and skills seeking a more comfortable life. By the turn of the century the city was a relatively compact settlement set in the midst of the vast Los Angeles basin. The ocean was some fifteen miles away, and only a few rich visitors had begun to establish villas in the hills overlooking the ocean and the plain. The city was particularly successful in attracting well financed businessmen who were determined to profit from its future. The most important of them for this discussion was Henry E. Huntington.

Son of one of the founders of the Southern Pacific Railroad and briefly president of the line himself, Huntington failed in his bid to dominate the Southern Pacific and instead turned his formidable wealth and organizing talents to creating a massive light rail system for the great metropolis he foresaw. Buying up franchises or laying his own tracks, he unrelentingly pushed his "Pacific Electric" system through the still empty foothills and valleys of southern California. Within twenty years of its founding in 1901, Pacific Electric was carrying over 250,000 passengers daily on 4,000 light rail cars over tracks that totaled more than a thousand miles.[7]

Huntington, however, never forgot that he was as much in the real estate business as in transportation. Before his lines pushed out into the orange groves or vegetable fields of the region he was careful to buy up as much as possible of the land that adjoined them. On this land, now conveniently accessible to downtown Los Angeles, he laid out building plots for dozens of suburban villages strung along the tracks. Independent developers had to pay Huntington and Pacific Electric a subsidy to ensure the all important rail service that alone could make their development a success. Many developers simply made Huntington a partner in their profits.[8]

The basic mechanism of these streetcar suburbs was the same as in the East and Midwest, but the urban structure that developed in Los Angeles was surprisingly different. In the older cities streetcar lines pushed out initially through preexisting urban areas; only the privileged few living in the suburbs at the ends of the lines were in contact with unspoiled countryside. In Los Angeles, however, the central city was relatively small and the streetcar routes enormously long. The cars moved swiftly over relatively empty countryside, making it possible to live in the midst of orange fields or on a quiet hillside and still be close to downtown.

In 1904 developer H. J. Whitley claimed that his homes nestled picturesquely in the Hollywood Hills were only twenty minutes on a westbound streetcar from the Pacific Ocean beaches, and only fifteen minutes on the eastbound car from downtown.[9] The cars, moreover, came every half hour. Even allowing for the inevitable exaggerations, Pacific Electric certainly meant that twentieth century Los Angeles was born decentralized. Nevertheless, the fact that all the streetcar lines converged at the downtown meant that the region had a genuine center that dominated employment, shopping, culture, and government.

The streetcar suburb thus universalized Los Angeles suburbia, giving not only the well-to-do but a large portion of the population the experience of living in a small town that was at once close to nature and close to downtown. Although many of the suburban homes still resembled those outside eastern and midwestern cities, others responded in their architecture to the climate and traditions of southern California. Herbert Croly observed in 1906 that many of the suburban homes "remind one of the lines and proportions of the ranch houses [of early California] . . . and in this respect they perpetuate the best available tradition. They tend to be one or two-story buildings, with long low lines, and with the roof overhanging and dominating the upright members."[10] Already the California ranch house was taking shape.

Prominent among the houses in the new developments was the bungalow, which Croly defined as a "picturesque variation on the type of the small suburban house." He praised the "simple and unaffected propriety" of the bungalows and emphasized that they were "within the means of all but actually poor and overworked people; and there are an inexhaustible number of charming spots, both on the sea-coast and in the hills and mountains, which are sufficiently accessible from the larger cities to invite their erection."[11] Thus, at a time that the automobile was still a rich man's plaything, Los Angeles had already made suburbanization a universal norm. The city had carried the streetcar concept to its logical extremes: a far-flung network of streetcar suburbs organized around a relatively compact downtown hub. For a brief moment the complementary extremes of city and country were reconciled in an urban form with benefits that were to be sought by all subsequent plans.

The Crisis of the Streetcar City

The streetcar metropolis was destroyed by its own success. It functioned well only when the Los Angeles basin was still a site for orange groves and vegetable fields. When congestion developed in the 1920s the city was forced to adopt a new strategy to preserve the advantages of the old.

The end of World War I was the beginning of a major period of growth. The movie industry had by this time firmly established itself in a region of such perpetual sunshine and mild climate that outdoor filming was possible in virtually all seasons. The oil industry expanded in response to the automobile, and many large firms—Firestone Rubber, for example—located their

West Coast plants in Los Angeles, providing an almost instant industrial base to match its strengths in agriculture.[12]

The biggest industry, however, was the business of growth itself: land speculation and house building based on the great expectations for the future. Throughout the region, developers borrowed heavily to build the roads, sewers, and streetlights that gave a piece of empty land the appearance of a community. They then sought to sell the lots as soon as possible, often to individuals who bought them for speculative resale. In 1923— the peak of the boom—714 subdivision projects were registered, comprising in all 17,300 acres and over 86,000 separate lots.[13] Observing this mania, Will Rogers commented that realtors will "sell you anything or anybody in the world so long as they can get a first payment. . . . Your having no money doesn't worry the agents. If they can get a couple of dollars down, or an old overcoat, or a shotgun, or anything to act as a first payment. Second-hand Fords are considered A-1 collateral."[14] Such headlong growth, however, soon threatened the conditions that had drawn people to the region.

The new developments were useless without good transportation, which at that time still meant access to the downtown area, where the bulk of specialized shopping and even jobs were still located. The Pacific Electric mass transit system was still strong, reaching its all-time peak in passenger miles in 1924.[15] But, especially near the core, its "big red cars" were slowed down by the region's automobiles. Even in the early 1920s Los Angeles had the highest ratio of automobiles to people of any city in the world.[16] In spite of its vast empty spaces Los Angeles still pulled the bulk of its people on the move into the business center where crowding was intolerable. By 1924 one report concluded, "The street traffic congestion problem of Los Angeles is exceeded by that of no other city."[17] Downtown, automobiles and Pacific Electric streetcars were trapped in a perpetual traffic jam. A crisis for the whole region was at hand.

The first solution was proposed by Pacific Electric, which had separated itself from the Huntington real estate interests and was now operating as a quasi-public utility company. They saw that their streetcars were competing with automobiles for space on the crowded streets, and therefore put forward a plan for the construction of a system of elevated lines running along their major routes. Downtown, the lines would go underground in subway tunnels and converge in a major new terminal, which would become the hub of the region.[18]

Simultaneously, a group of civic leaders organized around the Automobile Club of Southern California proposed a very different plan. They called for a massive investment in new roads: north–south and east–west boulevards capable of handling three lanes of traffic in each direction, with provisions for turning lanes at all major intersections.[19]

Both solutions were expensive, too expensive for them to be built simultaneously. The debate between them, largely confined to a small group of civic leaders, is especially interesting because there was ample recognition at the time that the option chosen would determine the city's future structure. The strongest point in favor of the mass transit solution was that it would save the downtown areas. Not only would congestion be largely eliminated by the extensive use of subways, but almost all travelers in the region would be pointed to the core as the natural focus of the whole system.

But mass transit tends to focus development along its corridors. One Los Angeles study of the time showed that over 80 percent of the Pacific Electric riders lived within two blocks of one of its lines.[20] If mass transit were to be the area's major transportation system, and if the road system were to remain relatively undeveloped, then population would naturally cluster along the new elevated lines. Land values would rise in those areas, and the single family house would become prohibitively expensive there. Los Angeles would thus develop into a series of corridor cities of apartment houses and bungalow courts clustered near the streetcar lines. The land remote from the lines would be only lightly developed or remain agricultural.

The proposed highway system would have a very different effect. Virtually every spot in the vast Los Angeles basin would be near a modern east–west or north–south boulevard, which would open up the whole region to immediate development. In the grid system of roads, every spot is accessible from every other spot without the necessity of passing through a central point, as in a radial mass transit system with a downtown hub. The road system thus implied a radical decentralization of the city, a threat not only to the mass transit system but to the vitality of Los Angeles's civic core.

In virtually any other city, such a threat would have met with a vigorous protest from civic leaders to save the downtown area. If they did not do so in Los Angeles, it was because the city's economy was so closely connected with real estate development that the sacrifice of the core and the mass transit system was a small price to pay for opening up vast territories to subdivision.

Indeed, the sale of lots and houses paid off in ways that were not available to developers of rental apartments. By the 1920s the essence of subdivision profitability was getting the customer to assume ownership. Most developers operated with almost no capital. They borrowed the initial outlay to construct roads, lighting, and drainage. Customers for lots generally obtained mortgages from the developers, who immediately resold the mortgages at a substantial discount to obtain cash to repay their initial outlays. The net effect of this system was that the lot owner was borrowing money from the ultimate purchaser of his mortgage at rates of 12 to 15 percent, an interest rate that drew money from around the country to Los Angeles.[21]

The system then repeated itself when the lot owner wished to build a house on his lot. Bank mortgages usually extended no more than ten years and covered no more than 50 percent of the value of the house. The homeowner paid only interest, and at the expiration date of the mortgage he was expected to repay the full amount of the loan. To raise this sum, he usually had to renegotiate a new mortgage, often on onerous terms. Moreover, these bank mortgages had to be supplemented with second and even third mortgages to cover the costs of construction. These mortgages were available from developers, but again at rates of interest that ranged from 12 to 15 percent.[22]

One can now understand why owning one's home was such an article of faith among real estate developers. To the substantial profits made from converting agricultural land to building land was added the opportunity to place well secured loans at high rates of interest. The salesman selling lots or the builder selling houses was simply one element in a system the ultimate purpose of which was to sell money—in other words, to sell mortgage commitments at highly profitable rates.

Only the lure of home ownership could induce consumers to assume the heavy burden of debt. Thus, any transportation system that threatened to raise the price of lots or to restrict the supply of land available for development of single family houses threatened the whole system of profitable real estate speculation. The civic elite had no doubt that roads served their interests better than mass transit. As the Los Angeles *Examiner* put it:

> Los Angeles needs wide streets, and lots of them.
> Los Angeles needs smooth streets, and lots of them.
> Los Angeles needs through streets, and lots of them.
> Los Angeles needs more streets, and lots of them.[23]

A somewhat more subtle analysis was put forward in a report to the influential Los Angeles City Club. The report maintained that Los Angeles was basically "a single family dwelling" city and that this "desirable situation" should be "maintained and encouraged." The low density of population made it virtually impossible for a mass transit system to pay for itself. Moreover, there was no point in subsidizing mass transit because it only led to a congested downtown area, and such centralization was becoming obsolete:

> Banking, industry, commercialized recreation, and even retail business are entering upon an era of decentralization. Business is pointing the way out of the intolerable congestion situation in our downtown areas. Branch banks are going out to the people, factories are seeking outside locations, neighborhood theatres are springing up all over the city, and some of our retail merchants are building, or have established branch stores in outlying sections.[24]

The report put forward a vision of the new city that was widespread at the time. The "city of the future will be a harmoniously developed community of local centers and garden cities,"[25] an environment of single family homes linked by highways. A resident could live in any section and work or shop in any other. No single spot would be privileged as the core, to which all citizens must resort. It was an updated version of the original Los Angeles vision, the whole basin to become a single great decentralized city without a center or boundaries.

In 1926, after a well organized campaign by civic organizations, Los Angeles voted overwhelmingly to approve the massive bond issue that made the road system a reality.[26] At the same time a proposal for a new central rail and trolley station—the only part of the mass transit proposals to reach the voters— was decisively defeated.[27] The results were soon obvious. The Pacific Electric system began its rapid deterioration, and by the late 1930s it had become the transportation choice of last resort. The Works Progress Administration's 1941 guide to the city described the system as "incredibly slow and antiquated," and plagued by "long waits and overcrowding." Service that once competed with the automobile in speed now took more than three times as long.[28]

The downtown area soon followed suit, growing ever shabbier as it lost its share of retail trade and commercial development to newer centers. Soon residents did not even realize that Los Angeles had once possessed a crowded, vital downtown, which had been a true center for the region. In 1922 the Automobile Club of Southern California had predicted that if the new roads were built, "the City of Los Angeles will be enabled to fulfill its destiny as a great world metropolis."[29] This decentralized destiny was now at hand.

The Creation of the Decentralized City

During the 1920s a group of sociologists at the University of Chicago confidently mapped the general form of the modern industrial city based on the model of concentric circles with the central business district occupying the center, industry and workers' housing in the middle rings, and suburbia forming the outermost ring.[30] At precisely the same time Los Angeles was creating a decentralized city that completely contradicted their assumptions. Functions were not classified by their distance from the center, which in any case was becoming increasingly irrelevant to the city. Instead, the grid system of roads made possible a distribution of formerly central elements throughout the metropolis. Where, then, was "suburbia"?

The answer, as I have suggested, is "everywhere." Developers could subdivide land at virtually any point, knowing that one of the new boulevards would allow the new residents to reach jobs and shopping anywhere in the city. Nevertheless, the different kinds of subdivisions were not evenly distributed throughout the city. The principal class distinction was no longer distance from the center—the poor living closer in, the rich further out—but elevation. The wealthy seized upon the hills as a sign of wealth and status, while more modest developments limited themselves to spreading along the endless flatlands—what Reyner Banham has called "the plains of Id."[31] For the wealthy, the high ground offered not only splendid views and purer air but also the exclusivity that distance had provided in the railroad suburb. As one realtor put it, "the hills . . . offer the only remaining areas that can and will be free from commercialism and business enterprise. The hills make it impossible for the vital things that make a home beautiful ever to be taken away."[32]

The archetypal hill suburb was, of course, Beverly Hills, perhaps the most successful (in terms of current land values) subdivision project ever attempted. It began, no doubt appropriately, in an oil speculation. A group of investors that included the ubiquitous Henry E. Huntington bought the 3,300 acre Hamel and Denker Ranch, hoping to find oil. When none was discovered, the "Amalgamated Oil Company" transformed itself into the Rodeo Land and Water Company and, in 1907, brought the New York landscape architect Wilbur Cook to the site to lay it out as an exclusive residential suburb. Cook's design had a grand symmetry and simplicity. Wide, gently curving streets—soon lined with trees—followed the slope of the land upward from the streetcar station into the hills, which overlooked the whole basin. The plan was protected when the company incorporated its still virtually empty tract as a separate city in 1913, adopting the name "Beverly Hills" from Beverly Farms, Massachusetts, an exclusive suburb and summer resort north of Boston, the success of which the company wished to emulate.[33]

But the magnificent sites remained virtually empty until after World War I, when Hollywood stars began to purchase homes in this exclusive enclave just west of Hollywood itself. When in 1921 Mary Pickford and Douglas Fairbanks built their estate, Pickfair, on the appropriately named Summit Drive, the success of Beverly Hills was assured.[34] And, as Beverly Hills filled with houses, developers began their march along the Santa Monica Mountains to the sea: Holmby Hills, modestly named for its developer's birthplace;[35] Westwood, which gained the prize of the new branch of the University of California; Bel Air, so exclusive behind its massive gates that its developer, Alphonzo Bell, refused to sell to "movie people";[36] the Brentwood Riviera, which claimed to surpass its French predecessor; and finally Pacific Palisades—originally Huntington Palisades, but the ocean eventually took precedence over the magnate—and the beaches of Malibu.

A similar march of affluence advanced along the foothills of the San Gabriel Mountains to Pasadena, San Marino, and Arcadia; but perhaps the most remarkable of all the hill suburbs was Palos Verdes. In 1913 the New York financier Frank Vanderlip had purchased the 16,000 acre Palos Verdes peninsula, some twenty miles south of downtown Los Angeles. The peninsula juts out high over the Pacific, with magnificent views of the ocean. Vanderlip decided to develop a portion of the site as a "high class residential district" and turned to Frederick Law Olmsted, Jr. to prepare a plan. World War I intervened, and Olmsted did not resume work until 1922, when Vanderlip assigned 3,200 acres to the speculator E. G. Lewis. Lewis was one of those individuals, part crank, part visionary, who seem fatally attracted to Los Angeles real estate. He soon went broke, but his salesmanship provided the impetus for his scheme of a city of 200,000 people on the Palos Verdes peninsula.

Olmsted's plan, only partially implemented, was a worthy successor to his father's Riverside, Illinois plan. The Palos Verdes design was a synthesis of the Riverside idea of community and the Llewellyn Park concept of the dramatic picturesque. Where Olmsted senior had only flat Illinois prairie to work with, Olmsted junior had a site overlooking the Pacific that far surpassed the Orange Mountains of New Jersey. He described the site as a "virgin tract of twenty-five square miles, with every advantage of climate, coast, and lofty intricacies of hills."[37] He had the technical means to achieve on a large scale the natural landscape of Llewellyn Park. He intended to cut curving automobile roads into the steep slopes that led down to the ocean, using as the aesthetic basis of his design the union of the house and its site. The whole development perches above the Pacific; a neat and well organized community juxtaposed with the most dramatic vistas of mountain and ocean.

What most distinguishes Frederick Law Olmsted, Jr. from his father, however, is the former's careful—no doubt too careful— social planning. His aim was to create a community "planned, guided, and controlled from the very start with the sole exclusive object of making it and keeping it, as a great cooperative enterprise, the pleasantest place to live that it can possibly be made."[38] As the best planning theory dictated, Palos Verdes was organized into separate neighborhood units, each grouped around an elementary school and local shopping areas. Within each neighborhood there was a calculated blend of large and small houses, as well as a strictly limited number of multifamily dwellings. Every detail was specified not only to achieve the proper residential and social environment, but also to prevent "deterioration" or "encroachment." As Olmsted wrote to the project's sales manager:

> The self-contained situation of the tract, its island of hills next to the ocean, safe from encroachment from any development of an adverse source surrounding it . . . gives an assurance of *stability* and *permanence* to the character of the community such as no residential area near the metropolis has had since the rapid flux and shift and uncertainty of modern developments set in.[39]

Olmsted even stipulated an "Art Jury" to judge all house designs and improvements in order to exclude anything in bad taste.[40] (The Jury still operates, though an examination of the approved designs shows that the Jury never discriminated against banality, especially when it came clad in stucco and a red tile roof.) Olmsted's aims nevertheless underline the irony of suburbia, especially in Los Angeles. The city was built on the possibility of instant change, of creating a community overnight where only empty land had been. Yet, once created, the new community must achieve stability and permanence, the only things the economic system that created suburbia could never provide. Like Riverside, Palos Verdes fell victim to a depression—the Great Depression—which restricted Olmsted's plan to a small portion of its original scope.[41]

As housing spread over the city, both in the exclusive suburbs and in the infinitely repeated lots and bungalows of the Plains of Id, industry and shopping also decentralized. Los Angeles never had an industrial zone as did the eastern and midwestern cities, and any tendency to develop one was defeated by the freedom of movement provided by the new road system. Factories were not forced to be near mass transit lines in order to attract workers. Even in the 1920s factory workers were automobile commuters, coming to their jobs from every section of the metropolis rather than from a single factory zone.[42]

Specialized shopping, that most zealously held prerogative of the central business district, also found new locations on the periphery. The trend is perhaps most significantly revealed in the so-called Miracle Mile of Wilshire Boulevard. In the 1920s, realtor A. W. Ross watched as affluent residents moved steadily westward along the hills away from the city center. His idea was simple, to move the great department stores to where their customers had gone. But behind this idea was, of course, the city's centrifugal impetus: there was no point in sacrificing to maintain a downtown area that was destined to decay. Ross purchased eighteen acres along the south side of Wilshire Boulevard, eight miles west of the downtown area, which he called the Wilshire Boulevard Center. His concept was from the start that this "center" would serve primarily shoppers traveling by automobile. The stores fronted on the boulevard, but behind them Ross provided large parking lots and elaborate entrances.[43]

Many merchants balked at the idea of placing a large department store in the middle of what was still a neighborhood of small suburban homes with open fields within sight. But Ross could show that most of the city's buying power now resided within a four mile radius of his center; that stores located there would intercept this buying power before it reached downtown. He was proved correct. The sidewalks on his Miracle Mile were deserted, but the parking lots were full. Downtown department stores hastened to establish elaborate branch stores on Wilshire Boulevard while letting their downtown stores run down. Decentralized, suburban shopping had come of age.[44]

By the end of the 1920s a new urban structure was in place in Los Angeles. Crucial metropolitan functions had exploded over the landscape, their scattering supported by an extensive network of roads that permitted multidimensional travel. This new sense of unlimited urban space was well illustrated in an article by E. E. East, the chief engineer of the Automobile Club of Southern California. Based on the club's research, he illustrated the day's driving of an affluent Beverly Hills family of four:

> The day for the X family, automotively speaking, starts at 7 AM with the arrival of the Mexican gardener from Belvedere. At 7:30 AM the

milkman arrives on his daily round from Culver City. Breakfast over, at 8 AM the son departs for classes at USC, and the daughter for a fashionable Pasadena school. At 8:30 the husband sets forth for his office in the Central Manufacturing District at Ventnor. At 11 o'clock the wife leaves for a shopping tour [of the Miracle Mile at Wilshire Boulevard]. . . . By 6 o'clock husband, son and daughter are back home. By 7 Mr. and Mrs. X have left again for dinner at the California Club, and an evening at the Hollywood Bowl. After dinner the son dashes over to consult a school mate in Hollywood, and the daughter scurries to Long Beach for a dance.[45]

In all, the family has covered more than 500 miles in their four cars. As East observes, none of these trips comes under the rubric of traditional commuting. None has its starting or ending point downtown. Instead, the family "has described a dizzy pattern" as their "paths crossed" and they "intercepted the journeys of countless thousands of others bent on similar missions." Traffic had become not only wide ranging but multidirectional. Each family was its own "core" in a decentralized city.

Freeways and Tract Houses: The Mature Suburban Metropolis

Los Angeles did not escape the Depression, which hit particularly hard at its main engine of growth: land speculation and house building. The underlying economy, however, remained strong, with agriculture, oil, and motion pictures as its mainstays and with aviation establishing itself as a significant new presence. The 1930s was thus a planning decade. Confidence in the future remained strong though actual growth slowed, so the new forms that were to dominate the 1940s and 1950s had time to mature. In particular, the two great symbols of postwar Los Angeles—the tract of endlessly repeated suburban houses and the freeway—were developed in the 1930s.

Both the tract house and the freeway were conservative in their inspiration. They attempted to maintain under changing conditions that commitment to a single family home and a decentralized environment which had characterized Los Angeles since the turn of the century. They carried to its logical, technological conclusion the premise that the whole metropolitan area must be amenable to single family houses, each with rapid automobile access to every other part of the city.

This impulse can perhaps be seen most clearly in the early history of the Los Angeles freeway system. In the 1920s the city had built the most extensive series of roads for its size in the world. They had their effect, but less than a decade later they were falling prey to the grave threat of congestion. The Automobile Club showed that each year the time required to reach virtually any destination was increasing. In what E. E. East called a "great, far-flung community that long since learned to depend on the automobile as its principal means of transportation,"[46] such delays could lead to a reconcentration that would drive up land values at the center and make the undeveloped land too remote for sale as housing.

If the Automobile Club was the first to document this threat, it was also the first to propose a solution. Continuing its status as the true planning organ of the city, the club's engineers devised a remarkably elaborate transportation plan based on a new form of road, the limited access, high speed expressway. Los Angeles did not invent the freeway; but in the 1930s such roads were new to the theory and practice of highway engineers. The limited access superhighway had evolved from the purely recreational parkways, like those which Robert Moses planned in the 1920s for Long Island, as well as from expressways designed to speed commuting to and from the central city. The Automobile Club's freeways resembled these predecessors in detail, but the overall purpose and conception of the freeway system were unique.[47]

The Los Angeles freeways were not intended to deliver traffic to a central spot. Instead, they were to be organized into a large grid superimposed over the denser 1920s grid of surface roads.

The freeways were truly to unite the whole region into one decentralized city, permitting rapid travel in any direction and between any two spots on the map. Once these high speed corridors were in place, even the vast distances of the Los Angeles basin could be covered in minutes. The traveler would then descend to the older grid of surface roads, which would deliver him to his destination.

What made the Automobile Club's plan—first presented in 1937—so remarkable was its completeness. It depicted more than five hundred miles of limited access freeways along with elaborate interchanges, a system that dwarfed the 1920s road plan. Nevertheless, the power of the automobile lobby and the fear of congestion were so great that this massive plan was officially adopted by the municipal and planning offices only two years after the Automobile Club proposed it. The only significant change involved a last-ditch effort by downtown interests to create a point of convergence—a modified hub—at the core.[48]

Unfortunately for downtown boosters, they were unable to suggest any way of handling the massive influx of automobiles that the convergence of offramps promised to deliver to their doors. One desperate plan pictured elevated highways running directly through specially constructed downtown skyscrapers, each with several floors of parking. The final plan omitted these odd visions. Although it did provide some convergence at the core, this expedient did nothing to halt the area's precipitate decline.[49] Mass transit, needless to say, was virtually ignored. One plan envisioned high speed buses traveling along the freeway, but where and how these buses would stop to pick up passengers was not considered.[50]

The proposed freeways were the most spectacular indications of planning for a substantial influx of population. Changes in the building and real estate industries were more subtle but perhaps even more decisive in maintaining the supremacy of the single family house. The Depression had dealt a mortal blow to the old system of underfinanced speculators and builders operating on a paper-thin margin of high priced credit. To save homeowners threatened by foreclosure, in 1933 the Roosevelt Administration created the Home Owners' Loan Corporation which refinanced over a million short-term mortgages and replaced them with a new form of home loan: the long-term mortgage whose equal payments spread over twenty to thirty years not only paid the interest but paid off (amortized) the principal as well. This crucial innovation was at the heart of the National Housing Act of 1934, which created the Federal Housing Administration (FHA). Title II of the Act authorized the FHA to insure mortgages, and its policies made the self-amortizing 25–30-year mortgage the norm throughout the nation. Whereas banks of the 1920s had limited their mortgages to no more than 50 or 60 percent of a home's value, the FHA insured mortgages of up to 90 percent of the value. No longer was a homebuyer forced to supplement an inadequate first mortgage with a high-interest second mortgage.[51]

These innovations rationalized the crazy quilt structure of mortgage financing left over from the 1920s. Moreover, the National Housing Act also created a stable and insured network of savings and loan institutions, where the deposits of small savers could flow directly toward home construction and mortgages. Nor were builders forgotten. They could draw upon FHA mortgage guarantees to get working capital to complete their projects. Developers, instead of struggling from one short term loan to the next, now had an assured supply of capital to undertake their initial work of street building, as well as assurances that customers for houses could find ample mortgage money with which to pay for their houses. This program, which was designed to stimulate modest growth for a moribund industry, in fact created the conditions for explosive suburban growth when the economy improved.

In particular, it allowed the subdivider to look beyond the rapid turnover of lots and make a longer term commitment to both subdividing the land and building the houses on it. A few developers in the 1920s, such as Harry Culver of Culver City, had taken that route, but relatively few possessed both the capital and the staying power to see it through. Instead, they reduced their risk by turning over the house building to other entrepreneurs prepared to take those risks on a house by house basis.[52]

The Federal Housing Administration loan guarantees made it possible for a single organization to undertake the complete task of turning an empty plot of land into a neighborhood of streets and houses. This change introduced both economies of scale and economies of speed into the suburbanization process. Lots could now be designed to fit the house built on them. A single crew of workers, using identical or highly similar plans, could rapidly erect a series of houses, utilizing wherever possible precut and prefitted elements that minimized labor costs on the site. Using this method in the late 1930s, a single developer in the City of Bell was able to build and sell 236 houses in twenty months.[53]

To suit this rapid pace of building, developers needed a simplified house design that would be both attractive to buyers and uncomplicated to build. The result was the California ranch house, which evolved from many different sources in the late 1930s. It was basically a throwback to the low California bungalow that Herbert Croly had seen and praised at the turn of the century. But the bungalow was now turned parallel to the street, its apparent size exaggerated by the addition of a connected garage. (In the automobile age there was no need to economize on street frontage.) The most prominent feature of the ranch house was the overhanging roof, a dominant motif in turn of the century ranch houses and bungalows, now brought back to prominence after the pseudocottage roofs of the 1920s. Some of the facade's details might lean toward colonial, Spanish, or American western styles, but the dominant impression was one of a modern simplicity. Within the house the open plan necessarily prevailed. A single, largely undifferentiated space included living, dining, kitchen, and recreation areas, while the bedrooms formed a right angle to the main space. A small patio was placed near the front door, while a much larger one sat at the back door.[54]

Through simplification, the "small California house," as

builders originally called it, had absorbed the main lessons of twentieth century modernism: forms and structure are one; inside and outside merge; and space within is open. (Frank Lloyd Wright, then an isolated figure, was building surprisingly similar "Usonian Houses" at the same time.) For a brief moment modernist architecture, populist aspirations, and the requirements of the market came together. For these houses were undoubtedly cheap. In the late thirties developers sold them for $3,000 to $4,500 each; with a Federal Housing Administration mortgage, this price meant a $50 down payment and a $30 to $50 payment each month.[55]

Housing reformers of the 1920s, like Lewis Mumford and Catherine Bauer Wurster, had seen an inherent contradiction between the requirements of modern building and living and the procedures of speculative house building. Bauer proclaimed that "the jostling small builders and the front-foot lots and the miserable straggling suburbs and the ideology of individual Home Ownership must go. And in their place must come a technique for building complete communities, designed and administered as functional units and constructed by large-scale methods."[56] It was not the communitarians but the speculators themselves who must successfully adopt the "large-scale methods" that Bauer had called for, and they used them not to build the modernist collective dwellings Bauer and Mumford advocated, but more efficiently constructed versions of that monument of "individual Home Ownership," the single family suburban house. The collective architecture and planning of the New Deal "Greenbelt Towns" remained a curiosity, while the suburban house gained new impetus from the most modern methods of functional mass production.

Los Angeles thus emerged from the 1930s still in touch with her original goals. The Los Angeles Master Plan of 1941 showed that 31 percent of the city's land was devoted to single family houses, with only 2 percent to multiple family dwellings.[57] With widespread automobile ownership—1.16 million cars in 1940, or 2.4 persons per vehicle[58]—and with the proposed freeway system (25 percent of the city was already given over to streets and highways), it still seemed possible to place these houses within a decentralized environment. The city plan predicted massive growth, but it also predicted that new residents coming to Los Angeles would continue to be accommodated in new suburban homes.

Apogee and Decline of the Suburban Metropolis

Los Angeles has never lacked publicity, but after World War II the city entered a new era as a symbol of postwar American culture. It became, in Asa Briggs's phrase, a "shock city," a city like Manchester in the 1840s, so new that it came as a shock to visitors and caused them to reconsider the meaning of a city.

Post-1945 Los Angeles was not so much a departure from the past as a fulfillment of its basic structure, a use of new means to safeguard the original end of a great city based on the single family house. The development of Los Angeles from 1940 to the present has meant the fleshing out of the bare bones constructed in the 1930s: the transformation of over 900 square miles of agricultural land into suburban tract developments, and the construction of almost 500 miles of freeways to forestall the congestion created by the new homes.[59] The city has thus seen a massive race between growth and congestion; each new freeway temporarily averted traffic paralysis, only to create new areas for growth that overwhelmed the freeway system anew.

It is an irony that the ideal of the suburban metropolis was perhaps most closely approximated in the very beginning of the period—1940—before the first freeway had been completed, and before the massive construction of tract houses had begun. Los Angeles then possessed a remarkable balance of urban and rural environments; it was the nation's leading agricultural county and ranked eighth in industrial production;[60] citrus groves and irrigated fields punctuated the landscape within sight of most homes. To the oil industry Los Angeles could add a significant proportion of the aircraft industry, as well as the movie studios at the height of their powers. The European war brought a remarkable group of cultural leaders to the city. At least temporarily, Los Angeles could claim to be at the center of western civilization.

Yet the city remained as its founders had wished: a collection of villages, devoid of the slums and overcrowding of the past, offering to almost everyone a suburban home on its own land. Spread out among the fields and groves, the houses provided access over a still uncongested road system to all that the region possessed: employment, entertainment, education, as well as miles of beaches and vast expanses of hills.

Postwar growth inevitably shattered this fragile equilibrium, swallowing up open space, congesting the highways, even poisoning the air (the first smog attack came in 1943).[61] Yet the process had attained a momentum of its own that accelerated in the years of prosperity. The San Fernando Valley, still largely rural in the 1940s, was the most prominent scene of hectic growth. Developments larger than the Levittowns of the East were easily accommodated within its vast plain. In 1950, for example, Louis H. Boyar bought 3,375 acres of farmland to build a new community which he called Lakewood Park. He built 17,000 houses for more than 70,000 residents.[62]

Growth had become a giant machine operating out of control, creating endless expanses of development that foreclosed forever the original vision of a community of homes set in a still verdant environment. Yet, for almost thirty years, the abundant space of southern California absorbed the increases. When the San Fernando Valley was filled, the focus of development shifted to Orange County, the original home of the citrus industry, or east along the foothills toward San Bernardino and the desert. Land remained relatively cheap, as the new freeways made more and more distant sites available for building; capital remained abundant, as a nationwide system of Federal Housing Administration financing poured savings deposits from across the country into the Los Angeles home building industry.

As late as the 1960s, the suburban metropolis appeared to be working.

The Watts riots of the mid 1960s were the first sign of serious trouble, proving that Los Angeles had indeed created a new form of slum: not the dark tenements of the older cities but the low density bungalow areas of the streetcar era that had been abandoned both by their original residents and by public transportation. In the late 1960s freeway building ground to a halt due to rising costs and opposition from homeowners "in the path of progress."[63] The energy crisis of the 1970s undermined the viability of a transportation system for a great city based so completely on the private automobile.

Gasoline shortages could be overcome, but the shortage of land could never be. As outward expansion reached its limits in the 1970s, desirable areas toward the center experienced an explosive boom in land values, which sometimes increased eight to ten times over the decade. This inflation would no doubt have gratified the salesmen who sold those lots in the 1910s and 1920s, but its effect was to eliminate the possibility of a single family home for every Los Angeles family. The two great safety valves of low density expansion—new land at the outskirts and more roads—had reached their end. There was no escaping congestion.

The recent history of Los Angeles has therefore been a history of reconcentration. Tract houses have given way to apartments and condominiums. High-rise buildings line the major boulevards. Perhaps inevitably, the downtown area has been reborn as the most logical site for a concentration of high-rise towers. E. E. East, the Automobile Club engineer, had concluded in 1941 that the "vision of a skyscraper city" downtown was dead forever.[64] In the late 1970s and 1980s that vision was restored as business and government leaders recognized the need for a centralized point of communication not dependent on long trips on congested roads. With the skyscraper city was also revived the idea of mass transportation. In September 1986, Los Angeles broke ground for the first four miles of a projected 150-mile subway system running out from old core through Hollywood and West Los Angeles and then to the San Fernando Valley. If this "Metro Rail" system is completed—funding for even the first small link remains in doubt—it would be only a small part of the same plan that had been advocated and rejected in the 1920s.[65] Los Angeles was, at tremendous cost, reinventing the wheel; or, more precisely, reinventing the centralized city based on a downtown hub and mass transit spokes.

If other great cities have come more and more to resemble Los Angeles, Los Angeles in turn has begun to resemble them. In Los Angeles the quest for a city based on the single family home came into conflict with the city's plans to be a great metropolis, a world center for finance, industry, and culture. Not even the great spaces of the Los Angeles basin could reconcile low density residential development with the centralizing, congesting tendencies of metropolitan growth. The suburban metropolis proved to be a contradiction in terms.

Yet the vision of a decentralized city that Los Angeles offered the world is by no means dead. It survives beyond the metropolis, not only beyond the densely built areas of the old cities but beyond the old suburban belts as well. In the newly developing sunbelt regions as well as in the areas of new construction on the periphery of eastern and midwestern cities, a new kind of city is taking shape. This new city—neither urban, nor rural, nor suburban in the traditional sense—is the true heir of the innovations introduced by Los Angeles in the 1920s and 1930s. It will be the subject of my concluding chapter: beyond suburbia.

CHAPTER 7

Beyond Suburbia:

The Rise of the

Technoburb

IF the nineteenth century could be called the Age of Great Cities, post-1945 America would appear to be the Age of Great Suburbs. As central cities stagnated or declined in both population and industry, growth was channeled almost exclusively to the peripheries. Between 1950 and 1970 American central cities grew by 10 million people, their suburbs by 85 million. Suburbs, moreover, accounted for at least three-quarters of all new manufacturing and retail jobs generated during that period. By 1970 the percentage of Americans living in suburbs was almost exactly double what it had been in 1940, and more Americans lived in suburban areas (37.6%) than in central cities (31.4%) or in rural areas (31%). In the 1970s central cities experienced a net out-migration of 13 million people, combined with an unprecedented deindustrialization, increasing poverty levels, and housing decay.[1]

Beyond Suburbia: The Rise of the Technoburb

As the central cities declined, the suburb emerged as a topic of national concern. For the first time in any society, the single family detached house was brought within the economic grasp of the majority of households. For most, this development was a cause for celebration. In Frank Capra's populist classic film of 1946, *It's a Wonderful Life*, the hero, George Bailey (played by James Stewart), is the manager of a building and loan society. He gives up his dreams of becoming an architect or engineer and creating vast new cities to stay in his home town and help his neighbors to buy their own houses. His proudest achievement is a suburban subdivision of tract houses, which he names Bailey Park. The villain, Mr. Potter (played by Lionel Barrymore), is a miserly banker whose selfish lending practices keep families paying rent for the tenements he owns. The film does much to explain American housing policy in the succeeding decades.

Others were less optimistic about suburbia than Capra. In the midst of an unprecedented building boom in the 1950s a scholarly debate over suburbia blamed the new patterns of living for the increasing conformity in American life. In the 1960s and 1970s that indictment was seconded by an analysis that held "white flight" responsible for the segregation and poverty of the inner cities. Yet both critics and proponents agreed that the most important aspect of the postwar environment was, in Kenneth Jackson's phrase, "the suburbanization of the United States."[2] Indeed, the phenomenon was so powerful that it was like a tide that washed over all precedents. It was as if suburbanization *began* in 1945.

In this concluding chapter I present a very different interpretation of postwar America. To me the massive rebuilding that began in 1945 represents not the culmination of the 200 year history of suburbia but rather its end. Indeed, this massive change is not suburbanization at all but the creation of a new kind of city, with principles that are directly opposed to the true suburb.

From its origins in eighteenth century London, suburbia has served as a specialized portion of the expanding metropolis. Whether it was inside or outside the political borders of the central city, it was always functionally dependent on the urban core. Conversely, the growth of suburbia always meant a strengthening of the specialized services at the core.

In my view, the most important feature of postwar American development has been the almost simultaneous decentralization of housing, industry, specialized services, and office jobs; the consequent breakaway of the urban periphery from a central city it no longer needs; and the creation of a decentralized environment that nevertheless possesses all the economic and technological dynamism we associate with the city. This phenomenon, as remarkable as it is unique, is not suburbanization but a *new city*.

Unfortunately, we lack a convenient name for this new city, which has taken shape on the outskirts of all our major urban centers. Some have used the terms "exurbia" or "outer city." I suggest (with apologies) two neologisms: the "technoburb" and the "techno-city." By "technoburb" I mean a peripheral zone, perhaps as large as a county, that has emerged as a viable socioeconomic unit. Spread out along its highway growth corridors are shopping malls, industrial parks, campuslike office complexes, hospitals, schools, and a full range of housing types. Its residents look to their immediate surroundings rather than to the city for their jobs and other needs; and its industries find not only the employees they need but also the specialized services.

The new city is a *techno*burb not only because high tech industries have found their most congenial homes in such archetypal technoburbs as Silicon Valley in northern California and Route 128 in Massachusetts. In most technoburbs such industries make up only a small minority of jobs, but the very existence of the decentralized city is made possible only through the advanced communications technology which has so completely superseded the face-to-face contact of the traditional city. The technoburb has generated urban diversity without traditional urban concentration.

By "techno-city" I mean the whole metropolitan region that has been transformed by the coming of the technoburb. The techno-city usually still bears the name of its principal city, for example, "the New York metropolitan area"; its sports teams bear that city's name (even if they no longer play within the boundaries of the central city); and its television stations appear to broadcast from the central city. But the economic and social life of the region increasingly bypasses its supposed core. The techno-city is truly multicentered, along the pattern that Los Angeles first created. The technoburbs, which might stretch over seventy miles from the core in all directions, are often in more direct communication with one another—or with other techno-cities across the country—than they are with the core. The techno-city's real structure is aptly expressed by the circular superhighways or beltways that serve so well to define the perimeters of the new city. The beltways put every part of the urban periphery in contact with every other part without passing through the central city at all.

For most Americans, the real center of their lives is neither an urban nor a rural nor even a suburban area, as these entities have traditionally been conceived, but rather the technoburb, the boundaries of which are defined by the locations they can conveniently reach in their cars. The true center of this new city is not in some downtown business district but in each residential unit. From that central starting point, the members of the household create their own city from the multitude of destinations that are within suitable driving distance. One spouse might work at an industrial park two exits down the interstate; the other at an office complex five exits in the other direction; the children travel by bus to comprehensive schools in their district or drive themselves to the local branch of the state university; the family shops at several different malls along several different highways; every weekend they drive fifty miles to a rural (but rapidly developing) area where they have a second house; all they need and consume, from the most complex medical services to fresh fruits and vegetables, can be found along the highways. Once a year, perhaps at Christmas, they go "downtown," but they never stay long.

The old central cities have become increasingly marginal,

while the technoburb has emerged as the focus of American life. The traditional suburbanite—commuting at ever increasing cost to a center where the available resources barely duplicate those available much closer to home—becomes increasingly rare. In this transformed urban ecology the history of suburbia comes to an end.

Prophets of the Techno-City

Like all new urban forms, the techno-city and its technoburbs emerged not only unpredicted but unobserved. We are still seeing this new city through the intellectual categories of the old metropolis. Only two prophets, I believe, perceived the underlying forces that would lead to the techno-city at the time of their first emergence. Their thoughts are therefore particularly valuable in understanding the new city.

At the turn of the twentieth century, when the power and attraction of the great city was at its peak, H. G. Wells daringly asserted that the technological forces that had created the industrial metropolis were now moving to destroy it. In his 1900 essay "The Probable Diffusion of Great Cities," Wells argued that the seemingly inexorable concentration of people and resources in the largest cities would soon be reversed. In the course of the twentieth century, he prophesied, the metropolis would see its own resources drain away to decentralized "urban regions" so vast that the very concept of "the city" would become, in his phrase, "as obsolete as 'mailcoach.' "[3]

Wells based his prediction on a penetrating analysis of the emerging networks of transportation and communication. Throughout the nineteenth century, rail transportation had been a relatively simple system favoring direct access to large centers. With the spread of branchlines and electric tramways, however, a complex rail network had been created that could serve as the basis for a decentralized region. (As Wells wrote, Henry E. Huntington was proving the truth of his propositions for the Los Angeles region.)

But there were other emerging networks, most notably electricity and the telephone. The electrical system gave every point in a region the same access to power as any other; the advantage of a central location was accordingly diminished. In an analogous way, the telephone provided instant communication from any point to any other point in a region, thus eliminating the need for a central location and face-to-face contact.

As Wells saw it, neither industry nor business needed the great city any longer, and both would inevitably melt away to cheaper, secluded locations. Not only could industry produce its goods more cheaply and more efficiently away from the core; but businessmen would invariably choose to live in quiet country towns and conduct their business by telephone. "Indeed, it is not too much to say that the London citizen of the year 2000 A.D. may have a choice of all England and Wales south of Nottingham and east of Exeter as his suburb, and the vast stretch of country from Washington to Albany will be 'available' to the active citizen of New York and Philadelphia before that date."[4]

Wells pictured the "urban region" of the year 2000 as a series of villages with small homes and factories set in the open fields, yet connected by high speed rail transportation to any other point in the region. (It was a vision not very different from those who saw Los Angeles developing into just such a network of villages.) The old cities would not completely disappear, but they would lose both their financial and their industrial functions, surviving simply because of an inherent human love of crowds. The "post-urban" city, Wells predicted, will be "essentially a bazaar, a great gallery of shops and places of concourse and rendezvous, a pedestrian place, its pathways reinforced by lifts and moving platforms, and shielded from the weather, and altogether a very spacious, brilliant, and entertaining agglomeration."[5] In short, the great metropolis will dwindle to what we would today call a massive shopping mall, while the productive life of the society would take place in the decentralized urban region.

Wells's prediction was taken up in the late 1920s and early 1930s by Frank Lloyd Wright, who moved from similar assumptions to an even more radical view. Wright had actually seen the beginnings of the automobile and truck era; he was, perhaps not coincidentally, living mostly in Los Angeles in the late 1910s and early 1920s. Wright, like Wells, argued that "the great city was no longer modern" and that it was destined to be replaced by a decentralized society.

He called this new society Broadacre City. It has often been confused with a kind of universal suburbanization, but for Wright "Broadacres" was the exact opposite of the suburbia he despised. He saw correctly that suburbia represented the essential extension of the city into the countryside, whereas Broadacres represented the disappearance of all previously existing cities.

As Wright envisioned it, Broadacres was based on universal automobile ownership combined with a network of superhighways, which removed the need for population to cluster in a particular spot. Indeed, any such clustering was necessarily inefficient, a point of congestion rather than of communication. The city would thus spread out over the countryside at densities low enough to permit each family to have its own homestead and even to engage in part-time agriculture. Yet these homesteads would not be isolated; their access to the superhighway grid would put them within easy reach of as many jobs and specialized services as any nineteenth century urbanite. Traveling at more than sixty miles an hour, each citizen would create his own city within the hundreds of square miles he could reach in an hour's drive.[6]

Like Wells, Wright saw industrial production inevitably leaving the cities for the space and convenience of rural sites. But Wright went one step further in his attempt to envision the way that a radically decentralized environment could generate that diversity and excitement which only cities had possessed.

He saw that even in the most scattered environment, the

crossing of major highways would possess a certain special status. These intersections would be the natural sites of what he called the roadside market, a remarkable anticipation of the shopping center: "great spacious roadside pleasure places these markets, rising high and handsome like some flexible form of pavilion—designed as places of cooperative exchange, not only of commodities but of cultural facilities."[7] To the roadside markets he added a range of highly civilized yet small scale institutions: schools, a modern cathedral, a center for festivities, and the like. In such an environment, even the entertainment functions of the city would disappear. Soon, Wright devoutly wished, the centralized city itself would disappear.

Taken together, Wells's and Wright's prophecies constitute a remarkable insight into the decentralizing tendencies of modern technology and society. Both were presented in utopian form, an image of the future presented as somehow "inevitable" yet without any sustained attention to how it would actually be achieved. Nevertheless, something like the transformation that Wells and Wright foresaw has taken place in the United States, a transformation all the more remarkable in that it occurred without a clear recognition that it was happening. While diverse groups were engaged in what they believed was "the suburbanization" of America, they were in fact creating a new city.

Fernand Braudel and his school of historians have called attention to the remarkable power of "structures" in history: deep patterns of economic and social necessity that operate with little regard for individual plans or government initiatives. Whatever its validity for history as a whole, this view has its value for explaining the emergence of the techno-city. Wells and Wright were powerless to bring about the new city they foresaw. Nevertheless, the inherent forces in twentieth century technology and society asserted themselves to form a new pattern of urban life.

Technoburb/Techno-City:
The Structure of the New Metropolis

To claim that there is a pattern or structure in the new American city is to contradict what appears to be overwhelming evidence. One might sum up the structure of the technoburb by saying that it goes against every rule of planning. It is based on two extravagances that have always aroused the ire of planners: the waste of land inherent in a single family house with its own yard, and the waste of energy inherent in the use of the personal automobile. The new city is absolutely dependent on its road system, yet that system is almost always in a state of chaos and congestion. The landscape of the technoburb is a hopeless jumble of housing, industry, commerce, and even agricultural uses. Finally, the technoburb has no proper boundaries; however defined, it is divided into a crazy quilt of separate and overlapping political jurisdictions, which make any kind of coordinated planning virtually impossible.

Yet the technoburb has become the real locus of growth and innovation in our society. And there is a real structure in what appears to be wasteful sprawl, which provides enough logic and efficiency for the technoburb to fulfill at least some of its promises.

If there is a single basic principle in the structure of the technoburb, it is the renewed linkage of work and residence. The suburb had separated the two into distinct environments; its logic was that of the massive commute, in which workers from the periphery traveled each morning to a single core and then dispersed each evening. The technoburb, however, contains both work and residence within a single decentralized environment.

By the standards of a preindustrial city where people often lived and worked under the same roof, or even of the turn of the century industrial zones where factories were an integral part of working class neighborhoods, the linkage between work and residence in the technoburb is hardly close. A recent study of New Jersey shows that most workers along the state's growth corridors now live in the same county in which they work.[8] But this relative dispersion must be contrasted to the former pattern of commuting into urban cores like Newark or New York. In most cases traveling time to work diminishes, even when the distances traveled are still substantial; as the 1980 census indicates, the average journey to work appears to be diminishing both in distance and, more importantly, in time.[9]

For commuting within the technoburb is multidirectional, following the great grid of highways and secondary roads that, as Frank Lloyd Wright understood, defines the community. This multiplicity of destinations makes public transportation highly inefficient, but it does remove that terrible bottleneck which necessarily occurred when work was concentrated at a single core within the region. Each house in a technoburb is within a reasonable driving time of a truly "urban" array of jobs and services, just as each workplace along the highways can draw upon an "urban" pool of workers.

Those who believed that the energy crisis of the 1970s would cripple the technoburb failed to realize that the new city had evolved its own pattern of transportation in which a multitude of relatively short automobile journeys in a multitude of different directions substitutes for that great tidal wash in and out of a single urban core which had previously defined commuting. With housing, jobs, and services all on the periphery, this sprawl develops its own form of relative efficiency. The truly inefficient form would be any attempted revival of the former pattern of long distance mass transit commuting into a core area.

To account for the new linkage of work and residence in the technoburb, we must first confront this paradox: the new city required a massive and coordinated relocation of housing, industry, and other "core" functions to the periphery; yet there were no coordinators directing the process. Indeed, the technoburb emerged in spite of, not because of, the conscious purposes motivating the main actors. The postwar housing boom was an attempt to escape from urban conditions; the new highways sought to channel traffic into the cities; planners attempted to limit peripheral growth; the government programs that did the most to destroy the hegemony of the old industrial metropolis were precisely those designed to save it.

This paradox can be seen clearly in the area of transportation policy. Wright had grasped the basic point in his Broadacre City plan: a fully developed highway grid eliminates the primacy of a central business district. It creates a whole series of highway crossings, which can serve as business centers while promoting the multidirectional travel that prevents any single center from attaining unique importance. Yet, from the time of Robert Moses to the present, highway planners have imagined that the new roads, like the older rail transportation, would enhance the importance of the old centers by funneling cars and trucks into the downtown area and the surrounding industrial belt. At most, the highways were to serve traditional suburbanization, in other words, the movement from the periphery to the core during morning rush hours and the reverse movement in the afternoon. The beltways, those crucial "Main Streets" of the technoburb, were designed simply to allow interstate traffic to avoid going through the central cities.[10]

The history of the technoburb, therefore, is the history of those deeper structural features of modern society first described by Wells and Wright taking precedence over conscious intentions. For purposes of clarity I shall now divide this discussion of the making of the techno-city into two interrelated topics—housing and job location.

Housing

The great American postwar housing boom was perhaps the purest example of the suburban dream in action, yet its ultimate consequence was to render suburbia obsolete. Between 1950 and 1970, on the average, 1.2 million housing units were built each year, the vast majority as suburban single family dwellings; the nation's housing stock increased by 21 million units or over 50 percent.[11] In the 1970s the boom continued even more strongly; twenty million more new units were added, almost as many as in the previous two decades.[12] It was precisely this vast production of new residences that shifted the center of gravity in the United States from the urban core to the periphery and thus ensured that these vital and expanding areas could no longer remain simply bedroom communities.

This great building boom, which seems so characteristic of post-1945 conditions, in fact had its origins early in the twentieth century in the first attempts to universalize suburbia throughout the United States. It can be seen essentially as a continuation of the 1920s building boom, which had been cut off for two decades by the Depression and the war. As George Sternlieb reminds us, the American automobile industry in 1929 was producing as many cars per capita as it did in the 1980s, and real estate developers had already plotted out subdivisions in outlying areas that were only built up in the 1960s and 1970s.[13]

But financially, organizationally, and technologically, the roots of the boom were in the 1930s, for it was then that the building industry streamlined itself. As we have seen in the development of Los Angeles, both the Federal Housing Administration mortgage and the mass produced tract house date from that era. Both reflected the need to reduce costs in order for the housing industry to survive in what appeared to be a drastically diminished market. As a result, the industry had already achieved a relatively efficient form just when demand for housing exploded.

Instead of developers and builders operating independently of each other as they had in the 1920s, each on his own shoestring and passing along the high costs of production and credit to the buyer, the postwar developer-builder could borrow large sums from savings and loan institutions to achieve industrial style economies of scale. William Levitt with his Levittowns was the most famous symbol of these industrial style planner-developer-builders, but the real impact came when medium and small builders were able to incorporate these innovations everywhere on the periphery.

The buyer, in turn, had easy access to the thirty year self-amortizing mortgages that the Federal Housing Administration had created in the 1930s and which private lenders soon matched. The federal government also ensured that housing would not have to compete with industry for the investor's savings. A federally insured "loop" directed the savings of small investors into savings and loan institutions, where they were channeled directly into short term loans for builders or mortgages for buyers. One might compare this system to Haussmann's "mobilizing" of capital through the Crédit foncier for the French building industry in the 1860s. The crucial difference was that, in nineteenth century France, large pools of money were brought together in order to create large "collective" buildings: the massive apartment houses that lined the French boulevards. In post-1945 America a massively financed and elaborately organized industry existed to make possible the detached single family house.

The streamlined financial and technical systems of the 1930s thus ensured that the overwhelming demand for new suburban housing in the postwar period would not bog down in high interest rates, inefficient building practices, or inflated land prices. Instead, the doubling of real median family income from 1950 to 1970 could be translated directly into the consumption of new houses. In that golden age of housing, new tract houses could be purchased for monthly payments that were often less than the prevailing rents in the central city.[14] George Bailey had finally vanquished Mr. Potter.

Even the late 1970s combination of stagnant real income with high interest rates, gasoline prices, and land values did not diminish the desirability of the new single family house. In 1981 a median American family earned only 70% of what was needed to make the payments on the median priced house; by 1986, the median family could once again afford the median house.[15] Single family houses still constitute 67 percent of all occupied units, down only 2 percent since 1970 despite the increase in costs;[16] moreover, a survey of potential home buyers in 1986 showed that 85 percent intended to purchase a detached, single family suburban house, while only 15 percent were looking at condominium apartments or townhouses.[17] The "single," as builders call it, is still alive and well on the urban periphery.

This continuing appeal of the single should not, however, obscure the crucial changes that have transformed the meaning and context of the house. The new suburban house of the 1950s, like its predecessors for more than a century, existed precisely to isolate women and the family from urban economic life; it defined an exclusive zone of residence between city and country. Now a new house might adjoin a landscaped office park with more square feet of new office space than in a downtown building, or might be just down the highway from an enclosed shopping mall with a sales volume that exceeds those of the downtown department stores, or might overlook a high tech research laboratory making products that are exported around the world. No longer a refuge, the single family detached house on the periphery is preferred as a convenient base from which both spouses can rapidly reach their jobs.

Without the simultaneous movement of jobs along with housing, the great "suburban" boom would surely have exhausted itself in ever longer journeys to workplaces in a crowded core on overburdened highways and mass transit facilities. And the new peripheral communities would have been in reality the "isolation wards" for women that critics have called them, instead of becoming the setting for the reintegration of middle-class women into the work force as they have. The unchanging image of the suburban house and the suburban bedroom community has obscured the crucial importance of this transformation in work location, the subject of the next section.

Job Location

As those who have tried to plan the process have painfully learned, job location has its own autonomous rules. The movement of factories away from the urban core after 1945 took place independently of the housing boom and probably would have occurred without it. Nevertheless, the simultaneous movement of housing and jobs in the 1950s and 1960s created an unforeseen "critical mass" of entrepreneurship and expertise on the perimeters, which allowed the technoburb to challenge successfully the two century long economic dominance of the central city.

Just as the workshops of nineteenth century America left the inner cities of their time to seek more room and cheaper land in the newer factory zones on the outskirts, so the twentieth century factories have deserted the factory zones for the industrial parks of the technoburb. This process was accelerated by the alteration in production methods, which emphasized a linear flow of production on a single level. These new methods rendered obsolete those four and five story reinforced concrete factories which were the monuments of the early twentieth century factory zone. In the New York City area, for example, factories built before 1922 occupied 1,040 square feet per worker, those built from 1922 to 1945 used 2,000 square feet, and those built after 1945 occupied 4,550 square feet.[18] This dramatic increase in size virtually forced factories out of the constricted city blocks of the inner city toward the open spaces of the technoburb.

At the same time, the growing importance of trucking meant that factories were no longer as dependent on the confluence of rail lines which existed only in the old factory zones. Workers had their automobiles, so factories could scatter along the periphery without concern about the absence of mass transit. (The scattering of aircraft plants and other factories in Los Angeles in the 1930s prefigured this trend.) The process gained momentum as a result of thousands of uncoordinated decisions in which managers allowed their inner city plants to run down and directed new investment toward the outskirts. In the Boston region, for example, 80 percent of new industrial building undertaken between 1954 and 1967 took place on the suburban fringes.[19] Nationwide from 1958 to 1967, central cities lost more than 338,000 manufacturing, trade, and service industry jobs, while the suburban areas around these cities gained more than 433,000.[20] As these trends continued through the 1960s, the 1970 census—which showed that suburban dwellers now outnumbered rural or urban population—was matched by a similar finding that jobs located in the suburbs now outnumbered those in the central city.[21]

These changes in job location during the 1950s and 1960s were, however, only a prelude to the real triumph of the technoburb: the luring of both managerial office employment and advanced technological laboratories and production facilities from the core to the peripheries. This process may be divided into three parts. First came the establishment of "high tech" growth corridors in such diverse locations as Silicon Valley, California; Silicon Prairie, between Dallas and Forth Worth; the Atlanta Beltway; Route 1 between Princeton and New Brunswick, New Jersey; Westchester County, New York; Route 202 near Valley Forge, Pennsylvania; and Route 128 outside Boston. The second step was the movement of office bureaucracies, especially the so-called back office, from center city high-rises to technoburb office parks; and the final phase was the movement of production-service employment—banks, accountants, lawyers, advertising agencies, skilled technicians, and the like—to locations within the technoburb, thus creating that vital base of support personnel for larger firms.

Indeed, this dramatic surge toward the technoburb has been so sweeping that we must now ask whether Wright's ultimate prophecy will be fulfilled: the disappearance of the old urban centers. Is the present-day boom in downtown office construction and inner city gentrification simply a last hurrah for the old city before deeper trends in decentralization lead to its ultimate decay?

In my view, the final diffusion that Wells and Wright predicted is unlikely, if only because both underestimated the forces of economic and political centralization that continue to exist in the late twentieth century. If physical decentralization had indeed meant economic decentralization, then the urban cores would by now be ghost towns. But large and powerful organizations still seek out a central location that validates their importance, and the historic core of great cities still meets that need better than the office complexes on the outskirts. More-over, the corporate and government headquarters in the core still attract a wide variety of specialized support services—law firms, advertising, publishing, media, restaurants, entertainment centers, museums, and more—that continue to make the center cities viable.

The old factory zones around the core have also survived, but only in the painfully anomalous sense of housing those too poor to earn admission to the new city of prosperity at the periphery. The big city, therefore, will not disappear in the foreseeable future, and residents of the technoburbs will con-tinue to confront uneasily both the economic power and elite culture of the urban core and its poverty. Nevertheless, the technoburb has become the true center of American society.

The Meaning of the New City

Beyond the structure of the techno-city and its technoburbs, there is the larger question: what is the impact of this decen-tralized environment on our culture? Can anyone say of the technoburb, as Olmsted said of the suburb a century ago, that it represents "the most attractive, the most refined, and the most soundly wholesome forms of domestic life, and the best application of the arts of civilization to which mankind has yet attained"?[22] Most planners in fact say the exact opposite. Their indictment can be divided into two parts. First, decentralization has been a social and economic disaster for the old city and for the poor, who have been increasingly relegated to its crowded, decayed zones. It has resegregated American society into an affluent outer city and an indigent inner city, while erecting ever higher barriers that prevent the poor from sharing in the jobs and housing of the technoburbs.

Second, decentralization has been seen as a cultural disaster.

While the rich and diverse architectural heritage of the cities decays, the technoburb has been built up as a standardized and simplified sprawl, consuming time and space, destroying the natural landscape. The wealth that postindustrial America has generated has been used to create an ugly and wasteful pseudo-city, too spread out to be efficient, too superficial to create a true culture.

The truth of both indictments is impossible to deny, yet it must be rescued from the polemical overstatements that seem to afflict anyone who deals with these topics. The first charge is the more fundamental, for it points to a genuine structural discontinuity in post-1945 decentralization. By detaching itself physically, socially, and economically from the city, the technoburb is profoundly antiurban as suburbia never had been. Suburbanization strengthened the central core as the cultural and economic heart of an expanding region; by excluding industry, suburbia left intact and even augmented the urban factory districts.

Technoburb development, however, completely undermines the factory district and potentially threatens even the commercial core. The competition from new sites on the outskirts renders obsolete the whole complex of housing and factory sites that had been built up in the years 1890 to 1930 and provides alternatives to the core for even the most specialized shopping and administrative services.

This competition, moreover, has occurred in the context of a massive migration of southern blacks to northern cities. Blacks, Hispanics, and other recent migrants could afford housing only in the old factory districts, which were being abandoned by both employers and the white working class. The result was a twentieth century version of Disraeli's "two nations." Now, however, the outer reaches of affluence include both the middle class and the better-off working class—a majority of the population; while the largely black and Hispanic minority are forced into decaying neighborhoods, which lack not only decent housing but jobs.

This bleak picture has been modified somewhat by the continued ability of the traditional urban cores to retain certain key areas of white collar and professional employment; and by the choice of some highly paid core workers to live in high-rise or recently renovated housing around the core. Compared both to the decaying factory zones and to peripheral expansion, the "gentrification" phenomenon has been highly visible yet statistically insignificant. It has done as much to displace low income city dwellers as to benefit them. The late twentieth century American environment thus shows all the signs of the two nations syndrome: one caught in an environment of poverty, cut off from the majority culture, speaking its own languages and dialects; the other an increasingly homogenized culture of affluence, more and more remote from an urban environment it finds dangerous.

If the fate of the poor caught in a decaying environment has been the major social cost of the techno-city, the homogenization of the new city has attracted equal concern. The 1950s in particular saw a remarkable outpouring of polemics on the so-called "suburban problem." To some degree they were critiques of American culture in general, which focused on suburbia as a relatively safe target. But two in particular, those of David Riesman and William H. Whyte, remain pertinent.

In an article called "The Suburban Sadness," Riesman raises the basic issue: is the low density of the new city destructive to all cultural diversity? He is concerned that the critical mass for a minority high culture simply cannot survive in the world of the outer city. His point of reference throughout is the classic industrial city, which certainly did focus the whole metropolitan area in a limited downtown area.[23]

This downtown core not only brought together the diverse classes and ethnic groups that formed the city, but through mass transportation it made the specialized cultures of the concert hall, the museum, the first-run movie house, and the theater available to all. The new city, Riesman fears, cannot generate this diversity. Culture is necessarily reduced to a lowest common denominator, the crass conformity of which will act as a barrier to individualism and freedom.

Conformity is very much the theme of William Whyte's analysis of Park Forest, Illinois—a suburb of Chicago—which forms part of Whyte's influential work of popular sociology, *The Organization Man*.[24] Much of the frantic socializing that Whyte found in Park Forest has proved to be atypical of suburbias in general, but the essential element of the analysis is less easily dismissed. Whyte identifies the basis of the new society in large organizations that can master space: in other words, that can distribute a narrow range of products over large areas. The suburb is the product of this world, both materially and socially.

Materially, it embodies large scale organization and mass production, in its relentless uniformity, its use of a narrow range of designs repeated endlessly without true variation or relief. Socially, it is dominated by "organization men," men whose personalities have been formed by the requirements of working smoothly in large organizations, and women who exist largely to provide the home environment these men need to exist.

The result—and here Riesman and Whyte are in essential agreement—is a crucial loss of texture in modern society, an end to the kind of individualism that has been at the heart of our culture. It is interesting that they draw exactly the opposite conclusions from decentralization that Frank Lloyd Wright did. Where Wright saw the city as the heartland of conformity and decentralization as the path to renewed individualism, Riesman and Whyte see decentralization as ultimately destructive of the density on which high culture depends.

One further element, which neither Riesman nor Whyte emphasized in their 1950s view, is television. Television has proved to be the perfect medium for the technoburb. Like the new city itself, television is inherently decentralized and home centered. It gives to those at the edge of a decentralized region exactly the same access to the central entertainment as those at the center. It bypasses the old centers of community—especially the downtown theater—to go directly to the home.

Since the 1950s television and the technoburb have been in alliance, each promoting the interests of the other. For television, the decentralized audience is the ideal audience, the perfect consumers of the standardized products that advertisements offer. In return, television has glorified the single family house as the standard American home, enshrined the low density neighborhood, and (perhaps not coincidentally) has provided an unrelentingly negative picture of the city as the haven of crime and deviance.

It is not difficult to wind up with a picture of the techno-city as a cultural wasteland, mired in standardization and conformity, unable to generate individuality. A mass migration to the new city can therefore be seen as a cultural disaster, a trivialization of American culture, and a destructive threat to the only environment in which culture can flourish.

In dealing with these concerns, we must acknowledge the essential truth that the new city will probably never be able to compete culturally with the old centers. There will be for the foreseeable future a division founded on choice between those who seek out even at great cost the kind of cultural excitement that can only be found in the center, and those who choose the family centered life of the outer city. Yet the issue still remains undecided, whether it is possible to create a truly decentralized culture, one in which the family centered life is compatible with a fair degree of choice. There is the irony that American society, which can find in these decentralized regions more than enough specialists in the most arcane engineering specialties, cannot hope to attract a large enough audience to support a chamber music concert.

Perhaps the only way to deal with these concerns is to see them as part of a larger evolution. As we have seen, the first organizations to flourish in a decentralized environment are indeed those which rest on standardization; but, in the world of high technology, at least, this standardization gives way eventually to a better balance of standardization and diversity. There is some evidence that this evolution is taking place culturally in the techno-city as well. It is no doubt a utopianism worthy of Frank Lloyd Wright to imagine that the new city will become the source of excellence in the arts, exporting its products to the city in the way that computers designed in campuslike laboratories find their way to the urban centers. Nevertheless, if the technoburb has its unique cultural mission for a decentralized nation, I believe it lies less in the areas of traditional culture than in that of the environment. Here I believe Wright was most truly prophetic in his determination to create a truly American landscape out of the materials of rapid and unlimited decentralization. "Broadacres," he wrote, "would be so built in sympathy with Nature that a deep feeling for the beauty of the terrain would be a fundamental qualification for the new city-builders."[25]

When applied to the realities of the peripheral city, these words have an uncomfortably ironic ring. One might conclude that the real qualifications for its builders and designers are a total disregard for nature and an overwhelming sympathy for the profit motive. Indeed, it is precisely the environmental impact of the techno-city that has drawn the most criticism, criticism best summed up in the inevitable word "sprawl." Architecture critic Ada Louise Huxtable has called the typical new settlements "slurbs" and has written that life there is "no voyage of discovery or private exploration of the world's wonders, natural and man-made; it is cliché conformity as far as the eye can see, with no stimulation of the spirit through quality of the environment."[26]

The case against the technoburb can easily be summarized. Compared even to the traditional suburb, it at first appears impossible to comprehend. It has no clear boundaries; it includes discordant rural, urban, and suburban elements; and it can best be measured in counties rather than in city blocks. Consequently the new city lacks any recognizable center to give meaning to the whole. Major civic institutions seem scattered at random over an undifferentiated landscape.

Even planned developments—however harmonious they might appear from the inside—can be no more than fragments in a fragmented environment. A single house, a single street, even a cluster of streets and houses can and frequently are well designed. But true public space is lacking or totally commercialized. Only the remaining pockets of undeveloped farmland maintain real openness, and these pockets are inevitably developed, precipitating further flight and further sprawl.

The case for the techno-city can only be made hesitantly and conditionally. Nevertheless, we can hope that its deficiencies are in large part the early awkwardness of a new urban type. All new city forms appear in their early stages to be chaotic. "There were a hundred thousand shapes and substances of incompleteness, wildly mingled out of their places, upside down, burrowing in the earth, aspiring in the earth, moldering in the water, and unintelligible as any dream." This was Charles Dickens describing London in 1848, in his novel *Dombey and Son* (chapter 6). As I have indicated, sprawl has a functional logic that may not be apparent to those accustomed to more traditional cities. If that logic is understood imaginatively, as Wells and especially Wright attempted to do, then perhaps a matching aesthetic can be devised.

We must remember that even the most "organic" cityscapes of the past evolved slowly after much chaos and trial and error. The classic late nineteenth century railroad suburb—the standard against which critics judge today's sprawl—evolved out of the disorder of nineteenth century metropolitan growth. First, planners of genius like John Nash and Frederick Law Olmsted comprehended the process and devised aesthetic formulas to guide it. These formulas were then communicated—slowly and incompletely—to speculative builders, who nevertheless managed to capture the basic idea. Finally, individual property owners constantly upgraded their holdings to eliminate discordant elements and bring their community closer to the ideal.

We might hope that a similar process is now at work in the postsuburban outer city. As a starting point for a technoburb aesthetic, there are Wright's Broadacre City plans and drawings, which still repay study for anyone seeking a vision of a modern yet organic American landscape. More useful still is the American New Town tradition, starting from Radburn, New Jersey, with its careful designs intended to reconcile decentralization with older ideas of community.[27] Already, New Town designs have been adopted by speculative builders, not only in a highly publicized project like James Rouse's Columbia, Maryland, but in hundreds of smaller planned communities, which are beginning to leave their mark on the landscape.

At the level of civic architecture there is Wright's Marin County Civic Center to serve as a model for public monuments in a decentralized environment. The multilevel, enclosed shopping mall has attained a spaciousness not unworthy of the great urban shopping districts of the past, while newly built college campuses and campuslike office complexes and research centers contribute significantly to the environment. Some commercial highway strips have been rescued from cacophony and have managed to achieve a liveliness that is not tawdry. (This evolution parallels the evolution of the nineteenth century urban core, originally a remarkably ugly cluster of small buildings and large signs, which was transformed into a reasonably dignified center for commerce by the turn of the century.)

Most importantly, there is a growing sense that open land must be preserved as an integral part of the landscape, through regional land use plans, purchases for parklands, and tax abatements for working farms. These governmental measures, combined with thousands of small scale efforts by individuals, could create a fitting environment for the new city. These efforts, moreover, could provide the starting point for a more profound diversification of the outer city. An increased understanding and respect for the landscape of each region could lead to a growing rejection of a mass culture that erases all such distinctions.

The techno-city, therefore, is still under construction, both physically and culturally. Its economic and social successes are undeniable, as are its costs. Most importantly, the new pattern of decentralization has fundamentally altered the urban form on which suburbia had depended for its function and meaning. Whatever the fate of the new city, suburbia in its traditional sense now belongs to the past.

The Legacy of Suburbia

In the midst of the techno-city small pieces of the old suburbia survive. Along a railroad line or perhaps a disused trolley line one can still see the characteristic forms, which go back ultimately to eighteenth century London and to the ideal that took shape on Clapham Common: a marriage of town and country, a reconciliation of nature and the man-made world.

Now, of course, "nature" is far away, and a newly built environment seems to stretch as far as the fields once did. Sometimes the old suburbs have remained as proud and protected enclaves in a world of shopping malls and superhighways. Like acolytes of a dying religion, a few of their residents maintain the old ritual of commuting by increasingly infrequent trains into the city. More frequently, the old suburbs have been swallowed up by the city they had once kept at bay: nineteenth century picturesque villages adrift in a decaying world of burned out apartment houses and closed factories.

Seen in historical perspective, suburbia now appears as the point of transition between two decentralized eras: the preindustrial rural era and the postindustrial information society. Suburbia originated when cities were strange juxtapositions of the very rich and the very poor; the mass of the population lived and worked in the decentralized world of the rural villages. Now both people and production are again forsaking the cities, leaving only those modern elite to share the central cities with their traditional urban neighbors—the desperately poor.

The residential suburb thus belongs to the Age of Great Cities, which has now reached its end. Suburbia was at once the most characteristic product of explosive urban expansion and a desperate protest against it. It permitted a bourgeois elite to enjoy all the advantages of the massive urban economy while escaping its perils. Now that the urban periphery is no longer the exclusive sanctuary of a privileged class we can better appreciate the lasting values embodied by the middle-class residential suburb during two centuries of industrialization and urbanization. Suburbia kept alive the ideal of a balance between man and nature in a society that seemed dedicated to destroying it. That is its legacy.

NOTES

Introduction

1. César Daly, *L'architecture privée au XIXe siècle sous Napoléon III*, 2 vols. in 3 (Paris: Morel, 1864), 1:20; my translation.

2. Chaucer, *Canterbury Tales*, Canon's Yeoman's Tale, lines 557–60:

> "In the suburbes of a town . . .
> Lurkynge in hernes and in lanes blynde,
> Whereas thise robbours and thise theves by kynde
> Holden hir pryvee fereful residence. . . ."

3. *Oxford English Dictionary*, s.v. "suburb."

4. Quoted in Pat Rogers, *Grub Street: Studies in a Subculture* (London: Methuen, 1972), 26.

5. John Strype in John Stowe, *A Survey of the Cities of London and Westminster and the Borough of Southwark* [orig. ed. 1598], "corrected, improved, and very much enlarged in the year 1720" by John Strype, 6th ed., 2 vols. (London: Innys & Richardson, 1754–55), ii, 76.

6. Anonymous article in *Old England* (London), 2 July 1748.

7. *Encyclopaedia Britannica*, 11th ed., s.v. "London."

8. Lawrence J. Stone, *The Family, Sex and Marriage in England, 1500–1800* (New York: Harper & Row, 1977), part 4.

9. Frederick Law Olmsted, "Preliminary Report upon the Proposed Suburban Village at Riverside, near Chicago" (New York, 1868); reprinted in S. B. Sutton, ed., *Civilizing American Cities: A Selection of Frederick Law Olmsted's Writings on City Landscapes* (Cambridge, Mass.: M.I.T. Press, 1971), 293.

10. H. G. Wells, "The Probable Diffusion of Great Cities" (1900), in *Anticipations and Other Papers*, vol. 4 of *The Works of H. G. Wells* (New York: Scribner's, 1924), 39. Wells himself attributes the phrase to George Gissing.

11. Adna F. Weber, *The Growth of Cities in the Nineteenth Century*, rev. ed. (Ithaca, N.Y.: Cornell University Press, 1963; orig. ed. 1899), 47.

12. Ibid.

13. Ibid., 39.

14. For the best scholarly analysis of the city's changing role over time, see Paul M. Hohenberg and Lynn H. Lees, *The Making of Urban Europe, 1000–1950* (Cambridge, Mass.: Harvard University Press, 1985).

15. Andrew Lees, *Cities Perceived: Urban Society in European and American Thought, 1820–1940* (New York: Columbia University Press, 1985), 136–88. As Lees emphasizes, these negative views were balanced by more positive evaluations of the impact of urbanization.

16. Kenneth T. Jackson, *Crabgrass Frontier: The Suburbanization of the United States* (New York: Oxford University Press, 1985).

17. Fernand Braudel, *Capitalism and Material Life, 1400–1800*, trans. Miriam Kochan (New York: Harper & Row, 1975), 373, for the concept of the city as "transformer."

Chapter 1. London: Birthplace of Suburbia

1. H. G. Wells, "The Probable Diffusion of Great Cities" (1900), *The Works of H. G. Wells: Anticipations and Other Papers* (New York: Scribner's, 1924), 4:39.

2. For the population of Paris and London in the eighteenth century, see E. A. Wrigley, "A Simple Model of London's Importance in Changing English Society and Economy 1650–1750," in Philip Abrams and E. A. Wrigley, eds., *Towns in Societies* (Cambridge: Cambridge University Press, 1978), 215–16. For London's population in 1800 see M. J. Daunton, "Towns and Economic Growth in Eighteenth Century England," in Abrams and Wrigley, *Towns in Societies*, 247, and B. R. Mitchell, *European Historical Statistics* (New York: Columbia University Press, 1978), 13.

3. John Stow, *A Survey of the Cities of London and Westminster and the Borough of Southwark* [orig. ed. 1598], "corrected, improved and very much enlarged in the year 1720" by John Strype, 6th ed., 2 vols. (London: Innys & Richardson, 1754–55), 1:3.

4. Daniel Defoe, *A Tour Thro' the Whole Island of Great Britain*, ed. G. D. H. Cole, 2 vols. (London: Peter Davies, 1927), 1:168, quoted in Max Byrd, *London Transformed: Images of the City in the Eighteenth Century* (New Haven: Yale University Press, 1978), 12.

5. See D. V. Glass, *London's Inhabitants Within the Walls, 1695* (Leicester, Eng.: London Record Society, 1966), for a detailed statistical study of London's social ecology based on records in the Corporation of London Records Office.

6. Norman G. Brett-James, *The Growth of Stuart London* (London: Allen & Unwin, 1935), 69.

7. Stow, *Survey of the Cities*, ed. Strype, 2:34.

8. Pierre Jean Grosley, *A Tour to London*, trans. Thomas Nugent, 2 vols. (London: Lockyer Davis, 1772), 1:33–4.

9. John Summerson, *Georgian London*, rev. ed. (Harmondsworth: Penguin, 1978), chap. 3.

10. Thomas Babington Macaulay, *The History of England* [orig. ed. 1849], 10 vols. (New York: Putnam, 1898), 1:29.

11. Ibid., 1:30.

12. John Gwynn, *London and Westminster Improved* (London: Dodsley, 1766), viii.

13. Ibid., vi.

14. The London bourgeoisie is best described in Nicholas Rogers, "Money, Land and Lineage: The Big Bourgeoisie of Hanoverian London," *Social History* 4 (1979): 437–54. See also Mary Dorothy George, *London Life in the Eighteenth Century*, 3rd ed. (London: University of London Press, 1951).

15. *Encyclopaedia Britannica*, 11th ed., s.v. "Chippendale, Thomas."

16. Rogers, "Money, Land and Lineage," 438–50.

17. Daniel Defoe, *The Complete English Tradesman*, 2d ed., 2 vols. (London: Rivington, 1727), chap. 23.

18. *Encyclopaedia Britannica*, 11th ed., s.v. "Lloyd's of London."

19. Defoe, *Complete English Tradesman*, chap. 23.

20. Ibid.

21. *Encyclopaedia Britannica*, 11th ed., s.v. "Theatre" and "Dance."

22. J. H. Plumb, "The New World of Children in Eighteenth Century England," *Past & Present* 67 (May 1975): 64–95. See also Rosamund Bayne-Powell, *The English Child in the Eighteenth Century* (New York: E. P. Dutton, 1939), chap. 10.

23. *Encyclopaedia Britannica*, 11th ed., s.v. "Vauxhall" and "Ranelagh."

24. Hannah More, *Cælebs in Search of a Wife* [orig. ed. 1808], 14th ed., 2 vols. (London: Cadell and Davies, 1813), 1:176.

25. Eric Pawson, *Transport and Economy: The Turnpike Roads of Eighteenth Century Britain* (New York: Academic Press, 1977).

26. Ian Watt, *The Rise of the Novel: Studies in Defoe, Richardson, and Fielding* (Harmondsworth: Penguin, 1963), 185.

27. George Orwell, *The Road to Wigan Pier* (New York: Harcourt, Brace, Jovanovich, 1958), 127.

28. Lawrence J. Stone, *The Family, Sex and Marriage in England, 1500–1800* (New York: Harper & Row, 1977), 7.

29. On the Evangelicals see Ian C. Bradley, *The Call to Seriousness: The Evangelical Impact on the Victorians* (New York: Macmillan, 1976); Ford K. Brown, *Fathers of the Victorians: The Age of Wilberforce* (Cambridge: Cambridge University Press, 1961); Standish Meacham, "The Evangelical Inheritance," *Journal of British Studies* 3 (1963): 88–104; and Catharine Hall, "The Early Formation of Victorian Domestic Ideology," in Sandra Burman, ed., *Fit Work for Women* (New York: St. Martin's Press, 1979), 9–14.

30. Quoted in Bradley, *Call to Seriousness*, 94.

31. G. M. Young, *Victorian England: Portrait of an Age*, 2d ed. (London: Oxford University Press, 1960), 1. Young gives equal influence to the belief in progress.

32. Robert Isaac Wilberforce and Samuel Wilberforce, eds., *The Correspondence of William Wilberforce*, 2 vols. (London: Murray, 1840), letter to Miss ____, 8 November 1787, 1:44.

33. Ibid., 1:45.

34. William Wilberforce, *A Practical View of the Prevailing Religious System of Professed Christians, in the Higher and Middle Classes of this Country, Contrasted with Real Christianity* [orig. ed. 1797], 11th ed. (London: Cadell and Davies, 1815), 365.

35. Ibid., 366.

36. Ibid., 366–67.

37. Ibid., 367.

38. Hannah More, *Strictures on the Modern System of Female Education*, in *The Works of Hannah More*, 7 vols. (New York: Harper & Bros., 1836), 6:204–6.

39. More, *Cælebs in Search of a Wife*, 1:239.

40. Ibid., 1:19.

41. Ibid., 1:21.

Chapter 2. Building the Bourgeois Utopia

1. Claude Lévi-Strauss, *The Savage Mind* (Chicago: University of Chicago Press, 1966), 16–33.

2. *Encyclopaedia Britannica*, 11th ed., s.v. "Gresham, Thomas."

3. Daniel Defoe, *The Complete English Tradesman*, 2d ed., 2 vols. (London: Rivington, 1727), 1:244–45.

4. London *Daily Advertiser*, 9 July 1774, quoted in Nicholas Rogers, "Money, Land and Lineage: The Big Bourgeoisie of Hanoverian London," *Social History* 4 (1979): 449. Compare F. M. L. Thompson, *Hampstead: Building a Borough, 1650–1964* (London: Routledge & Kegan Paul, 1974), 92, in which he describes the Haverstock Hill villa development at Hampstead in 1805, where each house "gives a perfect impression of a country estate in miniature."

5. Rogers, "Money, Land and Lineage," 443–52; the architectural, social, and economic history of the country house is brilliantly described in Lawrence Stone and Jeanne C. Fawtier Stone, *An Open Elite? England, 1540–1880* (New York: Oxford University Press, 1985), Part III, "Houses."

6. Defoe, *Complete English Tradesman*, vol. 1:108.

7. Pierre Jean Grosley, *A Tour to London*, trans. Thomas Nugent, 2 vols. (London: Lockyer Davis, 1772), 1:109.

8. *The Connoisseur*, 12 September 1754.

9. Ibid.

10. *The Connoisseur*, 26 August 1756.

11. *The Idler*, 29 July 1758.

12. *The Connoisseur*, 12 September 1754.

13. John B. Ward-Perkins, *Roman Architecture* (New York: Abrams, 1977), 51–58.

14. Quoted in Fernand Braudel, *The Mediterranean and the Mediterranean World in the Age of Philip II*, trans. Sian Reynolds, 2 vols. (New York: Harper & Row, 1972), 1:337.

15. James S. Ackerman, *Palladio's Villas* (Locust Valley, NY: Institute of Fine Arts, New York University, 1967), 17.

16. Andrea Palladio, *The Four Books of Architecture*, transl. Isaac Ware (1738; reprint ed. New York: Dover Publications, 1965), 46.

17. Ackerman, *Palladio's Villas*, 20.

18. W. S. Lewis, Warren Hunting Smith, and George L. Lem, eds., *The Yale Edition of Horace Walpole's Correspondence*, 48 vols. in 49 (New Haven: Yale University Press, 1937–83), 19:497.

19. Nikolaus Pevsner, *An Outline of European Architecture*, 7th ed. (Harmondsworth: Penguin, 1963), 337.

20. Ackerman, *Palladio's Villas*, 17.

21. Ibid., 2.

22. Kenneth Clark, *Landscape into Art* (London: Murray, 1949), 54.

23. Raymond Williams, *The Country and the City* (London: Chatto & Windus, 1973), 124.

24. For the significance of Pope's garden and villa see Maynard Mack, *The Garden and the City: Retirement and Politics in the Later Poetry of Pope, 1731–1743* (Toronto: University of Toronto Press, 1969).

25. Quoted in Pevsner, *Outline*, 347.

26. Daniel Defoe, *A Tour Thro' the Whole Island of Great Britain*, ed. G. D. H. Cole, 2 vols. (London: Peter Davies, 1927), 1:168.

27. Standish Meacham, *Henry Thornton of Clapham, 1760–1815* (Cambridge, Mass.: Harvard University Press, 1964); E. M. Forster, *Marianne Thornton, 1797–1887: A Domestic Biography* (New York: Harcourt, Brace, 1956). An interesting comparison to Clapham can be found in a study of Birmingham suburbia, Lenore Davidoff and Catherine Hall, "The Architecture of Public and Private Life: English Middle Class Society in a Provincial Town, 1780–1850," in Derek Fraser and Anthony Sutcliffe, eds., *The Pursuit of Urban History* (London: Edward Arnold, 1983), 326–46.

28. J. H. M. Burgess, *The Chronicles of Clapham (Clapham Common)* (London: A. V. Huckle & Son, 1929).

29. Charles Smith, "Perambulation of Clapham Common #27," in *Smith's Actual Survey of the Roads from London to Brighthelmstone* (London: Charles Smith, 1800).

30. *Kent's Directory* (London: Kent, 1797); I also used *Holden's Triennial Directory*, 2d ed. (London: Flint, 1799).

31. See, for example, the "Book of the Hoare Family," appendix C.VII in Burgess, *Chronicles of Clapham*. Henry Hoare, a Fleet Street banker, "built an elegant villa at Clapham Common, that he might be enabled, with greater convenience, to attend to his business in London without being obliged to sleep within its smoky atmosphere." Burgess has collected a remarkable store of such information, along with Clapham prints and drawings, which are now in the Guildhall Library, London.

32. William Cowper, *The Task* (1785), book 3.

33. For details of this genteel subdivision, see John Aiken, *The History of the Environs of London*, 3 vols. (London: J. Stockdale, 1811), 1:124; and Edward W. Brayley, *A Topographical History of Surrey*, 5 vols. (London: Dorking, Tilt, and Bogue, 1841–48), 3:280.

34. Samuel Thornton, vestry minutes, Clapham, 22 September 1795: Greater London Council Record Office, P95/TR11/6, p. 304. Samuel Thornton, a brother of Henry, owned his own Clapham villa and was "Lord of the Manor." This office, plus the control of the vestry by the genteel residents, gave the "suburbanites" control of local government.

35. Aiken, *Environs of London*, 1:124.

36. Forster, *Marianne Thornton*, 3–8.

37. Ibid., 18. A similar family sociability, though lacking the same serious content, has recently been shown for the rural gentry in this period: see Susan Lasdun, *Victorians at Home* (New York: Viking, 1981); both Lasdun and Mark Girouard, who wrote the introduction to her book, emphasize the contrast between the mixing of the Regency period and the greater social segregation of the Victorians.

38. Forster, *Marianne Thornton*, 13–26.

39. Bradley, *Call to Seriousness*, 180.

40. Forster, *Marianne Thornton*, 32.

41. Ibid., 18.

42. Hannah More, *Cælebs in Search of a Wife* [orig. ed. 1808], 14th ed., 2 vols. (London: Cadell and Davies, 1813), 1:91.

43. J. H. Plumb, "The New World of Children in Eighteenth Century England," *Past & Present* 67 (May 1975): 64–95.

44. Forster, *Marianne Thornton*, 20–38.

45. John Clive, *Thomas Babington Macaulay: The Shaping of the Historian* (London: Secker and Warburg, 1973), 21–35.

46. Forster, *Marianne Thornton*, 25.

47. Ibid., 24–25.

48. Marianne Thornton's letters to More were reprinted as "Letters from a Young Lady," in T. S. Ashton and R. S. Sayers, eds., *Papers in English Monetary History* (Oxford: Clarendon, 1953), 96–108.

49. Ibid., 32.

50. G. O. Trevelyan, *The Life and Letters of Lord Macaulay* [orig. ed. 1875], 2 vols. (London: Nelson, 1908), 1:40.

51. Forster, *Marianne Thornton*, 32.

52. Ibid., 8.

53. Ibid., 12.

54. Bradley, *Call to Seriousness*, 120.

55. Robert Isaac Wilberforce and Samuel Wilberforce, *The Life of William Wilberforce*, 5 vols. (London: Murray, 1838), 2:91.

56. *Encyclopaedia Britannica*, 11th ed., s.v. "London."

57. J. Hassell, *Picturesque Rides and Walks, with Excursions by Water, Thirty Miles Round the British Metropolis*, 2 vols. (London: printed for the author, 1817–18), 2.1:180.

58. John Nash, *First Report of H. M. Commissioners of Woods, Forests, and Land Revenues*, London, 1812, appendix XIIB. Reprinted as appendix III in John White, *Some Account of the Proposed Improvements in the Western Part of London*, 2d ed. (London: Reynolds, 1815).

59. *Oxford English Dictionary*, s.v. "suburb."

60. James Malcolm, *Anecdotes of the Manners and Customs of London*, 2 vols. (London: Longman, Hurst, 1810), 2:417. Italics in original.

61. Nash, *First Report*, xxx.

62. John Summerson, *Georgian London*, rev. ed. (Harmondsworth: Penguin, 1978), 175, links Shaw to the plan, which survives only as an engraved map in the Crace Collection of the British Museum that bears the names of Spurrier and Phipps, auctioneers. But, as Summerson observes, Shaw was only eighteen at the time. F. M. L. Thompson, "Introduction," in F. M. L. Thompson, ed., *The Rise of Suburbia* (Leicester: Leicester University Press, 1982), 9, attributes the plan to Shaw without hesitation.

63. Nash, *First Report*, xxxiv; for Regent's Park, see especially John Summerson, "The Beginnings of Regent's Park," *Architectural History* 20 (1977): 56–62.

64. John Nash, "Plan of Park Village," Public Record Office MPE/911.

65. Ibid.

66. *Dictionary of National Biography*, s.v. "Harford, John Scandrett, Jr." The author of this notice claims that Harford was the model for the priggish suitor in Hannah More's *Cælebs*.

67. J. N. Brewer, *Delineations of Gloucestershire* (1824), quoted in Nigel H. Temple, *John Nash and the Village Picturesque* (Gloucester: Alan Sutton, 1979), 72.

68. Uvedale Price, "Essay on Architecture and Buildings," in *Essays on the Picturesque* [orig. ed. 1794], 2 vols. (London: Mawman, 1810), 2:346–47.

69. *Discourse* (1786), quoted in Pevsner, *Outline*, 376.

70. John Summerson, *The Life and Work of John Nash, Architect* (Cambridge, Mass.: MIT Press, 1980).

71. Thomas Malton, *Essay on British Cottage Architecture* (London: printed for the author, 1804), 5.

72. J. Hassell, *Picturesque Rides and Walks*, 2 vols. (London: 1817–18), 1:13.

73. Pevsner, *Outline*, 378–79.

74. Karl Marx and Friedrich Engels, "The Communist Manifesto" (1848), in Robert C. Tucker, ed., *The Marx-Engels Reader* (New York: W. W. Norton, 1978), 475–76.

75. Charles Dickens, *Great Expectations*, chap. 36.

Chapter 3. The Suburb and the Industrial City: Manchester

1. Francis Sheppard, *London 1808–1870: The Infernal Wen* (Berkeley: University of California Press, 1971), especially chaps. 1–5.

2. William H. White, "On Middle Class Housing in Paris and Central London," *Royal Institute of British Architects Transactions* 28 (1877–78): 21–54.

3. For the continued vitality of the English urban row house, see Stefan Muthesius, *The English Terraced House* (New Haven: Yale University Press, 1982).

4. *Encyclopaedia Britannica*, 11th ed., s.v. "London—Suburbs."

5. The best guide to middle-class housing in London and its relationship to the city is the important work of Donald J. Olsen. See especially his *The City as a Work of Art: London. Paris. Vienna* (New Haven: Yale University Press, 1986); *The Growth of Victorian London* (New York: Holmes and Meier, 1976); *Town Planning in London: The Eighteenth and Nineteenth Centuries*, 2nd ed. (New Haven: Yale University Press, 1982); and "House Upon House: Estate Development in London and Sheffield," in H. J. Dyos and Michael Wolff, *The Victorian City: Images and Realities*, 2 vols. (London: Routledge and Kegan Paul, 1973), 1:333–58. See also two important studies of London suburbs, H. J. Dyos, *Victorian Suburb: A Study of the Growth of Camberwell* (Leicester: Leicester University Press, 1966) and F. M. L. Thompson, *Hampstead: Building A Borough, 1650–1964* (London: Routledge and Kegan Paul, 1974). In addition, shorter studies include J. M. Rawcliffe, "Bromley: Kentish Market Town to London Suburb," in F. M. L. Thompson, ed., *The Rise of Suburbia* (Leicester: Leicester University Press, 1982), 27–92; and Michael Kahn, "Suburban Development in Outer West London, 1850–1900," also in F. M. L. Thompson, ed., *The Rise of Suburbia*, 93–156.

6. Friedrich Engels, *The Condition of the Working Class in England*, ed. and trans. W. O. Henderson and W. H. Chaloner (Oxford: Blackwell, 1958), 50–78. For the importance of Engels for understanding Manchester, see Steven Marcus, *Engels, Manchester and the Working Class* (New York: Random House, 1974).

7. Thomas Bullock, *Bradshaw's Illustrated Guide to Manchester* (London: W. J. Adams, 1857), 7–8.

8. For eighteenth century population, see W. H. Chaloner, "Manchester in the Latter Half of the Eighteenth Century," *Bulletin of the John Rylands Library* 42 (Sept. 1959): 41–42; for the nineteenth century, Asa Briggs, *Victorian Cities* (New York: Harper & Row, 1965), 89; and B. R. Mitchell, *European Historical Statistics* (New York: Columbia University Press, 1978), 12.

9. J. H. Clapham and M. M. Clapham, "Life in the New Towns," in G. M. Young, ed., *Early Victorian England, 1830–1865*, 2 vols. (London: Oxford University Press, 1934), 1:244.

10. Chaloner, "Manchester," 40–60; Briggs, *Victorian Cities*, 88–138; François Vigier, *Change and Apathy: Liverpool and Manchester during the Industrial Revolution* (Cambridge, Mass.: M.I.T. Press, 1970), chaps. 5 and 6.

11. James Ogden, *A Description of Manchester* (Manchester, 1783), reprinted and ed. William E. A. Axon (Manchester: John Heywood, 1887).

12. James Butterworth, *The Antiquities of the Town, and a Complete History of the Trade of Manchester* (Manchester: C. W. Leake, 1822), 278.

13. Archibald Prentice, *Historical Sketches and Personal Recollections of Manchester*, 2d ed. (London: Gilpin, 1851), 360.

14. Samuel Brooks Papers, Manchester Central Library Archives, M/C 158; Leo H. Grindon, *Manchester Banks and Bankers* (Manchester: Palmer & Howe, 1887), 203–9.

15. Benjamin Love, *Manchester as It Is* (Manchester: Love and Barton, 1839), 200–201.

16. For the structure and architecture of the Manchester central business district, see *The Builder* 6 (Dec. 2, 1848), 577–78.

17. Prentice, *Historical Sketches*, 360.

18. George Saintsbury, *Manchester* (London: Longmans, Green, 1887), 105.

19. Briggs, *Victorian Cities*, 89–91.

20. Richard Parkinson, *On the Present Condition of the Labouring Poor in Manchester; with Hints for Improving It* (London, 1841); quoted in Briggs, *Victorian Cities*, 114.

21. Elizabeth Gaskell, *Mary Barton*, 2 vols. (London: Chapman and Hall, 1848), chap. 6.

22. Engels, *Condition of the English Working Class*, 55–56. On the subject of class segregation, see the important debate of David Ward, "Victorian Cities: how modern?" *Journal of Historical Geography* 1 (1975) and David Cannadine, "Victorian Cities: how different?" *Social History* 4 (1977). Against Ward's evidence of class mixing, Cannadine upholds the strong desire in the middle class to separate themselves from the working class.

23. Brooks Papers, M/C 158.

24. J. C. Loudon, *The Suburban Gardener, and Villa Companion* (London: published by the author, 1838), 32.

25. Alfred Lang, "Modern House-Building," *The Builder* 12 (Feb. 4, 1854), 74.

26. Joseph Perrin, *The Manchester Handbook* (Manchester: Hale and Roworth, 1857), 5.

27. H. G. Duffield, *The Stranger's Guide to Manchester* (Manchester: C. Duffield, 1850), 200–201.

28. For the details of speculative development and building see Great Britain, *Parliamentary Papers* (Commons), "Report of the Select Committee on Bank

Acts," 1857, 1, Evidence, Questions 5413–18; 5535–36. In Manchester land tenure was basically freehold subject only to a fixed "quitrent" which was paid to the original proprietor. In and around London landowners seldom sold freehold title and instead disposed of the land in 99-year leases for development. This created an even more complicated system of credit and borrowing. The best guides to this complicated subject are Dyos, *Victorian Suburb*, chap. 5; Muthesius, *The English Terraced House*, chaps. 3, 4, and 5; Thompson, *Hampstead*, 238–54; Olsen, "House upon House"; C. Treen, "The Process of Suburban Development in North Leeds, 1870–1914," in Thompson, ed., *The Rise of Suburbia*, 157–210; and Peter J. Aspinall, "The Internal Structure of the Housebuilding Industry in Nineteenth Century Cities," in James H. Johnson and Colin G. Pooley, *The Structure of Nineteenth Century Cities* (New York: St. Martin's Press, 1982), 75–106.

29. Manchester Central Library Archives, M/C 795, 15 September 1854.

30. Muthesius, *English Terraced House*, 24.

31. An interesting discussion of this phenomenon with regard to Edgbaston, Birmingham can be found in David Cannadine, *Lords and Landlords: The Aristocracy and the Towns, 1774–1967* (Leicester: Leicester University Press, 1980). See also Thompson, *Hampstead*.

32. J. C. Loudon, *The Suburban Gardener and Villa Companion*, 10.

33. H.S.G. [Henry Steenhauer Gibbs], *Autobiography of a Manchester Cotton Manufacturer* (Manchester: privately printed, 1887).

34. Alfred Lang, "Modern House-Building," 56.

35. R. J. Morris, "The Middle Class and the Property Cycle during the Industrial Revolution," in T. C. Smout, ed., *The Search for Wealth and Stability* (London: Macmillan, 1979), 91–113.

36. For Cobden's real estate investments, see Papers of the Cobden Family, Manchester Central Library Archives Department, M87/3/1 and M87/3/2.

37. For Victoria Park, see Maurice Spiers, *Victoria Park, Manchester* (Manchester: Manchester University Press, 1976).

38. Robert Rawlinson, *Report to the General Board of Health . . . on the Township of Rusholme* (London, 1850), 12.

39. Engels, *Condition of the Working Class*, 71.

40. Richard Cobden, *Incorporate Your Borough*, in *Cobden as a Citizen*, ed. William E. A. Axon (London: Unwin, 1907), 31.

41. J. C. Loudon, *A Treatise on Forming, Improving, and Managing Country Residences*, 2 vols. (London: Longman, Hurst, Rees, and Orme, 1806), 773. For Loudon's writings and influence, see John Archer, *The Literature of British Domestic Architecture, 1715–1842* (Cambridge, Mass.: M.I.T. Press, 1985), 500–536.

42. Ibid., 766.

43. J. C. Loudon, *The Suburban Gardener, and Villa Companion* (London: published by the author, 1838), 158.

44. Loudon, *Treatise on . . . Country Residences*, 845.

45. Donald Olsen, *The City as a Work of Art*, 101–13.

46. George Hadfield, *The Personal Narrative of one George Hadfield, M.P.*, bound MS, 1870, Manchester Central Library Archives, MS 923.2 H526, page 61.

47. Ibid., 60.

48. Ibid., 61.

49. Ibid.

50. Alexis Soyer, *The Modern Housewife* (New York: Appleton, 1850), 4.

51. Ibid., 336.

52. Ibid., 337.

53. Ibid., 338.

54. John Ruskin, *Praeterita* [1889], "Herne-Hill Almond Blossoms," reprinted in John D. Rosenberg, ed., *The Genius of John Ruskin* (Boston: Houghton Mifflin, 1963), 479–89.

55. John Ruskin, *Sesame and Lilies*, ed. Gertrude Buck (New York: Longmans, Green, 1905), 73.

56. Ibid., 85.

57. Ibid., 87.

58. Ibid., 90.

59. Ibid., 88.

Chapter 4. Urbanity versus Suburbanity: France and the United States

1. Olmsted, Vaux and Co., "Preliminary Report upon the Proposed Suburban Village of Riverside, near Chicago" (New York, 1868), reprinted in S. B. Sutton, ed., *Civilizing American Cities: A Selection of Frederick Law Olmsted's Writings on City Landscapes* (Cambridge, Mass.: M.I.T. Press, 1971), 295. This report will be referred to subsequently as "Riverside."

2. Daly describes his trip to London in "Maisons d'habitation de Londres," *Revue générale de l'architecture* 13 (1855), 57–63. His definitive statement on suburbs can be found in "Des Villas," in his *L'Architecture privée au XIXᵉ siècle sous Napoléon III*, 2 vols. in 3 (Paris: Morel, 1864), 18–27. See also Hélène Lipstadt, "Housing the Bourgeoisie: César Daly and the Ideal Home," *Oppositions* 8 (Spring 1977): 35–47; and Donald J. Olsen, *The City as a Work of Art: London. Paris. Vienna* (New Haven: Yale University Press, 1986), 165–71.

3. Laura Wood Roper, *FLO: A Biography of Frederick Law Olmsted* (Baltimore: Johns Hopkins University Press, 1973), chap. 6.

4. Ibid.

5. Olmsted, Vaux, "Riverside," 295.

6. David Pinkney, *Napoleon III and the Rebuilding of Paris* (Princeton: Princeton University Press, 1958), 8–11.

7. The periphery of an antebellum American city is perhaps best described in Henry C. Binford, *The First Suburbs: Residential Communities on the Boston Periphery 1815–1860* (Chicago: University of Chicago Press, 1985); pre-suburban Philadelphia is vividly evoked in Roger Miller and Joseph Sirey, "The Emerging Suburb: West Philadelphia, 1850–1880," *Pennsylvania History* 47 (1980), 102–4. See also Edward K. Spann, *The New Metropolis: New York City, 1840–1857* (New York: Columbia University Press, 1981), chap. 8; and Betsy Blackmar, "Re-walking the 'Walking City': Housing and Property Relations in New York City, 1780–1840," *Radical History Review* 21 (Fall 1979): 131–150.

8. Olsen, *City as a Work of Art*, chap. 4.

9. For an illuminating comparison of mid nineteenth century London and Paris, see Lynn Lees, "Metropolitan Types: London and Paris Compared," in

H. J. Dyos and Michael Wolff, *The Victorian City: Images and Realities* (London: Routledge and Kegan Paul, 1973), 1:413–28.

10. Pinkney, *Napoleon III*, 7.

11. Adeline Daumard, *Maisons de Paris et propriétaires parisiens au XIXe siècle* (Paris: Éditions Cujas, 1965), 96.

12. Pinkney, *Napoleon III*, 23.

13. William L. Langer, *Political and Social Upheaval, 1832–1852* (New York: Harper & Row, 1969), 346–50.

14. César Daly, "Maisons d'été des environs de Paris," *Revue générale de l'architecture* 17 (1859): 269–70.

15. Norma Evenson, *Paris: A Century of Change, 1878–1978* (New Haven: Yale University Press, 1979), 76–79; Pinkney, *Napoleon III*, 167–70.

16. Xavier Aubryet, "La Chaussée d'Antin," in *Paris Guide* (Paris: Librairie internationale, 1867), 2:1338–48.

17. Michel Gallet, *Stately Mansions: Eighteenth Century Paris Architecture* (New York: Praeger, 1972).

18. Olsen, *City as a Work of Art*, 42–44.

19. Daumard, *Maisons de Paris*, 90–91.

20. Olsen, *City as a Work of Art*, 94–96 and 114–25; Evenson, *Paris*, 200–201; and Daumard, *Maisons de Paris*, 99–100.

21. Louis Bergeron, *France Under Napoleon* (Princeton: Princeton University Press, 1968), 204.

22. Daumard, *Maisons de Paris*, 80–88.

23. See especially Pinkney, *Napoleon III*, chaps. 2–6. The cultural meaning of Haussman's plans is brilliantly described in Marshall Berman, *All That Is Solid Melts Into Air: The Experience of Modernity* (New York: Simon and Schuster, 1982), chap. 3, "Baudelaire, Modernism in the Streets."

24. Jeanne Gaillard, *Paris, la ville, 1852–1870* (Paris: Champion, 1970), 70–82.

25. Ibid., 77.

26. Bailleux de Marisy, "Des Sociétés foncières et leur rôle dans les travaux publics," *Revue des deux mondes* 34 (1861): 193–216.

27. Ibid., especially 194–200; also, Pinkney, *Napoleon III*, 193–206.

28. Bailleux de Marisy, "La Ville de Paris, ses finances et ses travaux publics," *Revue des deux mondes* 47 (1863): 775–836.

29. Daly, *L'Architecture privée*. See also William H. White, "On Middle Class Houses in Paris and Central London," *Transactions of the Royal Institute of British Architects*, Sessional Papers (1878): 21–55.

30. Ibid., 16–20; Olsen, *City as a Work of Art*, 124.

31. Daly, *L'Architecture privée*, 18–19.

32. Pinkney, *Napoleon III*, 165–66.

33. Evenson, *Paris*, 15–24; and Anthony Sutcliffe, *The Autumn of Central Paris* (London: Edward Arnold, 1970).

34. See for example the recent study by Michel Lacave, "Stratégies d'expropriation et haussmannisation: l'exemple de Montpellier," *Annales: économies. sociétés. civilisations* 35 (September–October 1980): 1011–25.

35. Carl E. Schorske, *Fin-de-siècle Vienna* (New York: Knopf, 1979), chap. 2; Olsen, *City as a Work of Art*, chap. 5.

36. Kenneth T. Jackson, *Crabgrass Frontier: The Suburbanization of the United States* (New York: Oxford University Press, 1985), 20–33.

37. See especially the Philadelphia villas now preserved in Fairmount Park.

38. Jackson, *Crabgrass Frontier*, 32.

39. Bainbridge Bunting, *Houses of Boston's Back Bay* (Cambridge, Mass.: Harvard University Press, 1967), 5–6.

40. For New York population, Jackson, *Crabgrass Frontier*, 27; for London, B. R. Mitchell, *European Historical Statistics* (New York: Columbia University Press, 1978), 13.

41. *Distinctive Private Houses* (1881), quoted in M. Christine Boyer and Jessica Sheer, "The Development and Boundary of Luxury Neighborhoods in New York, 1625–1890," paper presented to the "Culture of Cities" seminar, New York University, 1980, p. 100.

42. Ibid., 83. The best account of wealthy townhouse development in Manhattan, which emphasizes the commitment of the New York elite to the city, is M. Christine Boyer, *Manhattan Manners: Architecture and Style, 1850–1900* (New York: Rizzoli, 1985).

43. Miller and Sircy, "The Emerging Suburb," 103.

44. Frederick Law Olmsted to Henry H. Elliott, 27 August 1860, in *The Papers of Frederick Law Olmsted*, Charles Capen McLaughlin, ed. (Baltimore: Johns Hopkins University Press, 1980), vol. 3, *Creating Central Park*, Charles E. Beveridge and David Schuyler, eds. (1983), 262.

45. Ibid., 265. Olmsted's view of suburbia in the context of his larger urban vision has been thoughtfully analyzed in David Schuyler's important book, *The New Urban Landscape: The Redefinition of City Form in Nineteenth-Century America* (Baltimore: Johns Hopkins University Press, 1986), esp. chap. 8, "Urban Decentralization and the Domestic Landscape."

46. Ibid., 263.

47. Ibid., 260–61.

48. Jackson, *Crabgrass Frontier*, 61–67.

49. Kathryn Kish Sklar, *Catharine Beecher: A Study in American Domesticity* (New Haven: Yale University Press, 1973).

50. Ibid., 160. See also the important discussion of Beecher in Dolores Hayden, *The Grand Domestic Revolution: A History of Feminist Designs for American Homes, Neighborhoods, and Cities* (Cambridge, Mass.: MIT Press, 1981).

51. Sklar, *Catharine Beecher*, 159.

52. Andrew Jackson Downing, *Rural Essays*, ed. George William Curtis (New York: G. P. Putnam, 1853), xxviii. For this account of Downing I am much indebted to Phillida Bunkle, who allowed me to see her work on Downing in manuscript. Downing's significance for American domestic architecture is best assessed in Vincent J. Scully, Jr., *The Shingle Style and the Stick Style*, rev. ed. (New Haven: Yale University Press, 1971); and his significance for urban design in Schuyler, *The New Urban Landscape*.

53. Downing, *Cottage Residences* (orig. ed. 1842; reprinted from the 1873 ed. under the title *Victorian Cottage Residences*, New York: Dover Publications, 1981), ix. For discussions of American domestic ideology in this period, see especially Gwendolyn Wright, *Building the Dream: A Social History of Housing in America* (New York: Pantheon Books, 1981), chaps. 5–6; David Handlin, *The American Home: Architecture and Society, 1815–1915* (Boston: Little, Brown, 1979), chaps. 2–4; and Clifford Edward Clark, Jr., *The American Family Home, 1800–1960* (Chapel Hill: The University of North Carolina Press), chaps. 1–3.

54. For Downing's debts to Loudon, see Scully, *The Shingle Style*, xxviii; and John Archer, "Country and City in the American Romantic Suburb," *Journal of the Society of Architectural Historians* 42 (May 1983): 143.

55. Downing, *Cottage Residences*, ix.

56. Ibid.

57. Downing, *Rural Essays*, discussed in Schuyler, *The New Urban Landscape*, 153–156. Schuyler traces Downing's plan to his reaction against a developer's conventional grid plan for Dearman (now Irvington), New York.

58. Calvert Vaux, *Villas and Cottages* (New York: Harper, 1857).

59. Jackson, *Crabgrass Frontier*, 76–79; John Archer, "Country and City," 139–56.

60. Christopher Tunnard, *The City of Man*, 2d ed. (New York: Scribner's, 1970), 181–86; Schuyler, *The New Urban Landscape*, 157–60.

61. Walter L. Creese, *The Crowning of the American Landscape* (Princeton: Princeton University Press, 1985), 85.

62. Olmsted to Elizabeth Baldwin Whitney, 16 December 1890, *Papers of Frederick Law Olmsted*, 3:366.

63. Olmsted to Hartford, Conn. Board of Park Commissioners, draft ca. 1895, *Papers of Frederick Law Olmsted*, 3:41.

64. Roper, *FLO*, chaps. 12–13. See also the important insights on Olmsted in Thomas Bender, *Toward an Urban Vision: Ideas and Institutions in Nineteenth Century America* (Lexington: University of Kentucky Press, 1975).

65. Olmsted, Vaux, "Riverside," 295.

66. Ibid., 293.

67. Frederick Law Olmsted, "Public Parks and the Enlargement of Towns," *American Social Science Association* (Cambridge, Mass., 1870), reprinted in Sutton, ed., *Civilizing American Cities*, 66, 80.

68. Ibid., 93.

69. Ibid., 73.

70. Ibid., 80.

71. Quoted in Jackson, *Crabgrass Frontier*, 75.

72. Ibid., 294.

73. Olmsted to Edward Everett Hale, 21 October 1869, Olmsted Papers, Library of Congress, no. 01916. I am indebted to Charles E. Beveridge of the Olmsted Papers project for supplying me with the transcript of this letter.

74. Olmsted to Elliott, *Papers of Frederick Law Olmsted*, 264.

75. Olmsted, Vaux, "Riverside," 295.

76. Olmsted to Hale, Library of Congress, no. 01916.

77. Ibid.

78. Olmsted, Vaux, "Riverside," 292.

79. For Riverside, see especially Creese, *Crowning*, 219–40, "Riverside: The Greatest American Suburb"; and Schuyler, *The New Urban Landscape*, 162–66.

80. Olmsted, Vaux, "Riverside," 300.

81. Creese, *Crowning*, 227.

82. Olmsted, Vaux, "Riverside," 302.

83. Ibid., 301.

84. Olmsted to Hale, Library of Congress, no. 01916.

85. Olmsted, Vaux, "Riverside," 303.

86. Ibid., 299.

87. Creese, *Crowning*, 228.

88. Olmsted, Vaux, "Riverside," 303.

89. Ibid., 304.

90. Ibid., 296–98.

91. Olmsted, "Public Parks and the Enlargement of Towns," 74–75.
92. Ibid., 75.
93. Olmsted, Vaux, "Riverside," 292.
94. Olmsted to Hale, Library of Congress, no. 01916.
95. Creese, *Crowning*, 223.
96. Ibid., 224.
97. Ibid., 228.

Chapter 5. The Classic Suburb: The Railroad Suburbs of Philadelphia

1. See F. M. L. Thompson, *Hampstead: Building a Borough, 1650–1964* (London: Routledge & Kegan Paul, 1974), for an example of such exclusion.
2. The classic depiction of this system is Sam B. Warner, Jr., *Streetcar Suburbs: The Process of Growth in Boston, 1870–1900* (New York: Atheneum, 1974; orig. 1962).
3. Agnes Repplier, "Town and Suburb," quoted in John A. Lukacs, *Philadelphia: Patricians and Philistines, 1900–1950* (New York: Farrar, Straus, Giroux, 1981), 105.
4. Sidney J. Low, "The Rise of the Suburbs," *Contemporary Review* 60 (October 1891): 548.
5. These trends are clearly illustrated in the articles in F. M. L. Thompson, ed., *The Rise of Suburbia* (Leicester: Leicester University Press, 1982).
6. Robert A. M. Stern, *The Anglo-American Suburb*, special issue of *Architectural Design* 51 (October–November 1981), has generous selections of plans and photographs with short commentaries. For Scarsdale, see Carol A. O'Connor, *A Sort of Utopia: Scarsdale, 1891–1981* (Albany, N.Y.: State University of New York Press, 1982); for Brookline, Ronald Dale Karr, "Brookline and the Making of an Elite Suburb," *Chicago History* 13 (Summer 1984): 36–47; for Chicago suburbs, Michael Ebner, " 'In the Suburbes of Toun,' Chicago's North Shore to 1871," *Chicago History* 11 (Summer 1982): 66–77; and idem, "The Result of Honest Hard Work: Creating a Suburban Ethos for Evanston," *Chicago History* 13 (Summer 1984): 48–65; Warner, *Streetcar Suburbs*; and Joel Schwartz, "The Evolution of the Suburbs," in Philip C. Dolce, ed., *Suburbia: The American Dream and Dilemma* (Garden City, New York: Anchor Press/Doubleday, 1976), 1–36.
7. Sam B. Warner, Jr., *The Private City: Philadelphia in Three Periods of Its Growth* (Philadelphia: University of Pennsylvania Press, 1968).
8. Edward Teitelman and Richard W. Longstreth, *Architecture in Philadelphia: A Guide* (Cambridge, Mass.: M.I.T. Press, 1974), 1–3.
9. Ibid., 4–14.
10. Kenneth T. Jackson, *Crabgrass Frontier: The Suburbanization of the United States* (New York: Oxford University Press, 1985), 313–14; Theodore Hershberg, et al., "The 'Journey-to-Work: An Empirical Investigation of Work, Residence, and Transportation, Philadelphia, 1850 and 1880," in Theodore Hershberg, ed., *Philadelphia: Work, Space, Family and Group Experience in the Nineteenth Century* (New York: Oxford University Press, 1981), 129–73.
11. Teitelman and Longstreth, *Architecture in Philadelphia*, 116–27.
12. Warner, *Private City*, 79–157.
13. Teitelman and Longstreth, *Architecture in Philadelphia*, 200–201.

14. Ted Xaras, "A Time-Traveller's Trip on the Philadelphia, Germantown & Norristown Railroad," *Germantown Crier* 33 (Fall 1981): 82–87.

15. For the history of Germantown, see S. Hotchkin, *Ancient and Modern Germantown* (Philadelphia: Ziegler, 1889); Herbert Pullinger, *Old Germantown* (Philadelphia: David McKay, 1926); and Edward W. Hocker, *Germantown, 1683-1933* (Germantown: published by the author, 1933).

16. Mark Frazier Lloyd, "Germantown in the 1850s," *Germantown Crier* 31 (Spring 1979): 37. The transition from summer villas to full-time residences is clearly marked in Nicholas B. Wainwright, ed., *A Philadelphia Perspective: The Diary of Sidney George Fisher Covering the Years 1834-1871* (Philadelphia: Historical Society of Pennsylvania, 1967), esp. pp. 316 and 327.

17. For Houston see E. Digby Baltzell, *Philadelphia Gentlemen: The Making of a National Upper Class* (Glencoe, Ill.: Free Press, 1958), 118 and 206.

18. Ibid., 206–8. See also Willard S. Detweiler, Jr., *Chestnut Hill, An Architectural History* (Philadelphia: Chestnut Hill Association, 1969). Detweiler points out that the original Germantown rail line had already been extended to Chestnut Hill in 1854 (p. 22).

19. Teitelman and Longstreth, *Architecture in Philadelphia*, 238–53.

20. Baltzell, *Philadelphia Gentlemen*, 220.

21. Ibid.

22. Olmsted, Vaux and Co., "Preliminary Report upon the Proposed Suburban Village at Riverside, near Chicago" (New York, 1868), reprinted in S. B. Sutton, ed., *Civilizing American Cities: A Selection of Frederick Law Olmsted's Writings on City Landscapes* (Cambridge, Mass.: M.I.T. Press, 1971), 301.

23. Ibid., 296–303.

24. J. B. Jackson, quoted from a classroom lecture by Walter L. Creese, *The Crowning of the American Landscape* (Princeton: Princeton University Press, 1985), 235.

25. Herbert Warren Wind, "Shinnecock Hills and another Old-Timer," *The New Yorker* (August 4, 1986), 54–55. Other early courses included The Country Club, Brookline, Massachusetts (1893); Tuxedo Club, Tuxedo, New York (1889); and the Chicago Golf Club (1894). For Philadelphia clubs, see Baltzell, *Philadelphia Gentlemen*, 354–66.

26. Olmsted, Vaux, 301–2.

27. Clifford Edward Clark, Jr., *The American Family Home, 1800-1960* (Chapel Hill: University of North Carolina Press, 1986), chaps. 2–4.

28. Thomas Nolan, "The Suburban Dwelling and Country Villa, Recent Philadelphia Architecture," *Architectural Record* 29 (March 1911): 237–64; and John Taylor Boyd, Jr., "Philadelphia House Architecture," *Architectural Record* 42 (September 1917): 287–88. See also Alan Gowans, *The Comfortable House: North American Suburban Architecture, 1890-1930* (Cambridge, Mass.: MIT Press, 1986).

29. See especially the plans in Nolan, "Suburban Dwelling."

30. For the best analysis of the ideological and design conflicts of domestic architecture in this period, see Gwendolyn Wright, *Moralism and the Model Home: Domestic Architecture and Cultural Conflict in Chicago, 1873-1913* (Chicago: University of Chicago Press, 1980).

31. A "model" restrictive covenant was drawn up by the Olmsted Brothers in 1906 for their Druid Hills, Atlanta development. Olmsted Associates' papers, Library of Congress, no. 71.

32. An excellent analysis of this lower middle-class Philadelphia suburbia

can be found in Margaret S. Marsh, "The Impact of the Market Street 'El' on Northern West Philadelphia: Environmental Change and Social Transformation, 1900–1930," in William W. Cutler III and Howard Gillette, Jr., eds., *The Divided Metropolis: Social and Spatial Dimensions of Philadelphia, 1800–1975* (Westport, Conn.: Greenwood Press, 1980), 169–92.

33. Baltzell, *Philadelphia Gentlemen*, 201–5. See also J. W. Townsend, *The Old "Main Line,"* 2nd ed. (Philadelphia: privately printed for the author, 1922).

34. Gunther Barth, *City People: The Rise of Modern City Culture in Nineteenth-Century America* (New York: Oxford University Press, 1980) presents a very positive evaluation of the urban core and its institutions.

35. *Owen Wister out West*, quoted in Lukacs, *Philadelphia*, 251.

Chapter 6. Los Angeles: Suburban Metropolis

1. Stephen Bornson, "California—The Deluxe Subdivision," *Los Angeles Realtor* (May 1931): 11.

2. Richard J. Neutra, "Homes and Housing," in George W. Robbins and L. Deming Tilton, eds., *Los Angeles: Preface to a Master Plan* (Los Angeles: Pacific Southwest Academy, 1941), 191–201, at 191.

3. Ibid.

4. Regional Planning Commission, County of Los Angeles, *A Comprehensive Report on the Master Plan of Highways* (Los Angeles: Regional Planning Commission, 1941), 22.

5. Kelker, De Leuw and Co., *Report and Recommendations on a Comprehensive Rapid Transit Plan for the City and County of Los Angeles* (Chicago, 1925), 58. The "world's largest" refers to the number of track miles operated, 1,114.

6. Robert M. Fogelson, *The Fragmented Metropolis: Los Angeles, 1850–1930* (Cambridge, Mass.: Harvard University Press, 1967), chaps. 1–3.

7. Kelker, De Leuw, *Report and Recommendations*, 58. For the story of Pacific Electric, see Spencer Crump, *Ride the Big Red Cars* (Los Angeles: Crest Publications, 1962).

8. For evidence of such subsidies and deals, see the "Scrapbook" of developer H. J. Whitley, now in the Special Collections Rooms, UCLA Library, especially a cutting from the Los Angeles *Sentinel*, 1900.

9. Los Angeles *Examiner*, 7 May 1904. Whitley Scrapbook, UCLA.

10. Herbert D. Croly, "The California Country House," *Sunset* 18 (November 1906): 55.

11. Ibid., 56.

12. John Parke Young, "Industrial Background," in Robbins and Tilton, eds., *Los Angeles*, 61–73. See also Fred W. Viehe, "Black Gold Suburbs: The Influence of the Extractive Industry on the Suburbanization of Los Angeles," *Journal of Urban History* 8 (November 1981): 3–26.

13. *Los Angeles Realtor* (April 1929): 7.

14. *Los Angeles Times*, 1 July 1923. Quoted in Sherley Hunter, *Why Los Angeles Will Become the World's Greatest City* (Los Angeles: H. J. Mallen, 1923), 41.

15. Crump, *Ride the Big Red Cars*, 78.

16. Automobile Club of Southern California, *The Los Angeles Traffic Problem*

(Los Angeles, 1922), 10. For a scholarly treatment, see Mark S. Foster, "The Model T, the Hard Sell, and Los Angeles Urban Growth," *Pacific Historical Review* 44 (1975): 459–84.

17. Frederick Law Olmsted [Jr.], Harland Bartholomew, and Charles Henry Cheney, *A Major Traffic Street Plan for Los Angeles* (Los Angeles: Traffic Commission, 1924), 9.

18. Kelker, De Leuw, *Report and Recommendations.*

19. Automobile Club, *Los Angeles Traffic*; and Olmsted, Bartholomew, and Cheney, *Major Traffic.*

20. City Planning Commission [Los Angeles], *Mass Transit Facilities and the Master Plan of Parkways* (Los Angeles: City Planning Commission, 1942), 20.

21. The system is well described in Harry F. Hossack, "Helping the Client to Finance His Home," *Los Angeles Realtor* (March 1924): 7–30; and Charles E. Lindblade, "Home Financing—After the First Mortgage," *Los Angeles Realtor* (August 1925): 13–33.

22. Hossack, "Helping the Client"; and Lindblade, "Home Financing." Two important scholarly treatments of the question of home ownership, finance, and land use are Constance Perin, *Everything in its Place: Social Order and Land Use in America* (Princeton: Princeton University Press, 1977) and Matthew Edel, Elliott D. Sclar, and Daniel Luria, *Shaky Palaces: Homeownership and Social Mobility in Boston's Suburbanization* (New York: Columbia University Press, 1984).

23. *Los Angeles Examiner*, 20 July 1923.

24. Los Angeles City Club, *Report on Rapid Transit*, Supplement to *City Club Bulletin* 8 (30 January 1926), 4.

25. Ibid.

26. See David Brodsly, *L.A. Freeway: An Appreciative Essay* (Berkeley, Calif.: University of California Press, 1981), appendix, for an excellent discussion of this debate and its outcome.

27. Crump, *Ride the Big Red Cars*, 165–70.

28. Writers' Program, Works Progress Administration, *Los Angeles: A Guide to the City and Its Environs* (New York: 1941), 7.

29. Automobile Club, *Los Angeles Traffic*, 32.

30. Robert E. Park, Ernest W. Burgess, and Roderick McKenzie, *The City* (Chicago: University of Chicago Press, 1967; orig. ed. 1925).

31. Reyner Banham, *Los Angeles: The Architecture of the Four Ecologies* (Harmondsworth: Penguin, 1971), 161–77.

32. *Los Angeles Realtor* (March 1925): 28.

33. See Pierce E. Benedict, ed., *History of Beverly Hills* (Beverly Hills, Calif.: Cawston–Meier, 1934).

34. Ralph Hancock, *Fabulous Boulevard* (New York: Funk & Wagnalls, 1949), 171.

35. Ibid., 180. The developer was Arthur Letts.

36. Charles Blauvelt Hopper, *Memoirs of a Full Life* (privately printed, Los Angeles, 1963), 111, copy in the Special Collections Rooms, UCLA Library. The policy was discarded in the Depression.

37. Frederick Law Olmsted [Jr.], "Notes on the Palos Verdes Project, 1922," Olmsted Brothers Papers, Library of Congress, no. 5950.

38. Ibid.

39. Olmsted to Henry Clarke, sales director, Palos Verdes Project, 19 February 1924; reprinted in *Palos Verdes, the New City* (Palos Verdes: 1926), 4.

40. Palos Verdes Homes Association, *Protective Restrictions*, 1923. Blacks and Asiatics were excluded along with bad taste (p. 4).

41. Augusta Fink, *Time and the Terraced Land* (Berkeley: Howell-North, 1966).

42. Kelker, De Leuw, *Report and Recommendations*, 74.

43. Hancock, *Fabulous Boulevard*, 149–64.

44. Ibid., 163.

45. E. E. East, "Menace to Metropolitan Los Angeles," *Westways* (September 1937).

46. Ibid.

47. Automobile Club of Southern California, *Traffic Survey: Los Angeles Metropolitan Area*, Los Angeles, 1937. E. E. East, chief engineer. This publication contains the complete freeway system proposed by the club.

48. The Automobile Club suggestions were first incorporated in the Regional Planning Commission's *Report of a Highway Traffic Survey in the County of Los Angeles* (Los Angeles: Regional Planning Commission, 1937). They were then incorporated with modifications in Regional Planning Commission, County of Los Angeles, *Comprehensive Report on the Master Plan of Highways*, and idem, *Freeways for the Region* (Los Angeles: Regional Planning Commission, 1943).

49. Los Angeles Metropolitan Parkway Engineering Committee, *Interregional, Regional, Metropolitan Parkways* (Los Angeles: Metropolitan Parkway Engineering Committee, 1946). See Brodsly, *L.A. Freeway*, for the best account of the freeway system's evolution.

50. Los Angeles Metropolitan Traffic Association, *Express Motor Coach Service* (Los Angeles: Metropolitan Traffic Association, 1951).

51. George Sternlieb and David Listokin, "Housing: A Review of Past Policies and Future Directions," in George Sternlieb, ed., *Patterns of Development* (New Brunswick, N.J.: Center for Urban Policy Research, Rutgers University, 1986), 27–67; Jackson, *Crabgrass Frontier*, chap. 11.

52. Guy M. Rush, "Subdivision Financing," *Los Angeles Realtor* (February 1926): 17–40.

53. Young, "Industrial Background," in Robbins and Tilton, *Los Angeles*, 70.

54. See the houses in the special issue of *California Arts and Architecture* (June–July 1939) entitled "The Small California House" for an excellent sample.

55. Priestley A. Horton, "Small Homes and Small Budgets," *California Arts and Architecture* (June–July 1939): 16.

56. Catherine Bauer, "Slums Aren't Necessary," *American Mercury* (1934), quoted in Warren Susman, ed., *Culture and Commitment, 1929–1945* (New York: George Braziller, 1973), 288.

57. Regional Planning Commission, County of Los Angeles, *Comprehensive Report*, 23.

58. Ibid.

59. Brodsly, *L.A. Freeway*, 115–37.

60. Writers' Program, Works Progress Administration, *Los Angeles*, 11.

61. Marvin Briennes, "Smog Comes to Los Angeles," *Southern California Quarterly* 58 (Winter 1976): 515–79. The first attack, July 1943, was triggered by chemical plants and war industries as well as by automobile exhausts.

62. Remi A. Nadeau, *Los Angeles: From Mission to Modern City* (New York: Longman's, 1960), 275.

63. Brodsly, *L.A. Freeway*, chap. 4.

64. E. E. East, "Streets, the Circulating System," in Robbins and Tilton, eds., *Los Angeles*, 91–100, at 92.

65. *New York Times*, 30 Sept. 1986, 16.

Chapter 7. Beyond Suburbia: The Rise of the Technoburb

1. Louis H. Masotti and Jeffrey K. Hadden, eds., *Suburbia in Transition* (New York: New Viewpoints, 1974), editors' introduction, 5 and 99–100. For net outmigration and other figures from 1970 to 1980, see George Sternlieb and James Hughes, "The Uncertain Future of the Central City," in George Sternlieb, ed., *Patterns of Development* (New Brunswick, N.J.: Center for Urban Policy Research, Rutgers University, 1986), 109–121. The most recent population figures as well as a challenging interpretation of migration trends can be found in John Herbers, *The New Heartland: America's Flight Beyond the Suburbs* (New York: Times Books, 1986).

2. Kenneth T. Jackson, *Crabgrass Frontier: The Suburbanization of America* (New York: Oxford University Press, 1985).

3. H. G. Wells, "The Probable Diffusion of Great Cities," in *The Works of H. G. Wells*, vol. 4 (New York: Scribner's, 1924), 32.

4. Ibid., 41.

5. Ibid., 49.

6. I deal with Broadacre City at much greater length in my *Urban Utopias in the Twentieth Century: Ebenezer Howard, Frank Lloyd Wright, and Le Corbusier* (New York: Basic Books, 1977).

7. Frank Lloyd Wright, *The Living City* (New York: Horizon Press, 1958), 11.

8. George Sternlieb and Alex Schwartz, *New Jersey Growth Corridors* (New Brunswick, N.J.: Center for Urban Policy Research, Rutgers University, 1986), chap. 6.

9. George Sternlieb and James R. Hughes, "A Note on Information Technology, Demographics, and the Retail Revolution," in George Sternlieb, ed., *Patterns of Development*, 246–47.

10. Mark H. Rose, *Interstate: Express Highway Politics, 1941–1956* (Lawrence: University Press of Kansas, 1979). For further insights into the structure of the outer city see especially Peter O. Muller, *Contemporary Suburban America* (Englewood Cliffs, NJ: Prentice-Hall, 1981); Mark Gottdiener, *Planned Sprawl: Private and Public Interests in Suburbia* (Beverly Hills, Calif.: Sage Publications, 1977); Carl Abbott, *The New Urban America: Growth and Politics in Sunbelt Cities* (Chapel Hill: University of North Carolina Press, 1981); Mark Baldassare, *Trouble in Paradise: The Suburban Transformation in America* (New York: Columbia University Press, 1986); and Christopher B. Leinberger and Charles Lockwood, "How Business Is Reshaping America," *The Atlantic* 258 (October 1986): 43–63.

11. George Sternlieb and David Listokin, "Housing: A Review of Past Policies and Future Directions," in Sternlieb, ed., *Patterns of Development*, 46–48. The cultural significance of the housing figures is incisively described in Thomas Hine, *Populuxe* (New York: Knopf, 1986), chap. 3, "A New Place."

12. George Sternlieb and James W. Hughes, "Structuring the Future," in Sternlieb, ed., *Patterns of Development*, 11.

13. Sternlieb and Listokin, "Housing," 30–32.

14. Clifford Edward Clark, Jr., *The American Family Home, 1800–1960* (Chapel Hill: University of North Carolina Press, 1986), 222.

15. Philadelphia *Inquirer* (13 April 1986), 1-I.

16. Philadelphia *Inquirer* (6 April 1986), 2-J.

17. Philadelphia *Inquirer* (26 January 1986), 1-J.

18. Edgar M. Hoover and Raymond Vernon, *The Anatomy of a Metropolis* (Garden City, N.Y.: Doubleday, 1959), 27.

19. Brian J. L. Berry and Yehoshua S. Cohen, "Decentralizing Commerce and Industry: The Restructuring of Metropolitan America," in Louis H. Masotti and Jeffrey K. Hadden, eds., *The Urbanization of the Suburbs* (Beverly Hills, Calif.: Sage Publications, 1973), 442.

20. Ibid., 439.

21. Jack Rosenthal, "The Rapid Growth of Suburban Employment," in Masotti and Hadden, eds., *Suburbia*, 95–100.

22. Olmsted, Vaux and Co., "Preliminary Report upon the Proposed Suburban Village at Riverside, near Chicago" (New York, 1868), reprinted in S. B. Sutton, ed., *Civilizing American Cities: A Selection of Frederick Law Olmsted's Writings on City Landscapes* (Cambridge, Mass.: M.I.T. Press, 1971), 295.

23. David Riesman, "The Suburban Sadness," in William M. Dobriner, ed., *The Suburban Community* (New York: Putnam, 1958), 375–408.

24. William H. Whyte, *The Organization Man* (New York: Simon and Schuster, 1956). Whyte's book still retains its power and its pertinence, but it must be read in conjunction with Herbert J. Gans, *The Levittowners: Ways of Life and Politics in a New Suburban Community*, 2d ed. (New York: Columbia University Press, 1982). Gans effectively dispels the overstatements in Whyte with a model of careful observation based on his own residence in Levittown (now Willingboro), New Jersey. Also important is David Popenoe, *The Suburban Environment: Sweden and the United States* (Chicago: University of Chicago Press, 1977) based on careful observation in Levittown, Pennsylvania and a Swedish New Town.

25. Frank Lloyd Wright, *When Democracy Builds* (Chicago: University of Chicago Press, 1945), 58.

26. Ada Louise Huxtable, "An Alternative to 'Slurbs,'" in Masotti and Hadden, eds., *Suburbia*, 187.

27. See especially Daniel Schaffer, *Garden Cities for America: The Radburn Experience* (Philadelphia: Temple University Press, 1982), for a thorough review of the American New Town planning theory.

INDEX

abolitionist movement, 34–35, 60–61, 122
Ackerman, James, 50
Alsatia crime district (London), 8
Amalgamated Oil Company, 168
amusement gardens, 30–31, 33, 35
Anglican church, 34, 145
Anti-Corn Law League, 93
anti-Semitism, 154
apartment houses, 109, 110–16, 194
apprentices, 7, 29, 30, 61, 99
Archer, John, 125
archery, 147
architecture: civic, 205; domestic, 3–4, 13, 34, 65, 123–24, 148–50; historicism in, 68–70; urban, 4, 23–24; Victorian, 150
artesian wells, 158
associationism, 68, 70
Atlanta Beltway, 197
Austen, Jane, 28
Automobile Club of Southern California, 163, 166, 171, 172, 173–74, 180, 226n48

Back Bay, 118, 119
backyards, 146
badminton, 147
Baldwin, Christopher, 55
Baldwin Locomotive Works, 139
ballrooms, 30, 31
Banham, Reyner, 167

Barrymore, Lionel, 183
Bath, 42, 64
Battersea Rise, 52, 55–57
beaux quartiers, 111, 114
bedroom communities, 5, 17
Beecher, Catharine, 121, 122–23
Beecher, Lyman, 122
Bel Air, 168
Bell, Alphonzo, 168
Bergeron, Louis, 110
Beveridge, Charles E., 221n73
Beverly Hills, 167–68, 171–72
Birkenhead Park, 104, 124, 126
Blaise Hamlet, 67, 68, 70
Bornson, Stephen, 155
Boswell, James, 31
bourgeoisie, defined, 12
Boyar, Louis H., 179
Braudel, Fernand, 17, 189
Brentwood Riviera, 168
bricolage, 40, 45, 50
Briggs, Asa, 83, 178
Broadacre City, 188, 203, 204
Brogden, John, 53
Brooklyn Heights, 117
Brooks, Samuel, 81, 84–85, 89
broughams, 99
Brown, Lancelot "Capability," 48, 147
brownstones, 118, 128, 140
building and loan associations, 141, 183
bungalows, 161, 170, 176, 180
Bunkle, Phillida, 220n52